ANN ARBOR DISTRICT LIBRARY
31621014487025

Coaching BASEBALL Technical and Tactical Skills

American Sport
Education Program
with Tom O'Connell

D1299683

HUMAN KINETICS

Library of Congress Cataloging-in-Publication Data

Coaching baseball technical and tactical skills / American Sport Education Program.
p. cm.
Includes index.
ISBN 0-7360-4703-4 (soft cover)
1. Baseball--Coaching. I. American Sport Education Program.
GV875.5.C6195 2006
796.357'07'7--dc22

2005016082

ISBN-10: 0-7360-4703-4
ISBN-13: 978-0-7360-4703-6

Copyright © 2006 by Human Kinetics, Inc.

All rights reserved. Except for use in a review, the reproduction or utilization of this work in any form or by any electronic, mechanical, or other means, now known or hereafter invented, including xerography, photocopying, and recording, and in any information storage and retrieval system, is forbidden without the written permission of the publisher.

Notice: Permission to reproduce the following material is granted to instructors and agencies who have purchased *Coaching Baseball Technical and Tactical Skills:* pp. 13, 211-212, 214, 242, 245, 246, 247, and 250. The reproduction of other parts of this book is expressly forbidden by the above copyright notice. Persons or agencies who have not purchased *Coaching Baseball Technical and Tactical Skills* may not reproduce any material.

Acquisitions Editor: Amy Tocco; **Project Writer:** Tom O'Connell; **Developmental Editor:** Laura Floch; **Assistant Editor:** Mandy Maiden; **Copyeditor:** Bob Replinger; **Proofreader:** Joanna Hatzopoulos Portman; **Indexers:** Robert and Cynthia Swanson; **Permission Manager:** Carly Breeding; **Graphic Designers:** Bob Reuther and Nancy Rasmus; **Graphic Artist:** Sandra Meier; **Photo Manager:** Dan Wendt; **Cover Designer:** Keith Blomberg; **Photographer (cover and interior):** Dan Wendt; **Art Manager:** Kareema McLendon-Foster; **Illustrator:** Argosy; **Printer:** Versa Press

We thank Scripps Ranch High School in San Diego, California, for assistance in providing the location for the photo shoot for this book.

Copies of this book are available at special discounts for bulk purchase for sales promotions, premiums, fund-raising, or educational use. Special editions or book excerpts can also be created to specifications. For details, contact the Special Sales Manager at Human Kinetics.

Printed in the United States of America

10 9 8 7 6 5 4 3 2 1

Human Kinetics
Web site: www.HumanKinetics.com

United States: Human Kinetics
P.O. Box 5076
Champaign, IL 61825-5076
800-747-4457
e-mail: humank@hkusa.com

Canada: Human Kinetics
475 Devonshire Road Unit 100
Windsor, ON N8Y 2L5
800-465-7301 (in Canada only)
e-mail: orders@hkcanada.com

Europe: Human Kinetics
107 Bradford Road
Stanningley
Leeds LS28 6AT, United Kingdom
+44 (0) 113 255 5665
e-mail: hk@hkeurope.com

Australia: Human Kinetics
57A Price Avenue
Lower Mitcham, South Australia 5062
08 8277 1555
e-mail: liaw@hkaustralia.com

New Zealand: Human Kinetics
Division of Sports Distributors NZ Ltd.
P.O. Box 300 226 Albany
North Shore City
Auckland
0064 9 448 1207
e-mail: info@humankinetics.co.nz

contents

preface

If you are a seasoned baseball coach, surely you have experienced the frustration of watching your players perform well in practice, only to find them underperforming in games. In your playing days, you likely saw the same events unfold. Teammates, or perhaps even you, could tear the cover off the ball in batting practice and snag all of the ground balls in drills, but could not transfer that kind of performance to games. Although this book will not provide you with a magical quick fix to your team's problems, it will help you prepare your players for game day. Whether you are a veteran coach or are new to coaching, *Coaching Baseball Technical and Tactical Skills* will help you take your game to the next level by providing you with the tools you need to teach your team the game of baseball.

Every baseball coach knows the importance of technical skills. The ability of a player to field a fly ball, make a strong throw, block a pitch in the dirt, lay down a bunt, or throw a curveball can significantly affect the outcome of a game. The book discusses the basic and intermediate technical skills necessary for your team's success, including both offensive and defensive skills. You will learn how to detect and correct errors in your athletes' performance of those skills and then help them transfer the knowledge and ability that they gain in practice to execution in games.

In addition to learning about technical skills, the book focuses on tactical skills, including offensive skills like the sacrifice bunt, getting out of a rundown and stealing third base and defensive skills such as pickoff plays, defending the first-and-third double steal and double-play defenses. The book discusses the "tactical triangle," an approach that teaches players to read a situation, acquire the knowledge they need to make a tactical decision and apply decision-making skills to the problem. To advance this method, the book covers important cues that help athletes respond appropriately when they see a play developing, including important rules, game strategies and the strengths and weaknesses of opponents.

The book also covers planning at several levels—the season plan, practice plans and game plans. Sample games approach practice and season plans are offered. The season plan lays out a season based on the skills in this book and the practice plans include a description of eight practice sessions, covering elements such as the length of the practice session, the objective of the practice, equipment needed, warm-up, practice of previously taught skills, teaching and practicing new skills, cool-down and evaluation. Sample drills and games, as mentioned in both the games and traditional approach practice plans, can also be found in the *Coaching Baseball Technical and Tactical Skills* online course.

Of course, playing the games is what your practices eventually lead to. The book shows you how to prepare long before the first game, including dealing with issues such as communicating with players, parents, officials and the media, scouting your opponent and motivating your players. You will learn how to control your team's performance on game day by establishing routines and how to make decisions during the game, such as removing pitchers, making substitutions and setting a batting order.

PART I

Teaching and Evaluating

Being a good coach takes more than knowing the sport of baseball. You have to go beyond that and find a way to teach your athletes how to be better ballplayers. You also need to know how to evaluate your players to find effective ways to improve their performance.

In chapter 1 we will go over the fundamentals of teaching sport skills. We will first provide you with a general overview of your sport and talk with you about the importance of being an effective teacher. Next, we will define some important skills, helping you get a better understanding of technical and tactical skills and the traditional and games approaches to coaching.

We will build on the knowledge of how to teach sport skills with the evaluation of technical and tactical skills in chapter 2. We will discuss the importance of evaluating athletes, review the core skills that you should assess and describe how you can assess them. Chapter 2 stresses the importance of preseason, in-season and postseason evaluation and provides you with sample tools that you can use to evaluate your players.

By learning how to teach and evaluate your players, you will be better prepared to help them improve their performance.

chapter 1

Teaching Sport Skills

Although the rules and the look of the playing field have changed over the years, the basic concept of baseball has not—the team that scores the most runs wins. From its beginnings in the 18th century these basic concepts have become so ingrained into America that its terms are part of our everyday language. Many state judicial codes have "three strike" laws on the books for repeat criminals. Goofy people are said to be "out in left field." And when a young romantic says that he "struck out," everybody knows what it means.

A certain uniformity exists at all levels as far as rules are concerned, and a playing field in Indiana looks the same as a playing field in Oregon. Youth fields are merely shrunken versions of their high school and collegiate counterparts, with diamond-shaped infields and a fence in center field that is usually farther from the plate than the fence in left or right. The modern mound is 60 feet, 6 inches from the plate, and the pitcher has to keep one foot on the pitching rubber before throwing.

In the heyday of baseball, in the years when Babe Ruth and Joe DiMaggio were stars, seemingly every child in America learned the skills and the rules of the game at an early age. It would not have been necessary to explain the infield fly rule to children living in Brooklyn; they would have known it intuitively. But the teaching of baseball, like American society, has had to evolve. No longer can one assume that most Americans know the game; too many diversions are available to them. So, too, it cannot be taken for granted that youth will know how to perform the skills of baseball as soon as they step out of the cradle. Today those skills have to be taught.

Effective Teaching

A commonly held fallacy is that an athlete who excelled as a player can excel at coaching too. Great players often play instinctively and don't know why they do what they do. They just do it. Players who are not as skilled sometimes try to make up for their limited skills by becoming more knowledgeable about the tactics and techniques needed to become good baseball players. These players, although never able to perform at a high level themselves, learned enough about the game to know how to pass that knowledge of skills on to others. This is not to say that good players cannot be good coaches. Rather, you should realize that just because you were a good player you will not naturally become a good coach. You will need to work at it.

Good coaching is good teaching. There is no simpler way to put it! Coaches who discover the best way to help all their players succeed become the best coaches. Coaches must recognize this fact and be responsible for their athletes' learning. Coaching requires teaching.

Good coaches, then, not only teach the mechanics of the game but also understand the way that athletes learn. Rather than tell players how to play, good coaches teach them how to learn the game for themselves. This approach demands that you do more than just work with the *X*s and *O*s. The great player is the sum of many parts: technical skill, tactical skill, physical ability, mental acuity, communication proficiency and strength of character (Rainer Martens, *Successful Coaching, Third Edition*, Champaign, IL: Human Kinetics, 2004, pp. 186-188).) Although all these skills are important, this book focuses on the technical and tactical skills that you need to be aware of in coaching baseball. To learn more about other skills that should be part of the makeup of a great athlete, refer to Rainer Martens' *Successful Coaching, Third Edition.*

A baseball player could master literally thousands of technical and tactical skills. Covering every aspect of the game—from the simple act of gripping and holding a baseball to the complexity of successfully executing a bases-loaded pickoff play—would be impossible. Instead, this book focuses on the essential basic and intermediate technical and tactical skills, developed from a list of skills compiled with the cooperation and assistance of the American Baseball Coaches Association (ABCA).

Technical Skills

Everyone involved in coaching baseball knows the importance of technical skills. The way a player fields a ground ball, lays down a bunt, throws a curveball or executes a bent-leg slide has a big effect on the outcome of a game. Technical skills are "the specific procedures to move one's body to perform the task that needs to be accomplished" (Martens, *Successful Coaching, Third Edition,* p. 169). The execution of technical skills, the capability to teach athletes how to perform them, the flair to detect errors and correct them and the ability to recognize when those skills come into play in a game are all things that you will develop over time with the accumulation of experience. You may need years and hundreds of games to acquire the knowledge necessary to know instinctively what to do. This book will help you reach that stage more quickly, taking you from your current level of knowledge to a higher plane by showing you how to

- focus on the key points of the skill,
- detect errors in an athlete's performance of those skills,

- correct the errors that athletes make, and
- help athletes transfer the knowledge and ability that they gain in practice to execution in games.

Developed from the expertise of the ABCA, the plan outlined in this book will help you learn how to teach athletes to become masters of the basic to intermediate technical skills of baseball and will assist you in providing athletes with the resources necessary for success.

Tactical Skills

Although mastering the technical skills of baseball is important, it is not enough. Baseball players need to know not only how to play the game technically but also how to choose the tactics necessary to achieve success. Many baseball texts overlook the tactical aspects of the game. Coaches even omit tactical considerations from practice because they focus so intently on teaching technical skills. Teaching tactics is much harder and takes much more effort than teaching techniques, but the resulting dividends are substantial.

Tactical skills can best be defined as "the decisions and actions of players in the contest to gain an advantage over the opposing team or players" (Martens, *Successful Coaching, Third Edition,* p. 170). One way that coaches can approach teaching tactical skills is by focusing on three critical aspects, the "tactical triangle":*

- Reading the play or situation
- Acquiring the knowledge needed to make an appropriate tactical decision
- Applying decision-making skills to the problem

This book as a whole provides you with the knowledge you need to teach players how to use the tactical triangle. Part III covers important cues that help athletes respond appropriately when they see a play developing, including important rules, game strategies, and the strengths and weaknesses of opponents that affect game situations, as well as ways to teach athletes how to acquire and use this knowledge. Part III will help you teach athletes how to make appropriate choices in a given situation and will show you how to empower players to recognize emerging situations on their own and make sound judgments.

Anyone who has observed baseball for any length of time has witnessed players making errors in games on plays that they have practiced many times in training sessions. Such situations can cause tremendous frustration, for both players and coaches. As you will see, however, these errors can be prevented!

Traditional Versus Games Approach to Coaching

As mentioned previously, transferring skills from practice to games can be difficult. A sound background of technical and tactical training prepares athletes for game situations. But you can surpass this level by incorporating gamelike situations into daily training, further enhancing the likelihood that players will

---

*Reprinted, by permission, from R. Martens, 2004, *Successful Coaching*, 3rd ed. (Champaign, IL: Human Kinetics), 215.

transfer skills from practices to games. To understand how to accomplish this, you must be aware of two approaches to coaching: the traditional approach and the games approach.

Traditional Approach

Most coaches are comfortable with the traditional approach to coaching. This method often begins with a warm-up period followed by a set of drills, a scrimmage and finally a cool-down period. This approach can be useful in teaching the technical skills of baseball, but unless coaches shape, focus and enhance the scrimmages or drills, the athletes may not successfully translate the skills to game situations, leaving coaches to ponder why their team practices better than it plays.

Games Approach

Using the tactical triangle in practice supplies athletes with the tools they need to make appropriate and quick decisions. But unless they can employ these tools in game situations, they are of little value.

You have surely seen players jump into the batting cage in practice and tear the cover off the ball on the tees or the pitching machine but then have trouble making good contact after the game begins. This type of hitter has learned the art of performing well in drills but has not learned how to transfer those technical skills to tactical situations that occur during a game. Some people call this choking, but a more accurate description would be failure to adapt. The same sort of thing happens to the player who can field every ground ball flawlessly in practice but bobbles easy grounders in a game or lets them go through his legs.

The best way to prevent this scenario is to use the games approach to coaching, which provides athletes with real-time, gamelike situations in training that allow them to practice and learn the skills at game speed. This philosophy stresses the importance of putting technical skills rehearsed in drills into use in practice. You can drill players in a skill like bunting until they are sore, but if they never get the opportunity to use the skill in a gamelike setting, they will not be able to perform when it really counts—in an actual game. When players make mistakes in game-speed situations, they learn. You have to provide gamelike opportunities in which players can feel secure about making mistakes so that they can file those mistakes in the "baseball sense" parts of their brains. By doing so, the chances of their making the same mistakes in games will lessen.

The games approach emphasizes the use of games and minigames to provide athletes with situations that are as close to a real game as possible (Launder, Alan G., *Play Practice*. Champaign, IL: Human Kinetics, 2001). This approach requires more than just putting the team on the field, throwing them a ball and letting them play. Rather, according to Launder, the games approach includes three components that make each minigame educational:

1. Shaping
2. Focusing
3. Enhancing

Shaping play means modifying the game in a way that is conducive to learning the skills that you want to teach in that particular setting. The games approach shapes play by modifying the rules, the environment (playing area), the objectives of the game, and the number of players used (Launder, p.56). In a typical scrimmage situation, the stronger players dominate and the weaker players rarely get a chance to play an active role. When play is shaped—say, for example, by reducing the number of players—the weaker players are put into positions where they will have more opportunities to play active roles. But you cannot simply shape the play and expect miracles to happen. You need to focus your athletes' attention on the specific objectives that you are trying to achieve with the game. Young players are more apt to learn, or at least to reduce their reluctance to learn, if they know why you are asking them to grasp new tactical information.

Knowing how the tactic fits into the team's game plan or season plan also helps players buy into the tactic. You can assist your athletes with this phase by providing them with clear objectives and explaining how learning these objectives elevates their capability to play and helps their team win games. Shaping play and focusing players on objectives, however, cannot be successful unless you play an active role and work on enhancing their play. You can enhance minigames by adding challenges to make the contests between the sides equal. You can also enhance play by encouraging your players and give them confidence by frequently pointing out their progress. Minigames also give you an opportunity to stop the game whenever you recognize an opportunity to teach something that will improve their play even further.

Most coaches have used aspects of the games approach one way or another in their training sessions. Although you may already have a basic understanding of how to use this approach, this book takes the concept further by presenting a games approach season plan as well as sample practices for you to use with your team.

Both the traditional and the games approaches are sound coaching practices. Part IV examines both approaches to teaching the skills in baseball. Although both approaches have value, the philosophy of this book slants toward the latter. Providing athletes with game-speed, real-time situations that have clear objectives creates a productive, fun-filled learning environment. Athletes who have learned to think of training as a necessary evil will be more motivated to come to practice if they are engaged on a daily basis. More important, if they sense that they have ownership over what they learn in practice, they become more responsible team members. An added benefit is that baseball players who learn through the games approach will be better prepared for competition because they have already faced stiff challenges in their everyday practice sessions.

Knowing how to teach the technical and tactical skills of baseball is important, but you will never know how your players are performing unless you create good assessment systems. Next, you must learn how to evaluate players.

chapter 2

Evaluating Technical and Tactical Skills

Baseball players must master many technical skills and know how to apply those skills in tactical situations. Most of the focus in team practices and individual training sessions is the development and improvement of these baseball skills. Coaches, however, must also be concerned about objectively evaluating those individual skills and using the gathered information to aid in developing the team's season and game plans. For example, decisions about lineups, pinch hitters, relief pitchers, stealing bases, etc. can only be made if coaches have the necessary information at their disposal to make the "right call."

In order to gain competency in the decision making process, coaches must develop accurate measurement tools to help them assess their players. In addition to mechanical abilities, a vast array of nonphysical talents—mental capacity, communication skills and character training—overlay athletic performance, affect its development and should be considered (Rainer Martens, *Successful Coaching, Third Edition*). But, even though all of these skills are important, the focus here will be only on evaluating the technical and tactical skills of baseball. Please refer to *Successful Coaching, Third Edition,* to learn more about how to judge those other more intangible skills.

Guidelines for Evaluation

Regardless of the type of skill being measured and the type of tool being used to do the measuring, some basic guidelines should govern the evaluation process. These are:

- Understanding the purpose of evaluation
- Motivation for improvement
- Providing objective measurement
- Effectively providing feedback
- Being credible

Understanding the Purpose of Evaluation

Athletes need to know and understand the purpose of the test and its relationship to baseball. If the skill being evaluated is a technical skill, the correlation should be easy. But when you are evaluating physical skills, or when you are assessing mental, communication or character skills, you must explain the correlation between the skill and the aspect of the players' game that it will benefit. Doing so speaks to the importance of giving players ownership over their development.

Motivation for Improvement

The athlete must be motivated to improve. Understanding the correlation of the skill to baseball will help, but its game-time applications may at times seem far removed from practices and training. In the physical skills area, if you can create a gamelike atmosphere with lots of players watching as you conduct the testing, athletes will compete with more energy and enthusiasm than they will if you run the tests in isolation.

Still, the best motivation for players is to have them recognize their personal bests by comparing their current level of skill to a previous one. Working with players to compare past and present performances provides a graphic illustration of progress completely independent of the rest of the team. When players see themselves making progress, they will be more motivated to train harder. This concept, while focusing on the individual, is not antithetical to the team concept. You simply need to remind the team that if every player gets better every day, the team will be getting better every day!

Providing Objective Measurement

All evaluation and testing must be unbiased, formal and consistent. Athletes easily recognize flaws in the testing process and lose confidence in the results. You must be systematic and accurate and treat every player the same way for the test to have integrity. No player should receive credit for a test result on a skill if he does not execute the test regimen perfectly. You must mandate good form and attention to the details of the test. The same is true with evaluation tools that are not quantitatively measured. If you want to evaluate the technical skills of all your infielders, you must use the same tool for each and score them fairly and consistently if you expect them to trust the results, especially because most of the tests are highly subjective.

Effectively Providing Feedback

You must convey feedback to athletes professionally and, if possible, personally. Not wanting to fail, all athletes are self-conscious to a certain extent when they don't perform to their aspirations or the expectations of their coach. At the same time, all athletes have areas in which they need to improve, and you must be able to communicate those needs to the athlete, especially if he does not see the need for improvement! Private meetings with the athletes are crucial to the exchange of this information. Factual results, comparative charts ranking the athlete, historical records of previous test results and even study of videotape of the athlete's performances can all be effective in discreetly communicating both the areas of improvement and the areas where the athlete needs to make progress. You can accomplish these individual meetings in occasional and subtle ways: by asking an athlete to stay for a few minutes in the office after practice, by finding the athlete after practice or a workout in the locker room, by going out to practice early and creating an opportunity to talk to a player individually or by calling the player in to the office at random times just to talk. A visit to a player's class or cafeteria table during the school day can have great effect on his self-esteem. These in-person, one-on-one meetings are by far the best way to communicate the need to improve.

Being Credible

Finally, you must apply the principles that you are asking of your players to the process of evaluation. You must be an expert in the technical and tactical skills for the sport, so that you can accurately and consistently evaluate the skills of your players. You must understand the value and importance of the skills to convey the importance of these skills to the team. You must exhibit outstanding communication skills to be effective in teaching, and you must display those skills in your interaction with other staff members and coaching peers, especially in the presence of players, to establish credibility.

Evaluation Tools

Coaches have many tools to aid them in the evaluation process. As always, player and team statistics are readily available, but new formulas may prove a more well-rounded way of assessing them. Additionally, most schools have digital video cameras that you can and should use for evaluation purposes. Further, in recent years, many innovative charts have been developed to help coaches assess performance beyond what standard statistics may reveal. Let's look more closely at these tools.

Statistics

More than athletes in any other sport, baseball players are evaluated by comparative statistics. Baseball is a game of statistics—the .300 hitters, the RBI leaders, the 20-game winners. People constantly examine players based on their batting, fielding and pitching stats. Other forms of evaluation have recently come into prominence—namely, the use of video and computers to analyze players' swings, throwing motions or running forms—but statistics remain the main source of comparison and evaluation in the day-to-day workings of the game.

Recently, statistics that are more meaningful have come to the forefront in baseball thanks to the work of members of the Society for American Baseball Research (SABR). Their studies have convinced many people that on-base percentage ([walks

+ times hit by pitch + hits]/times at bat) should be weighted more heavily than batting average because the former more accurately measures a player's value to an offense. Slugging percentage has also taken on new luster, and OPS (on base + slugging) may be the preferred stat in the future. Sabremetricians have convinced coaches that a more useful evaluation of players results from tracking their batting average against right-handed and left-handed pitchers, with runners in scoring position, when ahead or behind in the game, and in a host of other hitting situations.

Photography and Video

Although videotaping of games is not as common in baseball as it is in other team sports, you should photograph or videotape all players throwing, hitting and fielding. You could show the video to the whole team on bad-weather days or use it as a discussion point during individual meetings with players. When sharing video with the whole team, be mindful that such viewing is more constructive if you hold the team accountable for review of the techniques and if they use the vocabulary of the coaching staff when they do so.

Rubrics

As Mark Twain said, "There are lies, damn lies and statistics!" Coaches sometimes read too much into statistics. For example, John may go one for four in a game, a .250 batting average, with one single and three groundouts, whereas Mike may be three for four in the game, a .750 batting average. If only statistics are used to evaluate these performances, Mike clearly outshines John, but a closer look at the game may reveal something else. What if two of Mike's hits were bloopers that got just over the outstretched arms of infielders and all of John's outs were crisply hit ground balls that the defensive players made nice plays on and just barely threw him out? Would you still say that Mike had a better game than John did? Probably not. This example illustrates the need for a more comprehensive and accurate way of evaluating the performance of a hitter, or any other player. Coaches need a system to evaluate the technical and tactical skills required for baseball on a detailed skill-by-skill basis. They need an instrument that allows them to look not only at the result, like batting average, but also at the key elements, whether mechanical or strategically related, that determine the player's ability to complete a task well.

Figure 2.1, *a* and *b*, provides an example of an uncomplicated rubric that allows you to isolate technical and tactical skills, skill by skill. By breaking down the whole skill into its component parts, the rubric also enables a more objective assessment of an athlete's performance in a skill than can be produced by statistics. You can use this rubric to evaluate basic technical skills, such as throwing a curveball, as shown in figure 2.1*a*. The rubric breaks down the skill into its component parts and provides a rating scale that you can use to evaluate performance on each of those parts. Also included is a sample for the related tactical skill of hit and run. This allows you to score players on their ability to recognize the cues and execute the skills necessary for a successful hit and run.

By their nature, rubrics are rather subjective because they ask the evaluator to rate on a 1-to-5 scale how well the infielder executes the basic elements of each technical or tactical skill. Each of those ratings would simply be the coaching staff's opinions based on observation. But you could add some statistical weight

Figure 2.1a Throwing a Curveball Technical Skill Evaluation

Key focal points	SKILL RATING Weak 1	2	3	4	Strong 5	Notes
Grip	1	2	3	4	5	
Wrist action	1	2	3	4	5	
Arm action	1	2	3	4	5	

From *Coaching Baseball Technical and Tactical Skills* by ASEP, 2006, Champaign, IL: Human Kinetics.

Figure 2.1b Hit and Run Tactical Skill Evaluation

Players' ability	SKILL RATING Weak 1	2	3	4	Strong 5	Notes
Avoid distractions as discussed in "Watch Out!"	1	2	3	4	5	
Read the situation	1	2	3	4	5	
Use the appropriate knowledge about the team strategy and the game plan	1	2	3	4	5	
Use the appropriate knowledge about the rules	1	2	3	4	5	
Use the appropriate knowledge about physical playing conditions	1	2	3	4	5	
Use the appropriate knowledge about opponents strengths and weaknesses	1	2	3	4	5	
Use the appropriate knowledge about one's self	1	2	3	4	5	

From *Coaching Baseball Technical and Tactical Skills* by ASEP, 2006, Champaign, IL: Human Kinetics.

to the process by scoring the player on each play when the skill came into use. For example, you could keep track during a game of the number of balls hit toward an infield position (sort of an expansion of the basic fielding average stat) and score the infielder on his quickness getting to the ball or starting to the ball and come up with a new statistic.

Fielding percentage simply grades the infielder on whether or not he cleanly fielded the ball and made an accurate throw, but by tweaking the stat, you can evaluate the infielder in a more useful way by pinpointing the area where the skill breaks down and analyzing each of the component parts. Knowing the exact part where the skill erodes can help you modify practices and help the player overcome the problem with the skill.

The process of scoring with rubrics may help you avoid the common trap of being preoccupied with the result of the skill (the out at first base) and coaching and evaluating only that outcome. Players know already that they are supposed to field the ball or make a good throw. They give themselves immediate feedback! Coaches must go beyond the result and focus their teaching on the process of fielding the ball, or the cues and knowledge needed to execute the tactics of the game, to alert the athlete to the portions of his technique that need improvement or where he may be lacking tactical expertise.

Critical Evaluation

An important corollary to this teaching and evaluation strategy is that even when the result is positive, the evaluation of the athlete's technique might be substantially critical. You need to be careful with criticism, however, and avoid purely negative comments. Athletes need to know that you care for them as individuals and are not just interested in *X*s and *O*s. The University of Michigan recently conducted a study of the expectations that high school athletes had of their coaches. The top three expectations were (1) don't show favoritism, (2) be concerned with the individual, not just winning, and (3) have a positive attitude. This finding shows that coaches should not neglect interpersonal skills when dealing with players.

Critical evaluation often must occur on the fly in the pressure of a game. A situation that can either have a disastrous effect on an athlete or be uplifting is a visit to the mound when a pitcher is in trouble. Pitchers already know that they should throw strikes, and they have been trying to do that. Telling the pitcher to throw the ball over the plate without giving him some positive feedback would be unlikely to help him. Instead of stating the obvious here, you should talk to the pitcher about where the skill is breaking down. You could tell the pitcher that you noticed that he wasn't keeping his weight over his back leg long enough or that his stride was too quick. Mentioning these sorts of things to a pitcher helps him concentrate on mechanics and may get his mind off the pressure of the situation.

Of course, you cannot do this for the athlete unless you know and understand those key elements. The following chapters in this book are designed to provide you with that information. Then, by using the technical and tactical skills outlined in parts II and III as a guide, you will be able to create evaluation tools like the one shown in figure 2.1, *a* and *b*, for each of the skills as you see fit during the season.

Figure 2.1, *a* and *b*, can also serve as a simple way to use the details outlined in the next two chapters by providing you and your players an outline and a graphic mechanism for understanding the areas where improvement is needed. You can adapt it to evaluate physical, mental, communication and character skills or any other skill set that you deem important.

Figure 2.1, *a* and *b*, can also be used as a summary exercise. After a game or after a week of practice, the athlete can score himself on all his essential technical and tactical skills, including all the cues and focal points, and on as many of the corollary skills as desired. You can also score the athlete and then compare the two score sheets. The ensuing discussion will provide you and the player with a direction for future practices and drills, and it will help you decide where the athlete needs to focus attention to improve performance. You should meet face to face several times during a season so that the athlete can look for improvement in the areas where he has been concentrating his workouts. As the process unfolds, a better correlation between the athlete's score sheet and your score sheet should occur.

Now is the time to learn more about the basic to intermediate technical and tactical skills of baseball. You will want to master these skills so that you can evaluate your athletes, help them master the skills and take your team to a higher level.

PART II

Teaching Technical Skills

Now that you know how to teach and evaluate sport skills, you are ready to dive into the specific skills necessary for success in baseball. This part focuses on the basic and intermediate skills necessary for your team's success, including offensive technical skills related to hitting, bunting, stealing and sliding and defensive technical skills related to throwing, catching, the basics for various positions and pitching variations.

Chapters 3 and 4 present the material in a way that is clear and easy to understand. More important, you can immediately incorporate the information into your practices. Whether you are a seasoned veteran or a new coach, you will find the presentation of skills in this part helpful as you work with your athletes.

For each skill, we first present what we call the "Key Points" for the particular skill. These points highlight the most important aspects of the skill, providing you and your players with a roadmap to proper execution of the skill. The remainder of the skill is a detailed explanation of these essential components, including instructional photos and diagrams to guide you along the way.

At the end of each skill we include a table to teach you to detect common errors and correct those errors in your athletes. To close each skill, we include a useful "At a Glance" section to guide you to other tools in the book that will help you teach your athletes this particular skill—whether it is another technical skill that they need to be able to perform, a tactical skill that uses this technical skill or a practice plan or drill that helps you teach the skill.

chapter 3

Offensive Technical Skills

This chapter will cover the offensive technical skills that you and your players must know in order to be successful. In this chapter, you will find:

Preparing to Hit

KEY POINTS

The most important components of preparing to hit are

- correct bat choice,
- strike zone knowledge,
- repeatable preswing routine,
- good contact position and
- comfortable batting stance.

Even before he has a turn at the plate, the hitter must understand many important elements. Unless the hitter has properly practiced and performed his preswing preparation, he is ill equipped for an at bat. Coaches often overlook and fail to teach these skills in a systematic and thorough manner.

You should address the following key points when preparing hitters for their turn at bat. After forming a clear picture of the techniques shown, examine the parts that go into finding a good stance and getting ready to hit. Keep in mind that each player is unique and may have an alternative approach that works for him.

CORRECT BAT CHOICE

Bats come in all sizes and shapes. Most youth and high school leagues today have rules that govern the weight of aluminum bats in comparison with their length. These rules were instituted for the sake of safety. Wooden bats do not have restrictions.

Players should choose a bat because it is the right weight and the correct balance and feel for them. When choosing a bat, players should consider the balance and feel rather than the color and design schemes.

The wrong bat can seriously diminish a hitter's capacity in the batter's box. If a player seems to be having problems swinging a bat, it may be too heavy or too long. If the barrel of the bat drops lower than the player's hands during the swing, especially if the player is experimenting with a wooden bat, it is usually a sign that the player cannot handle the bat. You should suggest that the player use a shorter bat. Recent changes in bat specification rules have eliminated much of the weight variations common in the past. Today all bats must conform to specifications created by the National Federation of State High School Associations (NFHS), the national governing body of high school sports. Coaches should check their state association rule book or the NFHS Web site (www.nfhs.org) for bat rules before recommending or buying bats.

STRIKE ZONE KNOWLEDGE

The rules of baseball define the strike zone as a 17-inch space over home plate, the top of which is halfway between the batter's shoulders and the waistline and the bottom of which is the knees, when the batter assumes his natural batting stance. This area is typically found from the top of the batter's knees to the letters on the uniform. The rules also state that any part of a baseball going through this imaginary area is a strike. Sounds simple, right? Well, not exactly.

Keep in mind that a baseball is about 3 inches in diameter. If any part of it crosses the strike zone, the pitch is a strike. The strike zone, then, is not 17 inches wide but more like 23 inches wide. The way that a batter takes his stance affects the size of his individual strike zone. Technically, it would seem that the strike zone, when you take into account variations in a batter's stance, should be the same for everyone. But it is not.

Many players forget to keep in mind that each has a personal strike zone geared exclusively to his stance, the kind of swing he has and the type of pitches he tends to hit. He should not swing at any pitch not in that personal strike zone, unless special circumstances dictate that he do so—such as a hit and run or a two-strike count. Ted Williams, whom many consider the best hitter ever to play the game, developed a color-coded "personal strike zone," which he used to guide his decision of whether or not to swing. In his book *The Science of Hitting* (Simon and Schuster; New York, 1982), Williams filled a strike zone with circles to represent balls and then colored the balls to represent the ones that he could hit well (using one color for the "hot" zone) and the ones that he couldn't hit well at all (using another color for the "cold" zone). Hitters should follow Williams' lead and create their own home zone, a color-coded strike zone for use at home. They can do this by measuring the distance between their knees and the midpoint of the area between the tops of their shoulders and their waist (see example shown in figure 3.1). They should then draw a rectangle of that height and 17 inches wide. Players can hang this rectangle on their bedroom or garage wall and visualize their home zone, making it easier for them to identify hot and cold opportunities when out on the field. Players who practice seeing their personal zones are better prepared—visually and mentally—for a trip to the plate.

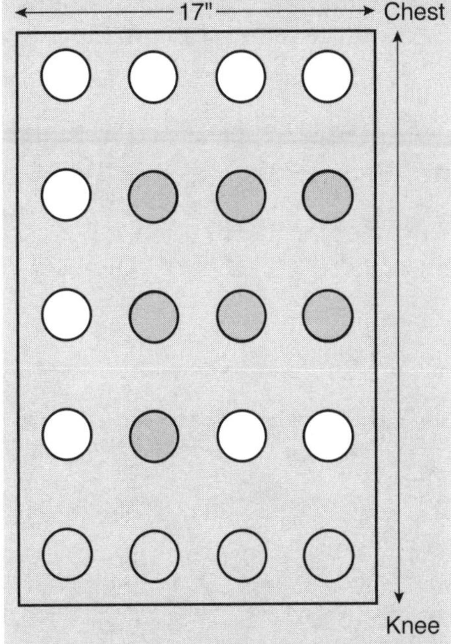

Figure 3.1 Home strike zone.

REPEATABLE PRESWING ROUTINE

Have you ever watched Derek Jeter when he steps into the batter's box? If you have, you might notice that he goes through a routine, or ritual, every time he gets ready to hit. This routine helps him visualize what he is going to do before he hits the ball and prepares his body for the actual swing. All baseball players need to develop a preswing routine which will help them get and keep their bodies relaxed and balanced in preparation for the upcoming pitch. All professional players go through the same phases and motions each time they step into the batter's box and before every pitch to get their bodies to feel the same balance while they mentally go through a preswing checklist. A player may go through a thought process while rocking forward and backward on his feet. A common preswing mental checklist might be "weight on balls of feet, knees bent, lean forward, loose and relaxed" and so on.

The good news is that a player's routine doesn't have to be long; it just has to be the same each time he steps into the box. Remember, repeatable actions lead to repeatable results. A routine might look something like this:

1. Place the right foot in the batter's box.
2. Look at the pitcher while keeping the bat on the shoulder.
3. Place the left foot in the batter's box.
4. Extend the arms away from the body with the bat and touch the far corner of home plate.

(continued)

5. Shift the weight from the back foot to the front foot and vice versa several times while taking several slow, controlled practice swings.
6. Stare at the pitcher all the time when doing this routine.

Every player, however, will have a somewhat different routine. The important thing for you to do is to remind players not to stand still in the batter's box between pitches. The more still they stand, the more tense they become. Swings need to be tension free, so you should promote movements, like swinging the bat forward and backward like a pendulum, that keep the body in motion.

Figure 3.2 Batter in good contact position.

GOOD CONTACT POSITION

It has been said that if a person doesn't know where he's going, he won't have the faintest idea how to get there. The same is true of hitters. Unless they have a firm concept in their heads of what their swing should look like when they make contact with the ball, they won't have any way of understanding how they should get there. Figure 3.2 shows a batter in what most would consider good contact position. With this positioning in mind, note the following:

- The bat is making contact with the ball out in front of the body.
- The head is centered, and the eyes are on the path of the ball.
- The front leg is straight.
- The hands are in the classic bottom-palm-down, top-palm-up position.
- The hips have rotated toward the pitch.
- The back foot has rotated and the back knee has been driven toward the front knee.

COMFORTABLE BATTING STANCE

To achieve perfect contact position, hitters must assume a comfortable stance with a strong base, as shown in figure 3.3. This stance allows them to see a pitch well and swing comfortably.

Although batting stances will vary, the successful batter will observe certain absolutes. Following are the key checkpoints that you should watch to be certain that hitters have a strong base:

Position in the Batter's Box

A common misconception of amateur players is that they have to stand deep in the batter's box to be effective. This positioning might help batters when facing pitchers who are throwing 90 miles per hour, but amateur hitters have no need to take this position routinely because few high school pitchers can throw that fast. Instead, to be ready to hit all pitches, hitters should assume a stance with the front foot (the one closest to the pitcher) even with the front of home plate. They should also stand somewhat away from the plate so that their hands are not in the strike zone.

Figure 3.3 Batter assuming a comfortable batting stance with a strong base.

Feet

The hitter should place the feet a little more than shoulder-width apart to provide a wide base from which he can feel balanced. The toes should be facing the plate, and the weight should be on the front half of the foot.

Ankles

The ankles should be flexible. Batters should be able to roll to either side with their ankles. If they can do this, they can be certain that their knees will be flexible and not locked in place.

Knees

The knees should be slightly bent. Overbending can lead to misdistribution of weight, which can inhibit a quick hip turn or make the batter "sit down," forcing the weight away from the plate. The hitter should also bend the knees so that they are positioned inside the feet.

Waist

The batter should bend forward slightly at the waist. Without bend in the waist, the hitter will have a stiff upper body and a less fluid swing.

Shoulders

The shoulders should be level and in line with the hips and knees. Leaving the shoulders on an angle, slanted either way, promotes either an uppercutting or a chopping motion in the swing. The batter should avoid both extremes of swinging.

(continued)

Hands and Arms

The hitter should hold the bat in the fingers and not grip it too tightly. Many high school players hold the bat too far back in their hands when they grip it. A good way to help players understand this is to stress that they are stronger with the bat in their fingers than they are with the bat in the palms of their hands. You can illustrate this by having players put the index finger of the throwing hand inside the palm of the other hand as shown in figure 3.4*a* and have them close the hand around the finger tightly. While gripping the throwing-hand finger as tightly as they can with the off hand, have them try to pull the finger out of the palm. They should be able to accomplish this easily. Next, have players put the throwing-hand index finger inside the fingers of the other hand as shown in figure 3.4*b* and repeat the same steps, tightening the off fingers around the throwing-hand finger and pulling. If they have held tightly and pulled as hard as they can, they will not be able to pull their finger out. This demonstration should prove that a grip is stronger in the fingers than it is in the palms.

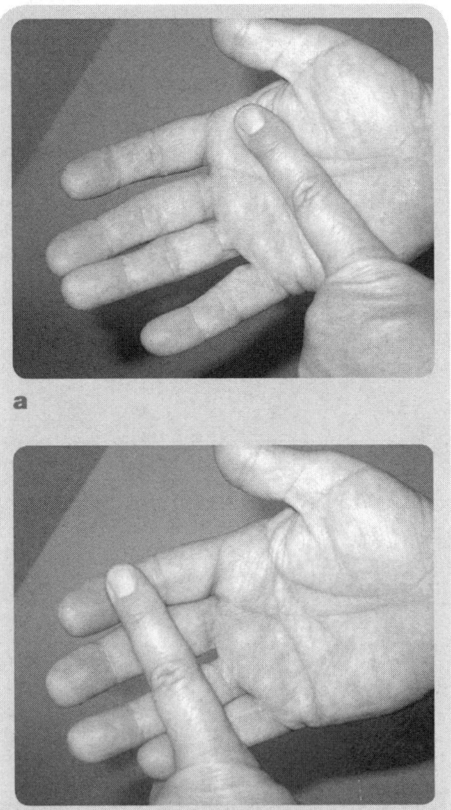

a

b

Figure 3.4 Gripping with *(a)* the palm and *(b)* the fingers.

A good way to get the arms in the correct position is to put the bat in the hands in the center of the body, lay the barrel of the bat on the back shoulder and then slowly move the bat off the shoulder and bring the hands horizontally back toward the back foot about 3 to 4 inches and away from the body about the same distance. When done in this manner, the arms and hands should be about letter high at the top of the strike zone and in a good launching position for a swing, as shown in figure 3.5.

Figure 3.5 Proper arm and hand positioning for the batter.

Head

The hitter's head should be turned toward the pitcher with the eyes level. The chin can even rest slightly on the front shoulder as a reminder to keep the head forward. The ball is easier to see when the eyes are level. If players don't understand the reason for this, ask them if they read books, watch TV or drive their cars with their heads tilted. They quickly find the answer.

At a Glance

The following parts of the text offer additional information on preparing to hit.

Bat Angle

The bat should be held at a 45-degree angle to the ground to allow for an easy swing. Holding the bat too straight up and down or slanted over the rear shoulder takes the bat away from the swing plane that the bat will follow when the batter decides to swing. The batter who holds the bat in either of those positions will have to make additional adjustments to get the bat into the right track. Some variation of this angle will occur in individual hitters, but you should make certain the variation is not too extreme. The more the batting stance varies from the norm, the better the player will have to be!

Overall Balance

When a hitter observes the previous points, the weight should be evenly distributed over the center of the body horizontally and vertically.

Common Errors

You may run into several common errors when teaching your athletes how to prepare to hit.

Error	Error correction
The player grips the bat tightly.	The player should keep the bat in the fingers, not in the palms.
The player uses a rigid stance.	To relax and stay balanced, the player should rock from the front foot to the back foot before the pitcher begins his motion. After the pitcher begins the motion, the player assumes a balanced stance. Players should go through the stance absolutes in their heads each time they step into the batter's box.
The player's knees are outside the feet.	This generally happens when the feet are not pointed forward. The feet must be facing the plate.

Swing and Follow-Through

KEY POINTS

The most important components of the swing are

- load position,
- swing and contact position,
- follow-through and
- timing and pitch selection.

After a batter has achieved a balanced, comfortable stance, the next step in the hitting process is awaiting the pitch and reacting to it by either not swinging, known as taking the pitch, or swinging at it. To examine the skill of hitting more closely, you need to pay close attention to some of the key points, or phases, of the swing, which in turn will help direct your attention to teaching the most important aspects of the skill. Keep in mind, too, that each player is unique and that a properly executed swing may look somewhat different for each person. When teaching the proper swing, keep in mind that the more extreme the swing, the better the hitter will have to be to make it successful.

Figure 3.6 Proper load positioning.

LOAD POSITION

Once the pitcher begins his motion to throw the ball, the hitter must react accordingly. This reaction, called loading, begins with a shifting of the weight toward the rear side of the body and a slight movement of the hands in the same direction, as shown in figure 3.6.

An old axiom in baseball was that "when the pitcher shows you his back, you show him yours." This meant that as soon as the pitcher reached his balance position (with the back turned to the hitter), the hitter began his loading technique by turning his back away. Although this adage may oversimplify the technique, it does imply the sense of the timing necessary for a good swing. John Malee, one of the up-and-coming hitting instructors in baseball, teaches that the load should be slow, easy and early. The hitter should begin the loading process early in the pitcher's motion. The load should be done slowly, with no herky-jerky, quick motions, and it should be easy, or tension free. You should also emphasize that the swing is a rotational movement, with the hips in the center, not a pendulum-like motion. The hips rotate slightly around a center of gravity; they do not slide backward and forward over it. The hips, however, are only one of several components of the loading action. Following are the key components of the load position:

Hands and Shoulders

The hitter's shoulders should turn slightly away from the pitcher as the hands move slightly back. The hands should move only slightly up or down from this initial position because any substantial movement can cause problems in the swing that lead to an uppercut or a chopping swing. The hands should also maintain their position at the top of the strike zone (for more information on the strike zone, refer to "Preparing to Hit" beginning on page 20) because a pitch in that area would be the highest pitch that a batter would want to swing at.

Front Foot

As the hitter's hands and shoulders move away from the pitcher, the front, or stride foot, should simultaneously reach slightly toward the pitcher. The term *reach* is preferable to *stride* because stride implies taking a step, which high school players often misinterpret to mean that they must lunge with a big step toward the pitcher. In contrast, the reach is a small, easy movement, more of a slide or stretch than a lift-and-place movement. This movement coils the body and prepares it to unleash the maximum amount of energy in the swing as the body unwinds.

Head

During the loading motion, the hitter's head should not move but should remain focused on the pitcher's release point.

SWING AND CONTACT POSITION

After the batter is in the load position, the body is ready to swing. The body is still balanced, and the head is focused on the pitch. Now, the batter must make the decision to swing or not to swing. If he makes the decision to swing, the body uncoils and launches the hands toward the ball. The first movement of uncoiling is crucial.

People disagree about what movement triggers the swing—some insist that it is the hands; some say it is the back knee. Whatever the case, both occur within milliseconds in slow-motion analysis of hitters. More important, the body senses that it is time to swing and begins a rotational motion toward the pitcher as follows:

1. The bottom hand moves the knob of the bat toward the ball, or moves toward a spot between the ball and the body, in a movement called staying inside the ball (see figure 3.7). This method is a much quicker

Figure 3.7 Hitter staying inside the ball.

(continued)

way of getting the bat to the ball than trying to bring the barrel to the ball, an approach known as casting the bat. When the hands move first, the elbows stay bent, allowing the arms to move quickly to the ball. When the barrel moves first, the elbows lock and slow down the arms. The hitter should aim for a short-to-long swing—that is, a swing that employs a quick movement of the knob directly to the ball with extension of the arms on contact and follow-through.

2. The hitter's back knee begins to move toward the front knee, starting the weight shift to the front foot.
3. The hips begin to uncoil when the back knee moves, thus starting the rotation of the swing.
4. The front leg locks to form a strong front side for the hips to rotate against.

If the hitter's judgment is correct about the pitch, these movements bring the body in good contact position as discussed in "Good Contact Position" on page 22. The front foot will be slightly closed; the front knee will be straight; the back knee will be close to the front knee; the back thigh will be straight, forming the classic L position with the back side; and the heel of the back foot, sometimes even the entire back foot, will be off the ground (see figure 3.2 on page 22).

On contact, the hitter must be sure that the hands have not rolled over until well after the bat has made contact with the ball. This means that the palm of the bottom hand on the bat is facing the ground while the palm of the top hand on the bat is facing the sky. This relationship is extremely important because if the top-hand wrist rolls over too soon, it will pull the bat away from good contact position. If a batter rolls over his wrists too early in the contact position, he will have a tendency to pull the ball, or hit it to his dominant field (more information on pulling appears in "Outfield Basics" beginning on page 114). Because of the circular action created by the swing, the dominant field for a right-hander is left field; for a left-hander it is right field. See figure 3.8, *a* and *b*, for incorrect and correct examples of a batter's hand position on contact.

a b

Figure 3.8 Batter's hand position on contact: *(a)* incorrect and *(b)* correct.

You should keep in mind that if the batter performs the swing correctly, he will hit the ball with the sweet spot of the bat. The sweet spot is the area of the bat where the contact between the ball and the bat results in the best hit. On a wood bat this area is about 3 inches long and is located 6 inches from the end of the barrel, opposite the part of the bat where the trademark is. The sweet spot on aluminum bats is much larger, between 7 and 9 inches long. When players are working on hitting, they should focus on contacting the ball with the sweet spot of the bat. One way that you can make players conscious of this is to put white athletic tape around the bat to coincide with the length of the sweet spot. Then, when players hit the ball in drills they will have a visual reminder about what part of the bat to use to hit the ball. Usually, though, especially in cold weather, a player's hands will let him know if he made contact on the sweet spot or not!

FOLLOW-THROUGH

After contact occurs, the hands continue slightly toward the ball, which allows the arms to straighten and extend before the wrists begin to roll over. The arms then continue into a position above the front shoulder and on the opposite side of the body from where they started, and the rear shoulder rotates until it is under the chin (see figure 3.9). At this stage of the swing, some players release the top hand from the bat. This technique is acceptable providing that they do not remove the hand before making contact with the ball. This motion finishes the "short to long" swing movement mentioned in the preceding section. If the hands, not the barrel, begin the swing, then the arms will naturally extend past and around the head in the follow-through. Another way of looking at this "short to long" movement is to be short (hands inside) *to* the ball and long (extend the arms after contact) *through* the ball. If, however, the batter has started his swing with the barrel of the bat, then he will not be able to extend through the ball and the hands will follow through very close to the body and below the head. This is what is described as a long to short swing.

Figure 3.9 Proper follow-through.

Sometimes at this stage of the swing, players will release their top hand from the bat. This is acceptable providing that they do not remove the hand before making contact with the ball. Hall of Famer George Brett perfected this technique of allowing his top hand to release after contact and won several American League batting crowns. He felt that this method enabled him to lengthen his swing even more, hit through the ball past the point of contact and drive the ball harder. Coaches should take care to make certain their hitters are not releasing the top hand too soon.

(continued)

Figure 3.10 Pitcher's arm reaching a spot above the shoulder at the release.

Also, the weight continues to shift toward the front side at this stage of the swing. The batter's rear foot should be up on its toes and the rear leg should be in the classic L position. Some hitters may shift their weight so dramatically that the rear foot will lose contact with the ground momentarily.

TIMING AND PITCH SELECTION

Swinging at pitches requires good timing of body movements in relation to the pitch. Even if a hitter possesses a flawless swing, he will not contact the ball if his timing is off. Consider one of the rules of pitching: If hitting is timing, the key to good pitching is *destroying* timing. With this in mind, remember that the coiling motion should begin early in the pitcher's motion—how early depends on how fast the pitcher throws. The coiling motion should consist of slow movements—deliberate, rhythmic movements that do not destroy timing—and it should be as free of tension as possible. A general rule for hitters is to begin loading or coiling when the pitcher's arm reaches a spot above the shoulder before the release of the ball (see figure 3.10). When using this spot as a starting point, most batters reach the contact point when the ball arrives.

Hitters should modify their load and swing movements according to the type of pitcher they are facing. The quicker the pitcher, the sooner in the delivery the hitter should begin the loading motion. Conversely, the slower the motion, the later the loading begins.

Additionally, hitters must also be judicious in selecting pitches to hit. In a typical six- or seven-pitch at bat, most pitchers throw only two or three pitches where they intend them to go, and they will likely make at least one mistake pitch. Of course, as the level of play improves—from freshman ball to varsity, for example—the number of pitches that the pitcher "locates" becomes higher.

At a Glance

The following parts of the text offer additional information on how to swing.

Preparing to Hit	p. 20
Hit and Run	p. 170
Situational Hitting	p. 172

Common Errors

You may run into several common errors when teaching your athletes how to swing.

Error	Error correction
The player throws the barrel of the bat at the ball (casting).	The swing must start with the lower hand and the knob of the bat, not the barrel.
The player wraps the bat too far behind the head in the loading position.	To avoid pushing the bat back too far, the player should concentrate on moving the bat back with the top hand instead of the bottom hand.
The player overrotates or turns his shoulders too much in the loading position.	With the player in his stance, place the bat in the crook of the player's arms and in front of his body (parallel to the player's shoulders). Ask the player to begin to coil, using the bat as a pointer. If the player is right-handed, the bat should not point any farther than where the second baseman would be play in the field. If the player is left-handed, use the shortstop as a guide.
The player moves his head back and forth during the swing.	This usually occurs because the body is moving as a pendulum instead of rotating. The player should focus on the idea that the body moves around the head, not the other way around.
The player moves his head forward over the front leg during the swing.	This may occur because the player is overstriding. Emphasize to the player that he should reach slightly toward the pitcher, not step.
The player overstrides.	The player should step on the big toe of the front foot in a reaching motion. If the player takes too big a step, he will not be able to land on the front part of the foot.
The player generates little power even though the swing looks good at contact position.	If the player is a top-hand releaser, he may be taking his top hand off the bat too soon. Emphasize keeping both hands on the bat through the hitting zone as long as possible. Players should be able to extend their arms without taking the top hand off the bat.
The player pulls the ball foul or swings late.	The player's timing is off. Have the player start his swing earlier or later depending on the results or have him slow down his loading motion.
The player's swing is slow and deliberate.	Make certain that the player is not gripping the bat too tightly. The grip should be in the fingers and relaxed. Tightening the grip on the bat makes the wrists less flexible and stiffens the forearm muscles. These conditions contribute to slow bat speed.
The player's back foot remains flat on the ground at contact position.	The player is using only his arms for the swing and is not rotating the hips.
The player hits the ball in the air.	The player is dropping his hands instead of moving them back in the loading position. Have the player focus on keeping the hands at the top of the strike zone and moving them backward slightly. Any other motion for this type of hitter promotes dropping the hands and causes a loop in the swing, which forces the player to uppercut the ball.

Bunting Basics

KEY POINTS

The most important components of bunting are

- body position,
- hand position,
- deadening and directing the ball,
- bunting strikes and
- deciding when to bunt.

In the early eras of baseball, the home run was not held in the esteem that it is today. Players were encouraged to bunt, steal, and hit and run—techniques considered to require more skill than hitting a ball 400 feet. Often called a forgotten art today, bunting is still an important technical skill in baseball, especially in high school baseball. Every well-coached team employs it frequently. Bunting can be used not only to advance base runners but also to surprise an opponent or to get runners on base against an extremely tough pitcher. Proper instruction in bunting is important because this skill, unlike regular batting, should be executed with little individual deviation in technique.

BODY POSITION

When bunting, players must get their bodies into a position that will allow them both to see the ball well and to place it where they want to on the field. When called on to bunt, players can assume two body positions, or stances:

Figure 3.11 Batter in square-around bunting position.

Square Around

If a bunt is called for, after receiving the sign from the coach, the batter should assume his normal position in the batter's box. After the pitcher has taken the sign from the catcher and comes to a ready position on the rubber, the batter should immediately shift into the bunting position. The batter moves his front foot back in the batter's box and moves his rear foot forward, thereby squaring his feet and legs to the pitcher as shown in figure 3.11. If the batter moves the front foot first, he may step on or outside the batter's box line. Any successful bunt hit from this position would be negated because according to the rules, a batter who hits the ball while a foot is out of the box is out and base runners have to return to the base occupied before the pitch. The batter should move the left foot first to avoid this violation.

After the feet are set, the batter bends both knees and bends forward at the waist, leaning slightly toward the plate and putting most of his weight on the foot closer to the plate. The bat should remain about letter high in the batter's stance so that the batter can easily move it downward (this will be discussed in more detail shortly). The head shifts to a point close to the bat so that the batter can follow the path of the ball better.

Pivot

As in the square-around position discussed earlier, the batter first assumes his stance, but when the pitcher begins his delivery, the batter pivots his body into bunting position without moving his feet. First, the batter pivots on the balls of both feet so that the feet point directly to the pitcher. As he does this, he bends both knees forward in the same direction and leans forward at the waist so that about 80 percent of his weight is on his front foot, as shown in figure 3.12. The hitter also lowers his head to a position that enables him to track the ball to the plate. From the waist up, the body is in the same position in both the square-around method and the pivot method of bunting.

Figure 3.12 Batter in pivot bunting position.

Whichever method is used—the square around or the pivot—when the bunt sign is given, the player should move up slightly in the batter's box. To avoid revealing his intentions, the batter should not make this move too obvious, but being closer to the pitcher will give him a better chance of keeping the bunt in fair territory.

HAND POSITION

Getting the body into a good position to bunt is important, but even more essential is positioning the hands and arms correctly. If the bat is not at the correct angle or the hands do not function properly, the bunt won't do its intended job of advancing the runner.

(continued)

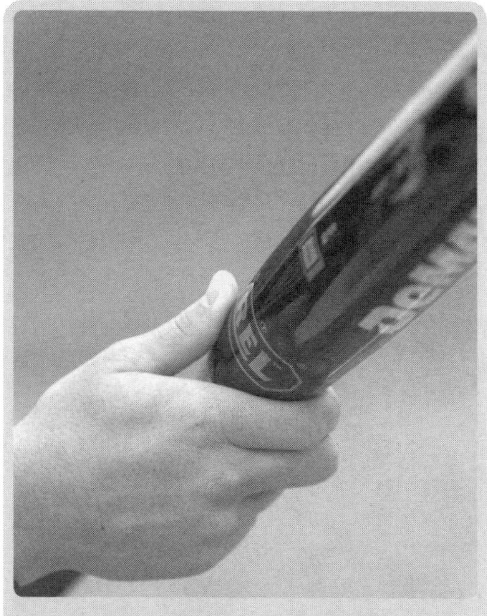

Figure 3.13 Hand position on the bat for the square-around and pivot bunts.

When preparing to bunt in both the square-around method and the pivot method, the batter must hold the bat the same way. As the feet are moving into position in both methods, the batter's top hand should slide up the bat so that it is near the brand trademark on wooden bats or, on aluminum bats, near the area where the bat begins to widen. The hand should pinch the bat loosely with the thumb on the top and the fingers on the bottom (see figure 3.13). Care should be taken to keep the fingers away from the side of the bat that will make contact with the ball. Players should bend the fingers at the first knuckle and place the fingernails against the bat rather than grab it as they would a can of soda pop in which they would expose the nails. The bottom hand can remain in the same position as it does in the regular batting stance, but the batter must not grip the bat so tightly that he constricts his muscles, which would make it harder for him to adjust to the location of the pitch.

For the square-around and pivot bunts, the batter should hold the bat at a 45-degree angle to the ground with the barrel at the top of the strike zone and the lower hand approximately 1 foot below (see figure 3.14). He should also hold the bat away from the body so that the sweet spot of the bat is in the strike zone area, extended away from the body and in front of the plate.

If the batter holds the bat over the top of the plate, he will create a bat angle that minimizes the chances for a successful bunt. This manner of holding the bat serves as a visual reminder to the batter that he should not bunt any pitch that is higher than the top of the barrel. Doing so would mean the bat is moving upwards, increasing the likelihood of the batter hitting the ball in the air. Also, any pitch above a barrel held at the top of the strike zone would be a ball. Batters, when preparing to bunt, should only go for strikes.

Figure 3.14 Bat position for square-around and pivot bunts.

DEADENING AND DIRECTING THE BALL

In a properly executed bunt, the batter moves the bat slightly backward toward the catcher at the point of contact. This technique deadens the ball off the bat so that it will not travel as far into the field as it would if the batter swung the bat at the ball. In a sense, the bunter tries to catch the ball with the bat, much as a fielder would. If a fielder were to stab at a ball without first giving a little with the glove hand, he wouldn't catch many balls. The ball would bounce off the glove onto the ground. Likewise, if the bunter doesn't give with the top hand as the ball contacts the bat, the bunt will be hit too hard and it will reach the defense sooner, lessening the chance for a successful sacrifice.

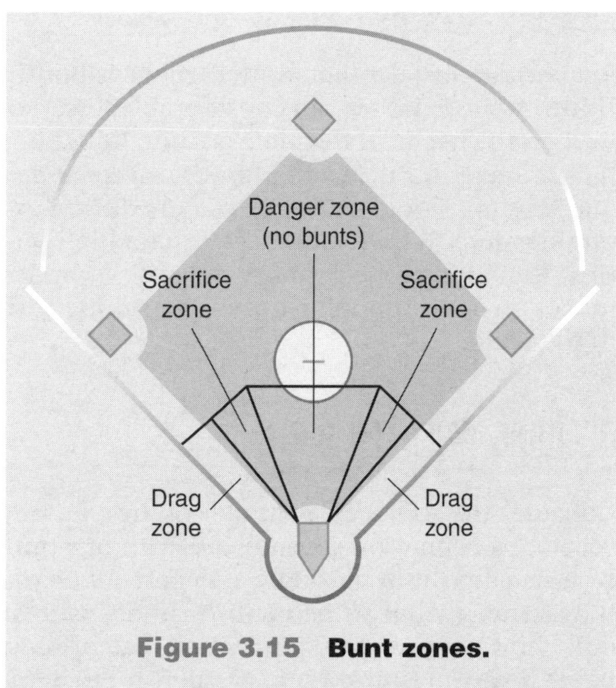

Figure 3.15 Bunt zones.

The deadening effect, however, is only one part of effective bunting. The other is being able to direct the ball away from oncoming defenders into successful bunt zones on the field (see figure 3.15). The bottom hand determines the direction of the bunt. If the bottom hand never moves the bat left or right, most bunts would travel directly toward the pitcher, who would then be able to make an easy force play, a result that would definitely not be desirable.

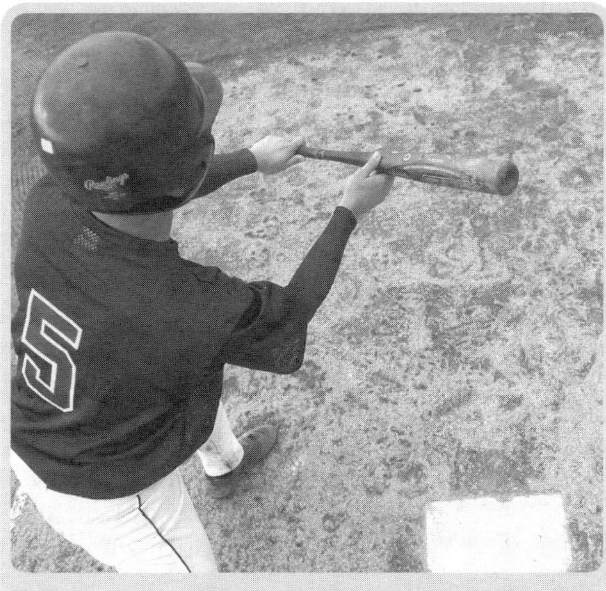
Figure 3.16 Bat positioning when bunting down the first-base line.

The bunter applies this directional force simply by moving the bottom hand in much the same way that a person would steer a motorboat by moving the handle of the engine. If the batter needs to bunt the ball down the first-base line (assuming that he is right-handed), he extends his left arm forward so that the hitting area of the bat is aimed toward the first-base side of the field, as shown in figure 3.16. A left-handed batter would pull his right hand closer to his body to accomplish the same thing. When contact occurs, the angle of the bat will direct the ball toward first base. If the bunter needs to hit toward third base, he would pull the left hand closer to the

(continued)

body (if right-handed), again changing the angle of the bat. Note that the bunter does not move the top hand much while steering with the bottom hand.

By practicing and perfecting these techniques, batters can put the ball onto the parts of the field that are hardest to cover defensively, as shown in the diagram of bunt zones in figure 3.15, thus greatly increasing the chances of advancing a runner.

BUNTING STRIKES

A common mistake that bunters make is bunting balls thrown outside the strike zone. Bunting poor pitches can considerably lessen the chances of a successful bunt. A pitch well off the inside of the plate is difficult to bunt because of the location of the bunter's hands and bat. Pitches high in the strike zone would be above the bunter's top hand, and bunters would find it extremely difficult to get the bat on the top half of the ball on this pitch. When bunters go after a high pitch they usually hit foul pop-ups or foul tips. Remember, the primary purpose of bunting is to advance runners. If the batter makes an out by popping up, runners don't advance and meaningless outs are charged to the team.

DECIDING WHEN TO BUNT

Consider the statistics: A runner on first base with no outs has a 43 percent chance of scoring; a runner on second base with one out, say one who has been advanced there by a sacrifice bunt, has only a 45 percent chance of scoring. So the sacrifice increases the chance by only 2 percent! A runner who successfully steals second base with no outs, however, has a 60 percent chance of scoring a run—decidedly better odds. This being noted, at times you may still want to bunt to advance the runner to the next base. When a game is tied in the late innings and good hitters are coming to the plate, you should probably bunt the runner to second to give your hitters a shot at driving the runner in. Another good time to bunt would be to squeeze a runner home from third with a weak hitter up in a must-score situation. These are just two of the many situations in which you might want to employ the bunt as opposed to the steal. A third option is to attempt a drag bunt instead of a sacrifice bunt to give the batter a better chance of being safe at first base.

You should also teach players to look for the bunt sign in late innings of close, low-scoring games because the tighter the game, the more pressure the defense feels. An anxious defender can mishandle a bunt in such situations.

The decision to bunt depends wholly on the team's overall philosophy about advancing runners. The coach should thoroughly discuss this philosophy with players before the season begins so that they can sense the importance of bunting and buy into that way of thinking right away.

At a Glance

The following parts of the text offer additional information on the basics of bunting.

Common Errors

You may run into several common errors when teaching your athletes the basics of bunting.

Error	Error correction
The player bunts the ball foul down the first-base or third-base line.	The player should hold the bat out in front of the plate so that the ball will stay in fair territory.
The player bunts foul tips or foul pop-ups.	The player is not trying to contact the top half of the ball or is holding his bat too low in the strike zone. Make sure that the player holds the bat at the top of the zone and never raises it during the bunting process.
The player bunts right back toward the pitcher's mound.	The player should use his lower hand as a rudder to steer the ball away from the pitcher.
The player bunts too hard.	The player probably isn't deadening the bat at the point of contact and may be swinging the top part of the bat at the ball. Emphasize "catching" the ball with the bat.

Sacrifice Bunting

KEY POINTS

The most important components of the sacrifice bunt are

- the concept of sacrifice,
- placing the bunt and
- suicide squeeze or safety squeeze.

The general mechanics of bunting were discussed previously and, as we learned, one reason for bunting is to advance runners. The intent of sacrifice bunting is to advance a base runner while allowing the batter to be thrown out at first base.

Successful execution of a sacrifice bunt requires more than correct mechanics. A mind-set and some basic field knowledge are also necessary. The batter must be willing to give up a chance to get a hit for the sake of advancing a teammate and perhaps helping his team win a game.

THE CONCEPT OF SACRIFICE

You shouldn't send a batter to the plate to bunt if the batter doesn't understand the meaning of sacrifice. The most important result of a sacrifice bunt is to advance a base runner to the next base. What happens to the bunter—whether he is safe or out—is of no consequence.

A player called on to hit a sacrifice bunt must understand that he is giving himself up for the good of the team. Bunters must stay in the batter's box until the bunted ball is on the ground. Bunters often begin to run before they have completed the bunt, with the result that the ball either goes foul or is hit to an area of the field where fielders can easily make the play and force the lead runner. The defense will be charging the plate after the batter squares to bunt to get a jump on the ball and make a good throw. For that reason, the hitter must hold his ground and bunt the ball to an area of the field that the defense has not covered.

PLACING THE BUNT

Look again at figure 3.15 on page 35 in "Bunting Basics." The noted areas are the ideal areas in which to bunt the ball to advance a runner. If you want to advance a runner on second base to third base, the ideal place to bunt would be to the shaded area on the third-base side of the field. Why? In most cases, the first baseman will be charging, so bunting the ball on the third-base side will make it harder for the first baseman to field and throw out the runner at third. Or, if the pitcher is very quick off the mound, especially if he is a left-hander, the batter should bunt the ball softly on the first-base side. If you are attempting to advance a runner from first to second base, the best place to bunt the ball would be to the area on the first-base side because the third baseman will be charging and attempting to make the play. By angling the bat, as explained in "Bunting Basics," beginning on page 32, the batter can place the bunt where it is most likely to advance the runner.

SUICIDE SQUEEZE OR SAFETY SQUEEZE

When a runner is on third base, the coach may call a bunt as a way to advance the runner to the plate and score a run. The team should attempt this play only with less than two outs. Most often, teams use the squeeze with one out. The bunter has two options in this situation:

Suicide Squeeze

In the suicide squeeze, the bunter must make contact with the ball no matter where it is pitched. Because the runner on third base will be running toward home as soon as the pitcher has committed to throw the pitch, the batter must attempt to hit any thrown ball, even those that are not strikes. If the batter does not bunt the ball or make contact, the runner will be dashing directly toward the catcher, who will have received the pitch and will be able to make an easy tag. The bunter must protect the runner from third at all costs. An exception would be on a pitch so high or wide that the catcher would be unable to catch it and still make a play on the approaching base runner.

Defenses are prepared to react to this bunting situation. If the defense throws a pitchout—a ball thrown deliberately out of the strike zone to give the catcher the opportunity to make a play on the runner—the bunter must step over the plate and deliberately leave the batter's box to hit the ball. Usually on a suicide squeeze the runner will be only a few feet from the plate when the pitched ball reaches the batter and will not be able to stop and retreat to third if the ball is missed. The catcher will easily tag him out. When the bunter steps over or on top of the plate, he will be called out, but the runner, who is in scoring position on third base, will not be out and will be allowed to return to third.

At a Glance

The following parts of the text offer additional information on sacrifice bunting.

Safety Squeeze

The safety squeeze is a less dangerous method of advancing the runner because the base runner does not advance to the plate until the batter bunts the ball on the ground.

When using the safety squeeze, the bunter should delay getting into bunt position to retain the element of surprise. Again, as with any sacrifice, the hitter must stay in the batter's box until the ball is on the ground to ensure success. The standard rules of bunting remain in place, including bunting only strikes. In the safety squeeze, unlike the suicide squeeze, the batter need not hit every pitched ball. The best place for a batter to bunt the ball is down the third-base line and away from the pitcher. If the bunt is successful, the runner will have a footrace with the third baseman and will usually win.

Common Errors

You may run into several common errors when teaching your athletes about sacrifice bunting.

Error	Error correction
The player begins to run before the ball is on the ground.	Advancing the runner is the most important aspect of a sacrifice bunt. The bunter may run before the ball is on the ground because he is more concerned about beating the throw to first base than advancing the runner.
On a suicide squeeze, the player backs away from inside pitches.	The player usually backs away because he is afraid of being hit with the ball. Teach players the technique of turning their backs to the pitch while ducking their heads and letting the pitch hit them in the big muscles of the back.

Drag Bunting

KEY POINTS

The most important components of drag bunting are

- batter intention and
- body movement.

Everyone loves the element of surprise. Who can deny the electricity that a great surprise play sends through the body? The drag bunt is a way to shock your opponent and excite your offense at the same time.

The basic philosophical difference between the drag bunt and the sacrifice bunt is that the former is used to get on base whereas the latter is used to advance a lead runner while giving up an out. The technique employed in the two bunts is also different. In the sacrifice bunt the batter shows the bunt early by getting into bunting position before the pitch is delivered, but the drag bunter tries to disguise the fact that he is bunting until it is too late for the defense to react. The batter waits until the pitcher's front foot hits the ground before he moves into bunt position, allowing him to keep the defense off guard and gain the edge he needs to beat the ball to first base.

Although a drag bunter's main goal is to get a base hit and perhaps start a rally, the technique varies from one side of the plate to the other.

BATTER INTENTION

A batter who intends to use the drag bunt should be careful not to give away his intentions beforehand. He must not pay undue attention to the third baseman, for example, by looking at him too much. Good third basemen watch hitters for any sign that seems out of the ordinary. More than one look might be considered unusual, for example, and a good third baseman might suspect a bunt and play a little closer to the plate. Batters should pay attention to the depth of infielders throughout a game, not just when they come to bat. If they notice that the corner infielders are playing deep and disregarding the bunt early in the game, they should file that information away and use it when they have a chance for a drag bunt. Knowing this information beforehand is what separates good baseball players from average ones.

BODY MOVEMENT

A left-handed batter has a distinct advantage over a right-handed batter when drag bunting because he is closer to first base. He is 3 feet closer based on his starting position in the batter's box, and because the drag bunt motion moves the body in the direction of first, by the time he bunts the ball, he is 6 to 7 feet closer to first base.

Right-handed batters, although they are farther from first base than left-handed hitters are, can achieve an edge by doing the following:

1. As the pitcher's front foot hits the ground, a right-handed batter should drop his right foot straight back behind him, toward the normal location of the on-deck circle. As he drops the foot back, the right hand should be sliding up the bat into bunting position (see figure 3.17*a*).
2. As the hand is sliding up the bat, the bat should be moved into bunting position out in front of the plate, letter high in the strike zone (see figure 3.17*b*). The bunter should be careful here not to swing the bat forward from the batting stance into bunting position because doing so could cause the ball to be hit too solidly.

a

b

c

Figure 3.17 Drag bunt for right-handed batter.

(continued)

Instead, he should move the bat into bunting position much in the manner that a person swings a hammer—in a downward motion.

3. The bat should be well out in front of the plate and usually angled toward the third-base line (see figure 3.17*c*). A bunt placed close to the third-base foul line is extremely difficult for a third baseman to play successfully.

As the pitcher's front foot hits the ground, a left-handed batter can achieve his edge by doing the following:

1. The left-handed batter should take a step directly at the pitcher with his left foot. As the batter is stepping forward with his left foot, the left hand should be moving up the bat into bunting position (see figure 3.18*a*).
2. When making contact with the ball, the player should have all his weight on his left leg. In most cases the right foot will be off the ground and ready to step toward first base as soon as the ball is hit (see figure 3.18*b*).
3. When the ball is hit, preferably down the third-base line, the batter should make his first step toward first base with the right foot (see figure 3.18*c*).

Like the right-handed batter, the left-handed batter has the option of bunting the ball to his pull side, down the first-base foul line or aiming it down the third-base line. If

a b

(continued)

Figure 3.18 Drag bunt for left-handed batter.

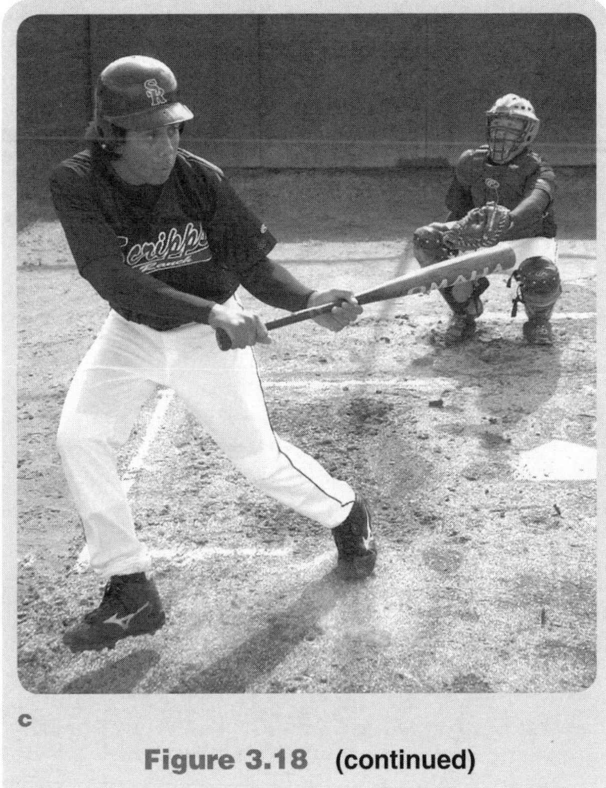

c

Figure 3.18 (continued)

At a Glance

The following parts of the text offer additional information on drag bunting.

the pitcher is right-handed, his follow-through will carry him toward the first-base foul line, so the left-handed batter would want to direct the ball toward third base, away from where the pitcher would be moving. If fielders suspect a bunt and are charging on the pitch, the batter who sees them moving can try to push the ball past one of them, usually the pitcher. Once the ball is past the pitcher, none of the other fielders will be close enough to make a play and the batter will be safe at first.

Common Errors

You may run into several common errors when teaching your athletes how to drag bunt.

Error	Error correction
The player bunts right back to the pitcher.	The player is not getting the bat out in front of the plate far enough. He should go back to the idea of using the bottom hand like a rudder on a boat to steer the ball.
The player fouls off too many bunt attempts.	The player may be moving his bat up and hitting the bottom part of the ball. Emphasize keeping the bat at the top of the strike zone and lowering it to the ball. Another reason for bunting foul is that the player may be letting the barrel of the bat drop below his hands on the drag bunt attempt. Remind players to keep the barrel above the hands.

Running Basics

KEY POINTS

The most important components of running are

- leg and arm movement,
- body angle,
- head position and
- aggressiveness.

Running is an integral part of baseball, but it is often ignored as a fundamental skill. Coaches don't pay enough attention to a player's running technique, instead leaving it up to the player to learn how to run. If players run incorrectly, whether running the bases or going after balls in the outfield, they waste valuable time and motion, thus increasing the chance of being called out or not getting to the ball in time to make a catch. In addition, players too often run the bases thinking only about getting to the next base. To play aggressive baseball, runners must think at least one base ahead. You should keep in mind that each player will have a unique running style.

Running involves the entire body. From the feet all the way up to the head, the body must work in synchronization for a player to run efficiently. All movement should be directed toward the runner's goal. For example, a player running to first base must direct all energy to that goal. No motion should take a player off course.

If you do not feel competent teaching basic running form, contact a track coach and have that person work with your team on the first day of training. Who better to teach running basics than a coach from a sport that treats running form as a science? Besides, most track coaches will gladly share their knowledge.

LEG AND ARM MOVEMENT

Running begins with short, choppy strides in which the lifting of the knees generates tremendous energy with pistonlike action of the legs. Long strides at the beginning of a run can cause loss of equilibrium. Overstriding forces a runner to run on his heels, destroying balance and causing the head to bounce up and down. A player in the field may then perceive the ball to be moving up and down. Runners should run on the balls of their feet, and the feet should hit the ground directly underneath the body.

As the legs are lifting and moving the body forward, the arms should also be churning. As the player is lifting a leg, the opposite arm should be thrusting forward in a right leg–left arm, left leg–right arm manner. If the right arm is stretching forward, the runner should drive the left elbow backward at the same time and vice versa. The hands should be closed in a fist, but not squeezed tightly, and the arms should be relaxed. Note that the arms should move in an up-and-down motion parallel to the side of the body, not across the front of the body. Many runners thrust their hands across their chests as if they were boxers. This motion defeats the purpose of straight-line running and tends to throw the runner off balance.

BODY ANGLE

Running should be as easy as standing. Note that sprinters get into an upright position as quickly as possible in races. Baseball runners should do the same. After the first push-off steps—what track coaches refer to as the acceleration phase—the runner should achieve an upright stance with a slight lean toward his target. Running hunched over uses too much energy and creates tension.

HEAD POSITION

The average human head weighs between 9 and 12 pounds. Keeping this in mind, running with the head up is more efficient than running with the head down. Running with the head down not only makes it more difficult to see but also pulls the body forward and off balance. The player should keep the muscles in the face loose. The less tension in the body, the quicker the athlete runs.

At a Glance

The following parts of the text offer additional information on running.

AGGRESSIVENESS

Aggressive running can put pressure on an opposing defense and force them into errors. Players should be taught to run thinking that on every hit ball, the defense is going to make a mistake, either mental or physical. Every time they run to first, they should be thinking about going to second. They should treat every single as if it is going to be a double, every double as a potential triple and so on. This way, players have an aggressive state of mind from the first step. Runners should even sprint to first base on a walk. You never know when the pitcher, catcher or infielders will drop the ball and allow the runner to reach second base. If the runner trots to first, advancing to the next base is impossible. In addition, each time players run in practice, they should run with aggressiveness in mind. This approach develops a gung-ho attitude to running. You should never make players run just for the sake of running; they should always run with a purpose.

You should teach players early to use their own judgment about being aggressive. If you continually stress smart baserunning, players will learn when to gamble and when not to gamble. Never chastise them for making an error of commission, that is, taking a chance on advancing to the next base if they did it aggressively. For more information on how to form an aggressive mind-set, see "Aggressive Baserunning" on page 156.

The following skills, "Running to First Base," "Rounding the Bases," "Stealing Second Base" and "Stealing Third Base" discuss running in detail, but with each phase of running, players should remember that being aggressive is the key.

Common Errors

You may run into several common errors when teaching your athletes how to run.

Error	Error correction
The player flings his arms across his body while running.	Emphasize to players the correct arm action of pumping the arms and moving the thumb of each arm in a pistonlike motion from back pocket to ear.
The player takes long strides when beginning to run.	Emphasize using short, forceful strides at the start like a sprinter in a 100-meter dash. Have the team watch a short video of sprinters at the start of a race.

Running to First Base

KEY POINTS

The most important components of running to first base are

- pushing out of the box,
- running outside the 45-foot line, and
- running through the base and looking right.

After hitting the ball, the batter–runner must not only use proper running form but also direct his energy flow toward first base and think aggressively. He should be thinking ahead about running beyond first base if the opportunity presents itself.

PUSHING OUT OF THE BOX

After hitting the ball, the batter's first step out of the box should be directly toward first base. He might take this step with either foot, depending on where he has transferred his weight on the follow-through of the swing. Most of the time, however, he will take this step by pushing off the rear foot (the right foot for right-handers and the left foot for left-handers) directly toward first base. The first few steps should be quick and get the hitter into top speed swiftly. The player should look ahead toward first base and should not follow the ball. Hitters who admire their handiwork are not being aggressive! After a few steps, the hitter can look briefly toward the field to see where the ball is so that he knows whether to run straight to the base or get ready to make a turn at first to continue to second.

RUNNING OUTSIDE THE 45-FOOT LINE

A runner should not move into the infield for the first few steps. The feet drive the legs toward first base in a straight line. The runner does this because the rules of baseball state that a runner must stay inside the 3-foot running lane when running to first base. This lane, usually marked by chalk on the foul side of the first-base foul line, is 3 feet wide and begins 45 feet from first base. Runners must remember that they could be called out for interference if the ball strikes them when they are to the fair side of this box when running to first. For example, on a bunted ball just fair to the first-base side, if the catcher fields and throws to first base while the runner is running on the grass side of the baseline and the throw hits the runner, the runner will be called out for interfering with the catcher's throw.

RUNNING THROUGH THE BASE AND LOOKING RIGHT

As a runner touches first base, his stride should continue. He runs through the base, not to it. To emphasize running through the base, teach your players that the sprint to first base is a 93-foot sprint, not a 90-foot sprint. Some runners make the mistake of jumping or lunging with their last step before hitting the base. This technique slows them down because to lunge, the body must gather momentum. Another gross mistake that runners make is sliding into first base when it is not necessary. Because a slide slows down the body, the runner should use it only when the first baseman has been pulled off the bag and will have to tag the runner to make the out.

After crossing first base, runners should slow down and look quickly to the right. Runners can slow down by shifting their weight from the balls of their feet onto their heels. At the same time they should lower their buttocks, which helps shift the weight to the rear and slow down the body.

As soon as runners cross the base, they should glance quickly to their right to see if the ball has passed the first baseman on an overthrow or a muffed catch. They shouldn't have to wait for the first-base coach to tell them to advance. If they are being aggressive, they will see for themselves the opportunity to advance. If this kind of defensive mistake occurs and the ball gets past the first baseman and rolls into foul territory, the runner should push off his right foot, resume proper running form and begin sprinting to second. Sometimes a bad throw will become apparent to the runner well before he reaches the base. If that happens, the runner should immediately begin rounding the base (discussed in "Rounding the Bases" beginning on page 48) and start for second. The runner should be cautious here because a hustling catcher will follow the runner to first base when no one else is on base and will be backing up the throw to first. If the catcher is in position to field the errant throw, the runner should not advance.

If no overthrow occurs, the runner should turn right after slowing down and return to first base. If a runner makes a move toward second base and then decides not to go, the defense can tag him out. He must hustle back to the base to avoid being tagged out.

At a Glance

The following parts of the text offer additional information on running to first base.

Running Basics p. 44

Rounding the Bases p. 48

Aggressive Baserunning p. 152

Common Errors

You may run into several common errors when teaching runners to run to first base.

Error	Error correction
The player lunges on the last step.	Emphasize running through the base, not just to it. Teach runners that they should sprint 93 feet, not 90 feet.
The player continues running well beyond first base.	Teach aggressiveness. The farther runners go toward the outfield, the less likely it is that they will be able to advance on an overthrow.
The player turns to the left after crossing first base.	Turning left is not a problem unless the player makes a definite move to second base. To avoid confusion among players and umpires, teach players to turn to the right and then return to first base.

KEY POINTS

The most important components of rounding the bases are

- making the turn,
- hitting the base.
- taking three steps toward second and
- running to the next base.

On a ball hit to the outfield, the batter becomes a base runner and should be thinking about advancing beyond first base. He cannot do this unless he knows how to make the turn at the base and get his body into position to go to second.

MAKING THE TURN

A runner needs to know where to start getting the body ready to make the turn at first. Willie Mays, considered one of the greatest base runners who ever lived, began his turn at first with his first move out of the batter's box. Instead of stepping directly toward first base, he angled out slightly into foul territory so that his path to first base was an arc that would take him directly to second base. Most players today are taught to make a question-mark turn at first base (see figure 3.19). To execute this turn, the player runs directly toward first base and then, on determining that the ball has gone into the outfield, pushes off hard into foul territory about halfway down the baseline. All the player has to do here is take a step to the right with the right foot to get the body far enough outside the line to set up a good angle to turn at first base.

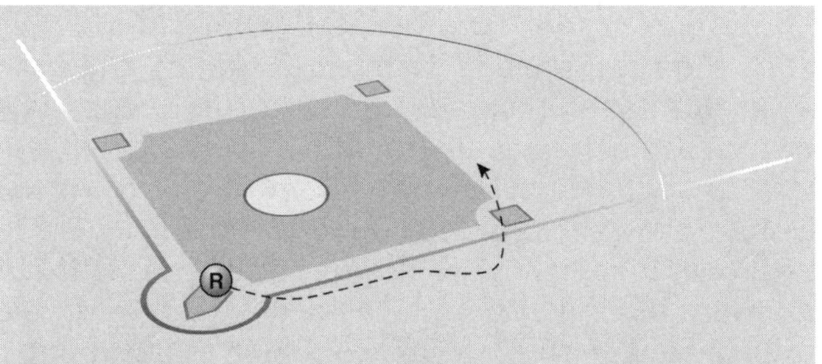

Figure 3.19 Runner making a question-mark turn at first base.

HITTING THE BASE

The best foot to use when hitting the base is the left foot. If runners hit first base with the left foot, they can push off the base and make a crossover step toward second with the right foot. But runners should not be too concerned about which foot hits the base. Hitting the base with the right foot is acceptable if the runners have not made too wide a turn going into the base. As players cross the base, they should lean toward second base, shifting their center of gravity and making it easier to redirect their path. Players should also thrust the right arm in the direction of second base to help redirect energy. By using these techniques, runners will avoid taking a big arc into the outfield and running additional distance to get to the next base.

TAKING THREE STEPS TOWARD SECOND

As a runner is crossing first base, he should be looking into the outfield in the direction that the ball was hit. As the ball is being fielded, he should take three steps toward second—right, left, right. As he lands on his third step, or right foot, he decides whether to continue to second or retreat to first.

If the defense muffs the ball, the aggressive runner, from this position in the baseline, automatically plants the right foot and goes full speed to second. If an outfielder mishandles the ball, he has to pick it up, get his feet underneath himself to throw and then make a good throw to the base. The infielder covering second has to field the ball cleanly and then make a good tag on the oncoming runner to get him out. The odds in this case favor the aggressive runner.

But if the defense fields the ball cleanly, the runner plants the right foot, stops his momentum toward second and turns to retreat to first base. In this case, the runner should not turn his head away from the play but should watch the ball as he retreats.

At a Glance

The following parts of the text offer additional information on rounding the bases.

RUNNING TO THE NEXT BASE

When base runners are on first or second base, they too should be thinking aggressively about moving beyond the next base. The only exception to this mind-set is when the batter hits a ground ball that forces the runner to the next base. In this case, the runner should run as hard as possible to the next base and make a good slide in an attempt to beat the force play.

If a runner is at first base and the ball is hit to the outfield, however, he follows the same routine as a batter who is headed toward first base. He first locates the ball and then makes the decision to advance or not to advance. If he decides to advance, his thought process should guide him into thinking that he can go to third base, not just second. The same is true of the runner who starts at second base. He should be thinking about scoring a run, not just advancing to third. In both cases, advancing beyond one base depends on the position of the ball and the outfielders' throwing abilities. See more about this in chapter 5, "Offensive Tactical Skills."

The runner should dip his center of gravity toward the next base when crossing over the base and thrust his right arm in that direction. The runner can cut more of the corner when rounding third base because the lead at second base will be deeper, allowing him to make a sharper turn at third. Find more about this in "Stealing Third Base," beginning on page 54.

Common Errors

You may run into several common errors when teaching your athletes how to round the bases.

Error	Error correction
The player makes wide turns at second or third.	Emphasize making the question-mark move when rounding the bases.
The player is timid about moving too far away from the base on fly balls.	Reiterate the importance of being aggressive and always thinking about the next base. Have the player run the bases during batting practice to get a better feel for all situations that can develop during a game.

Stealing Second Base

KEY POINTS

The most important components of stealing second base are

- getting the sign,
- taking the primary lead,
- body position on the lead,
- using the one-way lead,
- jab step and arm action,
- returning to first on a pickoff attempt and
- taking the secondary lead.

The aggressive team not only runs the bases well but also knows how to steal in case their hitting game fails them. Basically, stealing is getting a good jump on a pitcher's motion and beating the catcher's throw to second base. Stealing is an important technical skill in baseball.

GETTING THE SIGN

Any time a runner is on first base, a potential steal situation exists, and the player should focus on the signs from his coach at third base, looking specifically for the steal sign. As he is taking off his batting gloves and preparing to get his sign from the coach, he should be mentally reviewing the game situation—number of outs, inning, score and so on. When the runner takes the sign from the coach, he should be standing on the base with both heels on the corner closest to the pitcher. After the coach has flashed the signs to the runner, the runner should acknowledge that he has received the sign.

TAKING THE PRIMARY LEAD

Whenever a runner leads off any of the bases, the lead can be broken into two parts—primary and secondary. The primary lead is the first few steps the runner takes in order to take his basic lead off the base; the secondary lead is the advancement the runner makes toward the next base when the pitch is thrown (see "Taking the Secondary Lead" on page 53). A good primary lead gets a runner far enough off the base that he will be able to get a good jump if he is going to steal.

After getting his sign with both heels on the base, the runner should take a step with his left foot, followed by a step with the right foot, bend at the knees and the waist, and then take three short shuffle steps toward second base. This movement should create a good, balanced, 12-foot lead for the average high school player. After the first step is taken with the left foot (see figure 3.20*a*), the runner should pivot the foot so that it points toward the third-base line as the right foot is moving forward (see figure 3.20*b*). The three short shuffle movements that follow should be made by bringing the left foot in the direction of the right foot. Caution your players about bringing their feet directly together because doing so gets them off balance. When a pitcher with a good pickoff move sees a runner doing this, he will throw over to first as soon as the runner's feet come together. The pitcher who does this has a good chance of picking off the runner because, from this awkward, imbalanced position, he will have a tough time making a quick movement to dive back to the base.

Another fundamental of the primary lead, although rarely taught, is to have the runner lead off slightly to the inside of the baseline. This cuts the angle that the pitcher has of the runner and the base, bringing the runner closer to the pitcher, and making it seem as though the runner is closer to the base than he actually is. Also, warn your players not to begin their primary lead until the pitcher has taken his position on the pitching rubber.

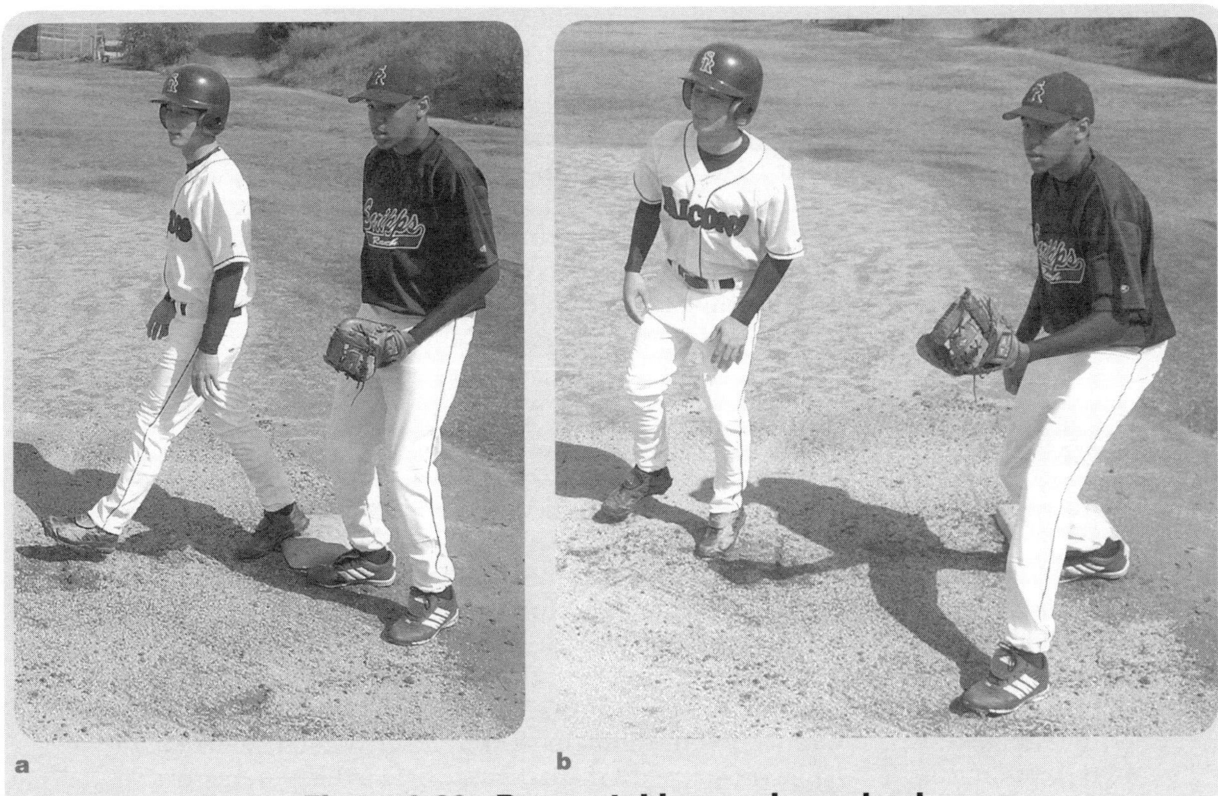

a b

Figure 3.20 Runner taking a primary lead.

BODY POSITION ON THE LEAD

When the runner has reached his primary lead, he should be in the basic athletic position. His feet should be at least shoulder-width apart, weight evenly distributed on the balls of the feet and knees flexed (see figure 3.21). The head should be up, the eyes focused on the pitcher and the back straight. This balanced position allows the runner to move in either direction—to steal second or dive back to first. As the runner takes his primary lead, he should never look back to first or down to the ground. If he takes his lead the same way every time, he should know intuitively how far he is from first base. Again, pitchers with good pickoff skills, especially left-handers whose heads are already facing the runner, will throw to first base as soon as the runner takes his eyes off of the pitcher. Advise runners to keep their eyes on the ball.

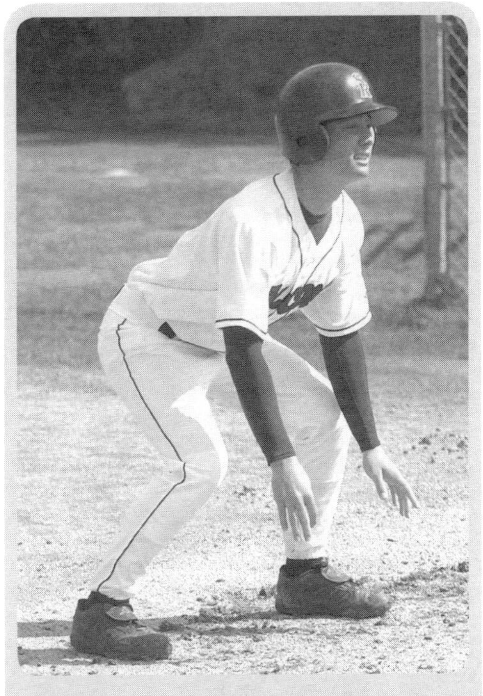

Figure 3.21 Basic athletic position for baserunning.

(continued)

USING THE ONE-WAY LEAD

Because stealing against left-handers involves ingesting and filtering many little things, base runners often find it easier to take one-way approach to stealing on a left-handed pitcher. As soon as the pitcher makes his first move to pitch—whether a leg lift, arm lift, leg swing or other movement—the runner, if he has received the steal sign, breaks for second base. Before a pitcher makes his first move, he has already decided what he will do—throw home or throw to first. Realize, too, that if the runner is picked off, the first baseman will often either throw high to avoid hitting the runner or hit the runner in the back with the throw. Both scenarios end with the runner safely at second.

JAB STEP AND ARM ACTION

After the runner has taken a balanced, comfortable lead and is ready to steal, he must get his body in motion toward second quickly. The best way to achieve this is with a short jab step with the right foot. From the primary lead, the right foot lifts slightly, opens toward second and then is jabbed into the ground with force to provide thrust for the body. As the jab step is occurring, the first movements of the arms help in getting the base runner to top speed quickly. As the right elbow thrusts back on the initial jab-step move, the left arm thrusts out toward second base (see figure 3.22*a*). This action is sometimes referred to as the quick draw, a reference to gunfights in the old Wild West. The arm action is similar to pulling a gun out of a holster with the left hand. The left leg then crosses over. The arms pump vigorously for a few steps, and the runner should then be at top speed (see figure 3.22*b*). Good base runners, when they know that they are going to steal, assume a wide stance and position the right foot slightly back and more toward right field than the left foot. This stance enables them to open their hips to second base quicker. They must be careful to make this subtle, however, because an observant infielder could pick this up and notify his pitcher that a steal is coming.

a b

Figure 3.22 Jab step.

RETURNING TO FIRST ON A PICKOFF ATTEMPT

If the pitcher throws to first base, the runner must be prepared to return to the base. If his body is balanced in the primary lead, ready to move in either direction, he should be able to get back to first base easily. On his return, he should use his left foot to touch the part of the base closest to right field. The runner can then swing his weight away from the first baseman by making a reverse pivot with the left leg and swinging the right leg away to avoid any tag. If the runner has a longer lead and the pitcher has a quick move, the runner will have to dive back to the base. To do this, he quickly changes his center of gravity by taking a quick jab step with the left foot toward the bag and diving and reaching with the hand for the back corner of the base. Aggressive base runners should not have to dive to get back to first base!

At a Glance

The following parts of the text offer additional information on stealing second base.

TAKING THE SECONDARY LEAD

If the runner is not stealing, on every pitch he should take a secondary lead, defined as a movement of a few hops toward second base as the ball is traveling home. The runner should stand up and shuffle several times toward second base while keeping his eyes on the ball and the catcher. If the ball is hit, the runner is already in motion toward the next base. If the hit is a line drive, the runner should stop and make sure that the ball is out of the infield before continuing to second. If the pitch is not hit, the runner should stop and begin running back to first base while watching the catcher in case he might throw to first on a pickoff attempt. The runner can also use another technique here, called the bluff run. In the bluff, the runner takes a few hard steps toward the next base and then quickly returns.

Common Errors

You may run into several common errors when teaching your athletes how to steal second base.

Error	Error correction
The player has a poor first step when stealing.	Emphasize the jab step and make certain that the player is using his arms enough. Use drills to teach good stealing jumps.
The player looks back at the base, measuring his lead.	Reemphasize the left, right, shuffle, shuffle, shuffle technique for the primary lead. If the runner does this the same way every time, he should be the same distance away from first base every time and will not have to look back.

KEY POINTS

The most important components of stealing third base are

- the straight-line leadoff,
- the angled leadoff and
- getting a bigger lead.

Knowledgeable baseball people say that stealing third base is easier than stealing second. Several reasons account for this. First, because the second baseman and the shortstop do not hold the runner on as a first baseman does, the runner can get a bigger lead. Second, the runner can break into a secondary lead sooner, creating momentum toward third base. Third, most pickoff moves require perfect timing to be successful.

On the other hand, the catcher has an easier throw to third base because it is 37.3 feet closer to home plate than second base is, so the runner must have a good jump on the pitch. Because the catcher has an easier throw and the runner at second is already in scoring position, some baseball pundits say that stealing third is unnecessary and too risky. But if a team wants to have an aggressive offense and continually put pressure on the defense, stealing third base is key to that philosophy.

STRAIGHT-LINE LEADOFF

Because the catcher can get the ball to third base quickly on stolen base attempts, the runner must do all he can to get a good lead. Most teams prefer to use a straight-line leadoff from second base. In this lead, the runner, after taking the signs from the coach, takes a lead to a position 20 feet (about seven steps) from second base on the baseline between second and third. While getting his lead, the runner must always keep his eyes on the pitcher and get additional help from the base coaches who should inform the runner of the location of the second baseman and shortstop.

If the middle infielders close the gap between themselves and second base, the base runner must shorten his lead to avoid being picked off. After walking a few strides, the runner should break down into the basic primary lead stance that he assumes when leading off first base. From this position, when the ball is pitched, the runner can either break to steal third base or take a secondary lead (see "Stealing Second Base" on page 50) and return to second if he decides not to steal. Fielders and runners often play a game of cat and mouse here as the fielders try to keep the runner close and the runner tries to get a bigger lead.

ANGLED LEADOFF

Another type of lead used at second base is the angled lead, used in the Dodgers organization and popularized by former Dodgers infielder and major league manager Davey Lopes, who stole over 40 bases seven times in a 15-year career. In this aggressive leadoff technique, the runner begins by taking a five- to seven-step lead as he would in the straight-line lead, but he does so on an angle that is three or four steps back from the baseline toward left field. When the pitcher is in set position, the runner walks slowly directly toward the pitcher. As the pitcher turns his head to look to the plate, the runner shuffles into his secondary lead. When the runner has made the decision to steal, he walks toward the pitcher on a little more of an angle and then breaks for third base as soon as the pitcher looks away from him. As with the straight-line lead, the runner must focus on the pitcher and be attentive to the instructions of the base coaches. This type of lead has several advantages. First, the runner has a bigger lead by the time the pitcher releases the ball, thus increasing the chances of a successful steal. Second, because the leadoff takes the runner directly toward the shortstop's normal playing position, the shortstop is less able to sneak behind the runner on a pickoff attempt. Third, because the runner has a running start before the pitcher releases the ball, he reaches sprint speed more rapidly.

At a Glance

The following parts of the text offer additional information on stealing third base.

GETTING A BIGGER LEAD

Because the runner must have a good lead at second base, he should continually try to stretch the lead farther each time he reaches the base during a game. While focusing on the pitcher, the runner should edge closer to third base with small steps. Here, the base coaches are extremely important in helping runners get good leads.

The first-base coach can aid the runner by moving down the first-base line into a position with which the runner can align. The coach then uses first base as a spot that matches second base. If the coach is 10 feet from first base, the runner can likewise be 10 feet from second base. When done correctly, this technique gives the runner a visual key, in addition to the audible one, to a good leadoff. If the shortstop or second baseman starts to move closer to the base, the first base coach moves back toward first, visually cuing the runner to return as well.

Common Errors

You may run into several common errors when teaching your athletes about stealing third base.

Error	Error correction
The player looks back at the base to see how far he is away from the base.	Emphasize that players should intuitively know how far off the base they are without looking. They should focus their attention on the pitcher and learn to listen and use their peripheral vision to detect movement from the middle infielders.
When using the Lopes' lead, the player begins his movement toward the pitcher before the pitcher has looked back to check him.	Emphasize to players that they should take their primary lead and hold it. They should move into the secondary lead only as the pitcher turns his head. Moving too early destroys the timing and usually causes the runner to get too big a lead and then feel as if he has to retreat when the pitcher looks back. When this happens, stealing third becomes virtually impossible.

Bent-Leg Slide

KEY POINTS

The most important components of the bent-leg slide are

- sitting into the slide,
- the three-point sliding stance,
- pop-up variations and
- preventing injuries.

The most commonly taught method of sliding is the bent-leg slide. Some teams use this slide exclusively because of the misconception that it is safer, although doing so discounts the human nature to dive into things and is psychologically not as aggressive. In contrast to the headfirst slide, the bent-leg slide is a foot-first slide in which the lower portion of the body leads the way.

SITTING INTO THE SLIDE

Players must perform the bent-leg slide assertively. The runner will be traveling at top speed when beginning the slide. As the runner nears the 10-foot area where the slide begins, he simply begins to sit down as he would if a chair were present. As the lower part of the body begins this sitting motion, the sliding leg—the leg that touches the base—kicks out toward the base and the bottom leg tucks underneath. The momentum from the run leading up to the slide is sufficient to make this an easy motion for the runner. Coaches should alert their players that the wetter the field is, the later the runner should begin his slide. This is true for any of the slides players may use.

THREE-POINT SLIDING STANCE

Figure 3.23 Bent-leg slide.

The bent-leg slide requires a three-point sliding stance as shown in figure 3.23. After the runner has thrust out his sliding leg and begun to sit down, the slide takes place on three parts of the body. The bottom foot contacts the ground on the top outside part of the shoe, the bottom knee and leg hit the ground at the same time and slide along the ground and the buttocks contact the ground, allowing the player to sit down in a good sliding position. When the heel of the outstretched leg hits the base, the knee bends and the energy of the slide decreases.

Remind players to keep their hands up and away from the ground to avoid dragging them and possibly causing injury. Players must sit on their bottoms, not on their sides, when doing the bent-leg slide. Sliding on the side of the thigh or hip can cause nagging “strawberry” contusions that can take a long time to heal.

POP-UP VARIATIONS

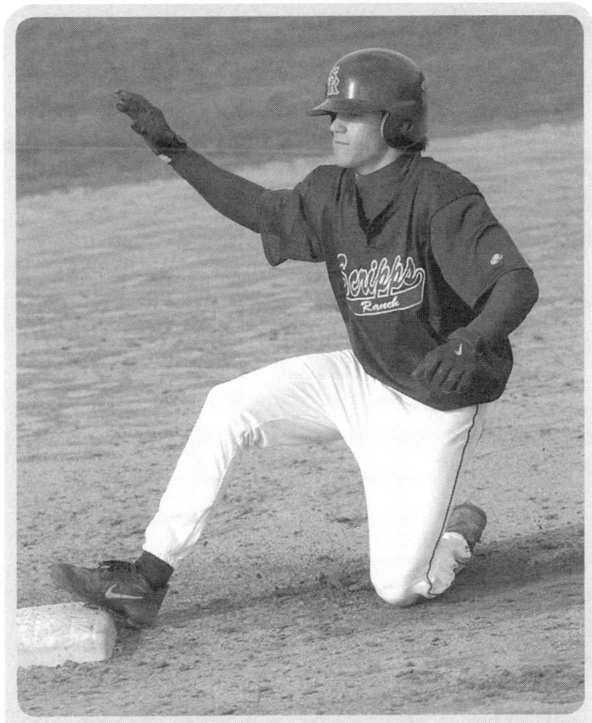

Figure 3.24 **The extended leg on a pop-up slide provides leverage.**

A variation of the bent-leg slide is the pop-up slide. As its name implies, the runner pops upward into a standing position after sliding. This technique enables the runner to get quickly to his feet and be in a position to run to the next base on a defensive mistake because the momentum caused by the lead foot hitting the base forces the runner to get up. Two variations are the top-leg technique and the bottom-leg technique.

In the top-leg technique, the pop-up slide begins as a basic bent-leg slide, so the top, or sliding, leg will hit the base with the heel. To get up more quickly and run after a pop-up slide, runners should slide with the right leg extended. This technique puts the body closer to the next base and forces the first motion to be in that direction. If runners slide with the left leg extended, the pop-up occurs in the opposite direction and moves the weight away from the baseline rather than toward it. Remind runners to always keep their heads up when sliding feet first so that they are able to see the play developing. If runners lay back too far with their upper body, they won't have a good view of the action and be able to make quick running decisions.

Because of the momentum created by the slide, the pop-up is easy to do. After the heel of the right foot hits the base, the runner should bend the ankle forward so that the front of the foot makes contact with the base and provides leverage to lift up the sliding runner (see figure 3.24).

This action transfers the weight to the front of the foot and forces the right leg to begin lifting the body. In addition, the weight should shift slightly toward the inside of the right foot, facilitating quicker explosion from the base by creating a push-off point. These slight movements, combined with the forward motion of the slide itself, help lift the body off the ground.

No matter which pop-up technique is used, the following absolutes of sliding should be adhered to. First, the outstretched leg should be kept slightly bent to prevent the leg from jamming into the base. Secondly, the runner should keep his upper body in a more or less upright position. This keeps the majority of the weight centered on the bent leg and the buttocks and allows for a more balanced sliding position. And third, the slide should be started closer to the base than normal. Instead of starting the slide 10 feet from the base, the runner should start the slide about 8 feet away. This makes the runner's slide into second have more energy and enables him to pop up more quickly.

(continued)

PREVENTING INJURIES

The runner must be certain to keep the sliding leg off the ground during the slide. If he drags this foot on the ground, the spikes of the shoe could catch the ground before the base, causing injury. He must not lean back with the upper body and drag the hands on the ground. He should hold the hands up with the thumbs inside the fingers and the hand closed around them.

Players should learn to begin their slides early, approximately 10 feet from the base. This routine helps them avoid indecision. Of course, field and weather conditions determine where a runner should start the slide. For example, when the field is wet, moist soil will grab a runner, making it more difficult to slide, so runners may not be able to start their slides until they are closer to the bases. Conversely, on a slick sliding surface, runners should start their slides farther from the base because the loose soil will cause them to slide farther and faster.

Runners should also learn to relax while sliding. Tensing up the body often leads to jamming the feet into the base rather than giving a little when they hit. Tightened muscles become less flexible and cause the player's actions to be slower and stiffer. When relaxed, the runner will flow into the slide and glide into the base. Most sliding injuries occur when players are uncertain about whether to slide or not to slide or because they are genuinely fearful of getting injured while sliding. Coaches can help alleviate this uncertainty by making sliding practice a key element in their daily practice plans. One good way to teach sliding safely is to have players practice sliding in the outfield grass or some other similar area in their stocking feet. There is little chance of injury sliding this way because there is nothing to catch the feet and twist an ankle, the major fear of hesitant sliders. Coaches should be cautioned, however, that they may have some "angry" moms on their hands who have to wash those grass-stained uniforms!

Runners should refrain from using the pop-up variations when sliding into second base on a force play. In this situation, popping up might put the runner in jeopardy of injury by getting in the way of the infielder's throw to first base. Recent rules interpretations have given umpires great leeway in being able to call an "automatic" double play if they determine that the sliding runner at second base, by virtue of his pop-up slide, interfered with the fielder's attempt to make a throw to first base. Popping up in this situation may be costly, especially if the batter running to first would have beaten the throw.

One final word needs to be added regarding sliding and injury. Any true baseball fan that listens to or watches major league baseball has heard announcers, players and coaches often talking about "breaking up the double play." By this they mean the common professional practice of sliding into second base in such a way as to disrupt the pivot man's balance and hopefully prevent him from completing the double play. This is often accomplished by sliding not at the base, but in the direction of the fielder, no matter how far from the base he may be! And even though the main purpose of this "take out" slide may not be to injure the fielder, many fielders at all levels of the game have been injured severely. This technique—while common in professional baseball—should never be used in the high school game.

At a Glance

The following parts of the text offer additional information on the bent-leg slide.

Stealing Second Base	p. 50
Stealing Third Base	p. 54
Aggressive Baserunning	p. 152
Knowing When to Steal Second	p. 162
Knowing When to Steal Third	p. 166

Common Errors

You may run into several common errors when teaching your athletes how to use a bent-leg slide.

Error	Error correction
The player dives into the slide.	Emphasize keeping the weight forward while running and lowering the body into the slide instead of jumping into the slide.
The player does not keep his head up while sliding.	Show the importance of knowing where the ball is so that on an overthrow the runner can quickly get to his feet and begin running to the next base.
The player's slide ends short of the base.	This player has begun his slide too soon. Emphasize getting to about 10 feet from the base before lowering into the slide.
The player gets "strawberry" burns on the side of the thigh.	This player is not sliding on the buttocks but is instead sliding on the side of his leg. Emphasize sitting down on the "biggest part of the body."
Momentum carries the player into center field on a pop-up slide into second base.	Emphasize sliding with the right foot extended. This puts the body in the proper position for good pushoff toward the next base.
The player stops dead on the slide and has to use his hands to get up.	In this case, the player is probably starting his slide too soon or is slowing down. The momentum of the slide should allow the runner to hit the base and lift his body. Emphasize going into the base at full speed.

Headfirst Slide

KEY POINTS

The most important components of the headfirst slide are

- running into the slide,
- body contact points and
- preventing injuries.

To be successful in most stealing attempts, players must slide into the base being stolen. In high school, the average runner with a 12-foot lead at first base will reach second base in approximately 3.5 seconds. If a pitcher, from the first movement he makes in his stretch position, can deliver the ball to home plate in 1.5 seconds, then the catcher must get the ball to second base in less than 2 seconds to throw out the runner. Because any time less than 2.1 seconds glove to glove is a good time to second base for a catcher, most runners have to slide into second to be safe. Even if runners will beat the throw easily, they should slide to avoid overrunning the base and being tagged out. Another good reason for sliding is that umpires have a tendency to call runners out when they don't slide because coming in standing up makes the play look closer than it is.

Good base stealers in the game today prefer the headfirst slide, a more aggressive slide than the bent-leg slide and a quicker way of reaching the base.

RUNNING INTO THE SLIDE

In preparing to slide, many runners make the mistake of slowing down immediately before beginning to slide. Just as runners should slide every time they steal a base, they should continue running hard and gradually lower themselves into the base, not stopping and jumping or leaping at the base. Rickey Henderson, the most proficient base stealer in major league history, said that when he was stealing, he felt as though he were falling toward second base the whole time. By leaning their weight forward as they run, runners can then simply lean a little more forward to begin the slide. This technique is easier than the backward lean required in the bent-leg slide.

BODY CONTACT POINTS

So the slide begins with the runner beginning to fall toward the base. When done correctly, the player's chest and thighs contact the ground at about the same time. The player extends his arms toward the base, making certain to point the fingers slightly upward to avoid jamming them into the base on contact (see figure 3.25). When sliding, the player should also keep his head up so that he can see the situation. For example, if the player sees that a tag is going to be applied to his left hand, he could roll slightly to his right side and pull the hand away, perhaps avoiding the tag and being called safe instead of out.

Discourage jumping to the base or belly flopping. These techniques slow the runner by causing a downward force of the body rather than an outward force.

PREVENTING INJURIES

Coaches are often concerned about player safety with the headfirst slide. When exercising proper precautions, however, this technique is safe. As mentioned earlier, players should slide every time they steal a base. Most sliding injuries occur when runners are

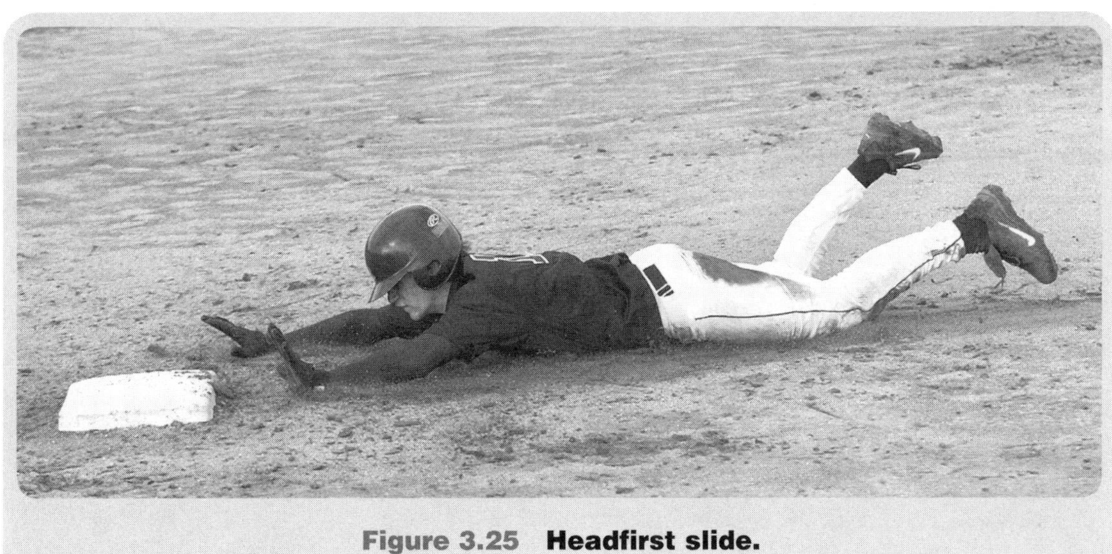

Figure 3.25 Headfirst slide.

indecisive about whether to slide. Eliminate indecision and injury by having players slide every time. As shown in figure 3.25, teach your players to point their fingers slightly upward to avoid jamming them into the base on contact. Note that runners should never slide headfirst into a catcher wearing shin guards. In this situation, sliding feet first is safer.

At a Glance

The following parts of the text offer additional information on sliding headfirst.

Stealing Second Base	p. 50
Stealing Third Base	p. 54
Aggressive Baserunning	p. 162

Common Errors

You may run into several common errors when teaching your athletes how to slide headfirst.

Error	Error correction
The player dives into the slide.	Emphasize keeping the weight forward while running and lowering the body into the slide instead of jumping into the slide.
The player does not keep his head up while sliding.	Show the importance of knowing where the ball is so that on an overthrow the runner can quickly get to his feet and begin running to the next base.
The player's slide ends short of the base.	This player has begun his slide too soon. Emphasize getting to about 10 feet from the base before lowering into the slide.

chapter 4

Defensive Technical Skills

This chapter will cover the defensive technical skills that you and your players must know in order to be successful. In this chapter, you will find:

Throwing Basics

KEY POINTS

The most important components of throwing are

- grip,
- arm action,
- upper-body action,
- lower-body and foot action, and
- throwing variations by position.

Throwing is perhaps the most important technical skill in baseball. Unless players throw properly, the ball will not get to its intended location. Besides the implications that correct throwing has on the outcome of the game, incorrect throwing can also lead to physical problems, which may eventually force players to discontinue playing the game.

Unfortunately, many coaches adhere to that oldest of baseball maxims, "If it ain't broke, don't fix it." This kind of thinking exists because coaches sometimes place winning above player development at an early age. Players can have improper arm action while playing in youth leagues and have an advantage because of their size, but as they move up the ladder, the inability to throw properly becomes a detriment and slows their development.

The most important defensive skill in the game, throwing, should not be left to chance. Coaches must stress proper throwing mechanics and good arm action every day in practice and games. The four main areas of emphasis when teaching throwing are the grip, the arm action, the upper-body action and the lower-body and foot action. Variations according to the different positions also need to be considered.

GRIP

Figure 4.1 Throwing grip.

For most throws, the player should grip the ball across the seams at their widest gap. The first and index finger should be approximately three-quarters of an inch apart, resting on top of the ball. The inside of the thumb should be placed directly opposite these fingers underneath the ball (see figure 4.1). A piece of black electrical tape wound around the circumference of the ball is a good teaching aid for players at all levels. The tape forces them to place their fingers in the proper positions. Using the tape as a guide, the fingers on top of the ball straddle the sides of the tape and the thumb is directly centered on the tape. This positioning centers the thumb between the fingers and enables a good grip. Gripping the ball with the fingers across the wide seams of the ball allows the ball to travel in a straighter path than it would if the fingers grip the ball along the seams. Placing the fingers farther apart might seem to help a player control the ball better, but having the fingers in this arrangement reduces the speed of the thrown ball. Placing the fingers closer together will enable a faster throw but will sacrifice accuracy. Players have to find the spot on the ball where they can throw with the best combination of accuracy and speed. This location will vary from player to player.

Players should not hold the ball too deeply in the hand. They should hold the ball with pressure out on the fingertips and with a noticeable space between the ball and the crook of the first finger and thumb (see figure 4.2). The fingers should not grip the ball too tightly. Players should hold the ball in the same manner in which a person would hold an egg, with just enough pressure so that it does not fall out of the hand, but not so much pressure so that the shell would break.

Figure 4.2 Gripping the ball so that it is not held too deeply in the hand.

ARM ACTION

You should teach players to start the throwing motion with their hands together on every throw. With the exception of the throw after fielding a slow rolling ball on the run, baseball throws begin with the player taking the ball out of the glove—the hands are together. The throwing-arm action after the ball is taken from the glove can be abbreviated as taking a path down from the glove, back, up to the sky and over the shoulder, or "down, back, up and over." Later skills sections that discuss throws by position will also use this phrase.

To allow proper arm action, the wrist must remain loose when the fingers grip the ball and throughout the throwing motion. The first movement of the arm and hand is down and away from the glove (see figure 4.3*a*). The arm then makes a circular motion away from the center of the body and upward (see figure 4.3*b*). Care should be taken when making this arc to keep the elbow of the arm relaxed and bent at about a 55- to 60-degree angle. The arm then swings upward to its apex, a point at which the elbow is even with or above the shoulder (see figure 4.3*c*). The elbow begins to move toward the target, forcing the forearm to lie back into a position where it can move forward, reach the release point and eventually follow through (see figure 4.3*d*).

Essentially, the arm can assume two different slots, or angles, at the release point—the overhand slot in which the arm and hand are held almost directly above the shoulder, and the three-quarters arm slot in which the arm and hand throw from a path on an angle of approximately 45 degrees from the shoulder. As long as the elbow stays above the shoulder, any angle between the two just described is acceptable, and players will eventually find a comfortable slot from which to throw. Coaches should not allow players to throw from what is called the sidearm slot, in which the arm and hand find a slot 90 degrees out from the shoulder. Throwing from this position leads to bad mechanics and arm damage because the arm moves across the body and puts undue pressure on the tendons in the elbow.

(continued)

a b c d

Figure 4.3 Proper arm action for a throw.

Throughout the beginning of the throwing motion, the fingers should stay on top of the ball. For this to happen, the wrist must swing to allow the fingers to point away from the target at the longest part of the arm arc. If this wrist swing doesn't occur, the fingers will move to a position under the ball too early in the arm action, causing the player to throw more with the shoulder than with the arm.

UPPER-BODY ACTION

While the arm is swinging down and away from the glove, the upper body must turn so that the shoulder opposite the player's throwing arm points directly to the target. This is the main reason that coaches should insist that players keep both hands together when learning the skill of throwing. In the case of a right-handed thrower, the upper body has to rotate enough so that the left shoulder can point at the target. Care should be taken not to let the hands get too far from the body as shown in figure 4.4*a* or to wrap too far behind the body as shown in figure 4.4*b*. Both of these irregularities lead to improper arm action. In the first, the arm circle is too small and the throw loses power. In the second, the body overrotates away from the target and follows a longer arc, causing the player to throw across the body and adding tension. The shoulders should remain level to the ground throughout the throwing motion.

a b

Figure 4.4 Thrower's hands *(a)* too far away from the body and *(b)* wrapped too far behind the body.

(continued)

LOWER-BODY AND FOOT ACTION

Almost everything in baseball begins with the feet, including throwing. As a player is receiving the ball, he should begin turning his rear foot (the foot on the side of the throwing arm) so that the instep of the foot is facing the target as he catches the ball. A good visualization technique for this skill is to have players imagine that they have an arrow extending straight out of their instep as shown in figure 4.5. To make this step with the foot, they would have to turn that arrow so that it points at their target. After making this movement, the hips can begin to rotate, leading to the closing of the front shoulder.

Next, as the player is pulling the ball out of the glove, the front foot strides toward the target (see figure 4.6). Ideally, the foot should point slightly closed to the target, but not too much left or right of it. If a right-hander's foot points to the left, the shoulders won't rotate properly, preventing a full arm arc in the throw. If the foot points too far to the right, the player will be throwing across his body, decreasing his throwing speed and adding unwanted movement to the ball. During the throw, the body weight shifts from the middle of the body to the rear leg and then finally to the front leg. When the weight shifts to the front leg, the rear foot lifts off the ground, allowing the arm to finish its arc and follow through across the body (see figure 4.7).

THROWING VARIATIONS BY POSITION

Although the throw is basically the same no matter what position a player plays, there are a few differences. Note, however, that the arm action stays the same no matter what position the throw is made from. The variations of a throw according to position follow.

Infielders

Because an infielder must field a ball and throw it quickly and accurately to one of the bases, the arc of the throwing arm will naturally be somewhat shorter than described previously. Instead of moving the arm considerably down out of the glove, the infielder should move the arm more backward than down. The hand will reach the apex quicker, and the infielder will be able to release the ball faster. In addition, the lower-body action will be different because the stride will be shorter to permit a quicker throw.

Outfielders

Outfielders because of their location usually have the longest throw on the field, so they obviously need to have great power and strength behind their throws. The outfielder's arc will thus be longer than that of other players and the stride with the lead leg will also be much longer to facilitate the longer throw. When preparing to throw, the outfielder should use a specific technique called the "crow hop" before he takes his long stride. This technique enables the outfielder to use his body to help the arm in making the

Figure 4.5 Player must turn the instep of the pivot foot toward the target to initiate the throw.

Figure 4.6 Player's front foot strides toward the target as he pulls the ball out of the glove.

Figure 4.7 Shifting of player's weight so that the arm can finish its arc and follow-through.

throw. Instead of just subtly moving the front foot forward as in the normal throwing motion, the outfielder's first step after he catches the ball should instead be a forceful jump upward and forward (see figure 4.8, *a-c*) with the throwing-side foot. This crow-hop motion forces the outfielder's body into action so that he can get more push off his back leg, thereby assisting the arm in making the throw.

(continued)

a b c

Figure 4.8 **Crow hop.**

Catchers

The catcher's arm arc is the shortest of all players on the field. Because the catcher may have to make an extremely quick pickoff throw to first or third base or to get a runner trying to steal second, the ball must reach its apex immediately.

Catchers may have very little arm arc, but the action of the throwing arm is the same. First, the wrist and arm swing the ball so that it faces away from the catcher's target. From that point forward, the catcher uses the same arm action—the elbow leads, the forearm lays back, the shoulder rotates and the forearm and wrist explode toward the target. The catcher's lower-body action must be quick and forceful, so he must rapidly transfer his weight from the rear foot to the front foot. The quickness and force with which the catcher must execute this throw make it the most violent throw in baseball. Even catchers who do not possess strong arms can still "gun" out opposing runners if they work hard on their mechanics and shorten their arm arc. Just taking a tenth of a second off the time it takes to get the ball from the mitt into launching position can make the catcher's throw exponentially more effective.

Pitchers

A pitcher's throw is similar to an outfielder's throw except that the pitcher isn't able to get a running start. He will use a long arc in the arm action, but the stride will not be as drastic as an outfielder's stride because the pitcher must be careful to get his body in the maximum effective throwing position on each pitch. An overlong stride will lead to other mechanical problems, especially with off-speed pitches. Early baseball rules allowed the pitcher to get a running start before throwing the ball to the batter so long as he stayed within the "pitcher's box" much as the "bowler" does in the game of cricket. Modern pitching mechanics have evolved as trainers looked for a way for a pitcher to throw as hard from a still starting position as he could when running.

For a more detailed exploration of throwing, look at "Catching a Throw," which begins on page 72. Also, for more information on pitches, refer to the section on pitching skills found on pages 94 through 101.

At a Glance

The following parts of the text offer additional information on the basics of throwing.

Common Errors

You may run into several common errors when teaching your athletes how to throw.

Error	Error correction
The player's throws often curve on their way to their target.	Check the player's grip. Most likely, the fingers are not staying above the ball or the grip is on the wrong part of the ball. Also, make sure the player's arm path is three-quarters to overhand to give the ball the proper rotation. A sidearm motion will cause improper rotation on the ball and make it move away from its target.
The player seems to be using his shoulder too much in his arm action.	This occurs when there is no bend in the elbow and the arm gets too straight. Caution players to keep their elbow bent and relaxed throughout the throw.
The player seems to push the ball rather than throw it.	Pushing the ball can occur for several reasons. First, the player is likely taking the ball up out of the glove. Second, the fingers are probably underneath the ball. Stress keeping the fingers on top and the ball down.
The player's throws seem to travel in a rainbow arc rather than in a straight line.	This problem can occur when the player's elbow is not reaching a point even with or above the shoulder. Emphasize keeping the elbow up.

Catching a Throw

KEY POINTS

The most important components of catching are

- selecting a glove,
- wearing the glove properly,
- positioning the throwing hand and
- positioning the body.

Like throwing, catching a ball is a basic technical skill in baseball. Whenever a ball is thrown, whether on a relay, steal attempt, pickoff or in the simple act of tossing the ball around after an out, someone has to catch it. Even the catcher, who admittedly has the most difficult receiving position in baseball, still just catches the ball when the pitcher throws it. But unless the player is cognizant of the focal points of catching, this seemingly easy task becomes difficult and could have disastrous effects on the outcome of a game.

SELECTING A GLOVE

Gloves are not created equal. In this age of specialization, players should choose a glove because it serves its function well, not because it looks cool. They should be more concerned that the glove is functional and fits their hands properly.

Outfielders need larger gloves—12 1/2 inches is the norm—so that they can extend their reach. Middle infielders need smaller gloves, 11 to 11 1/4 inches, so that they can get the ball out of the pocket faster. Pitchers and third basemen should have slightly larger gloves than middle infielders do, at 11 1/2 to 11 3/4 inches.

No coach would expect a catcher to sit behind the plate wearing an infielder's glove; the coach would supply a proper catcher's mitt. Likewise, if an athlete is going to play first base, insist that he buy a first baseman's glove specifically for the kinds of catches that he will need to make at first. Don't let a first baseman wear a regular fielder's glove!

WEARING THE GLOVE PROPERLY

A glove should essentially be an extension of a player's hand. Shoving the fingers of the hand too deeply into the glove fingers inhibits their ability to bend. Instead, the hand should be inserted into the glove so that easy flexion of the player's fingers makes the glove's fingers bend quickly, enabling them to close easily on a thrown or hit ball. The glove back should not be tightened too much for the same reasons. It should just fit the hand snugly.

POSITIONING THE THROWING HAND

When a ball is thrown to a player, he should await the ball with his elbows bent and his hands held near the top of the chest. The throwing hand should be held next to the glove hand so that the player can catch the ball with "two hands." Perhaps the worst habit in baseball is catching the ball with only the glove hand and holding the throwing hand loosely at the side.

As the thrown ball reaches the receiver, he should extend his hands for the catch but should not lock his elbows (see figure 4.9). This method allows him to give slightly with the glove as he catches the ball, creating the movement necessary to bring the ball and glove back toward the body and into throwing position. The player should also try to catch the ball near or in the webbing of the glove so that the fingers can close easily around the

Figure 4.9 Receiver's hand positioning when making a catch.

ball. If the throw reaches the player below the waist, he should rotate his glove wrist counterclockwise and catch the ball with the fingers of the glove pointing down. Likewise, the throwing hand should be rotated so that the fingers are pointing to the ground. A key here is to keep the wrists of both hands bent a little so that they are loose and flexible and to not extend the arms too far. This allows quick movements to adjust to throws.

At a Glance

The following parts of the text offer additional information on catching a ball.

Throwing Basics	p. 64
Catcher Basics	p. 74
Reacting As a Catcher	p. 90
Defensive Positioning	p. 178
Pitcher Pickoffs	p. 190
Rundowns	p. 202
Wild Pitches	p. 204

POSITIONING THE BODY

As a thrown ball nears, the receiving player moves the foot on his throwing side toward the ball. This action enables him to gather momentum to make the succeeding throw and allows him to position his body so that he will be catching the ball on the throwing side of the body. He should time this movement so that when he is catching the ball, he is planting the throwing foot. As soon as he catches the ball, the throwing hand reaches in and pulls the ball out. Also, whenever possible, the receiver should try to get his chest in front of the ball.

Common Errors

You may run into several common errors when teaching your athletes how to catch a ball.

Error	Error correction
The player tries to snag the ball as if he were using the glove as a net.	Emphasize having the elbows bent when receiving the ball and cushioning the ball toward the chest, not pushing it away.
A right-hander catches the ball consistently on his left side with one hand or with two hands (vice versa with the left-hander).	Point out to the player that after catching the ball, he will have to throw it. Have the player stand in one spot and throw to a wall 30 feet away after catching the ball. Time the player catching on the wrong side of the body and then on the correct side. Do the same with the player catching the ball with one hand and with the throwing hand down on the side and then with the throwing hand in proper position. The results will be surprising.

Catcher Basics

KEY POINTS

The most important components of the catcher are

- ideal catcher attributes,
- equipment and protection,
- mental acuity,
- positioning the mitt,
- giving signs,
- stance with no runners on base,
- stance with runners on base and
- framing pitches.

Besides the pitcher, no one controls the ball more during a game than the catcher does. Because all action in a game takes place in front of him, the catcher has the responsibility of directing the defense. In addition, the catcher has to signal the pitches that the pitcher throws and must be observant of opposing hitters and their tendencies. In short, he is the defensive leader. For these reasons, catching is the most important technical position in baseball.

IDEAL CATCHER ATTRIBUTES

Most high school athletes do not grow up wanting to become catchers. As youngsters, all players want to be pitchers, shortstops or center fielders—the glamour positions. Many players become catchers because they may have been the only player on their team not afraid to be hit, and hit often, or because they were too slow of foot to play other positions well. Instead of choosing slow or big players, however, astute coaches should identify players who exhibit leadership skills and turn them into catchers. Look at the great World Series teams throughout the years. Most had great catchers who were also great leaders—Johnny Bench, Yogi Berra, Thurman Munson, Bill Dickey and most recently, Ivon "Pudge" Rodriguez.

To be great leaders, catchers must have the right character. They must be able to take charge. They have to settle the team down when things get out of hand. They have to make crucial decisions and tell fielders where to throw the ball on plays in front of the plate. They have to be able to judge outfield throws to the plate and tell the cutoff man what to do with the ball when it gets to him. When dealing with pitchers, they have to know each pitcher's strengths, weaknesses and eccentricities and use that knowledge to help them stay composed.

Besides leadership ability, catchers should have memories like elephants. Catchers have to pay attention to the position in the box where each hitter normally stands. They have to remember what pitches the hitters hit well and which ones they don't so that they can call the pitches without using guesswork. They have to be aware of bunt or steal situations. They have to be able to sniff out trick plays. All these things are possible for a catcher who focuses on the game.

Catchers should also be quick footed. They don't have to run fast—even in the big leagues most catchers are slow—but they should be able to move quickly within the catcher's box to keep balls from getting past them and to shift their feet for throws. Catchers also need to have quick hands so that they can easily move the glove from one side of the strike zone to the other.

The ability to do all this helps the catcher make his pitchers feel confident. Catchers have to treat the area behind the plate as their domain. You should tell the catcher that the catcher's box is his castle and that he should allow nothing to escape from it. This advice imbues the catcher with a sense of pride for his realm. By blocking balls in the dirt even with no one on base, the catcher not only gains practice in the skill but also gives the pitcher confidence.

EQUIPMENT AND PROTECTION

When it comes to catching equipment, one size definitely does not fit all. Too many catchers have been injured and have lost playing time because they were wearing improperly fitting equipment. The shin guards should fit comfortably and cover all areas that need protection—the shins, knees, calves and even the top of the shoes. Guards come in lengths ranging from 11 to 17 1/2 inches, and you should make sure that the ones that your catchers use cover all areas that need protection. The same is true for chest protectors. Not everyone's torso is the same length, so protectors range in size from 12 to 18 1/2 inches. Catchers should wear protectors that thoroughly cover their vulnerable upper-body areas. Additionally, catchers at every playing level should wear protective cups.

Recent NFHS rules changes regarding catcher's equipment state that high school catchers must wear a helmet and mask combination that provides full throat and ear protection and meets the standards of the National Operating Committee on Standards for Athletic Equipment (NOCSAE). The hockey-style mask shown in figure 4.10 is probably the safest for game use because it incorporates the throat protector and helmet right into the face protector. Players may still use the classic mask, but it must now be firmly attached to the helmet.

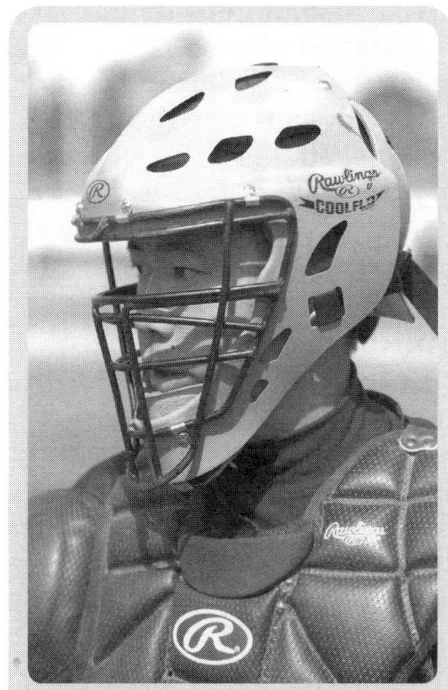

Figure 4.10 Hockey-style face mask.

Catcher's mitts of the 21st century have more in common with a first baseman's mitt than they do with catcher's mitts of 50 years ago. The new two-piece, extended-palm gloves make catching a pitched ball much easier, but they can also promote bad technical habits, such as one-handed catching, so you should always stress proper fundamentals with your catchers.

Catchers should keep their equipment clean and check straps on shin guards and chest protectors daily for signs of wear. The inside padding on helmets and other gear should also be cleaned regularly to prolong use. Catchers should be as careful with their gear as they are with their gloves and bats.

MENTAL ACUITY

Even today, some coaches refer to catching gear as the "tools of ignorance." This phrase harkens back to the day when slowness of foot, big physical size and the willingness to let balls be hit off the head, chest and knees was equated with being dumb! This is no longer the case. Catchers must be fearless, not dumb. They sometimes may have to give up their bodies for the sake of the team. This is not a position for the faint of heart.

The catcher has to be the coach's eyes, mouth and brains on the field. You should communicate daily with your catcher regarding strategy and the reasons behind the strategy. If the catcher knows your intentions, fewer problems will occur on the field.

(continued)

As touched on in a previous point, catchers must also become students of human nature, especially the nature of the pitchers on the staff. You can visit a pitcher only so many times per inning or game, so the catcher has to be able to call time and talk to the pitcher when he senses a loss of rhythm or faulty mechanics. The catcher should also inform you when he senses that a pitcher is losing it. In fact, at the end of each inning before the catcher gets comfortable on the bench, you may want him to provide a progress report on the pitcher.

After every out or play in a game, the catcher should move out in front of the plate and let his teammates know the situation. He can do this by standing in front of the plate, signaling the number of outs with his fingers and pointing to the base or bases on which his teammates should be focusing. Doing this helps his teammates concentrate on the tactics of the game.

Catchers have to scrutinize what players do in the batter's box: Where does the hitter stand? How does he hold his bat? Does he lunge? Does he step away from the ball? What pitches does he like to swing at? Catchers also have to be aware of who can run and who can't. This information can assist them in making decisions about pitch selection. Even if you call the pitches during the game, the catcher should be aware of the reasons why the pitch is being called and remember the situation in which it's being used.

POSITIONING THE MITT

The catcher should receive the ball tension free with soft hands. Many times, catchers needlessly tense up the receiving hand and lose the flexibility needed to move the mitt, adjust quickly to the flight of the ball and then softly catch it. Tension-free catching begins when the catcher puts on his mitt. The mitt is merely an extension of the hand; it doesn't replace the hand. Therefore, the hand should not be jammed into the mitt. The mitt should be worn comfortably so that it closes easily when the fingers move. If the hand is jammed into the mitt, it is more difficult to close quickly and softly.

When giving the pitcher the target, the catcher should hold the gloved hand out away from the body with the hand bent slightly up at the wrist as shown in figure 4.11*a*.

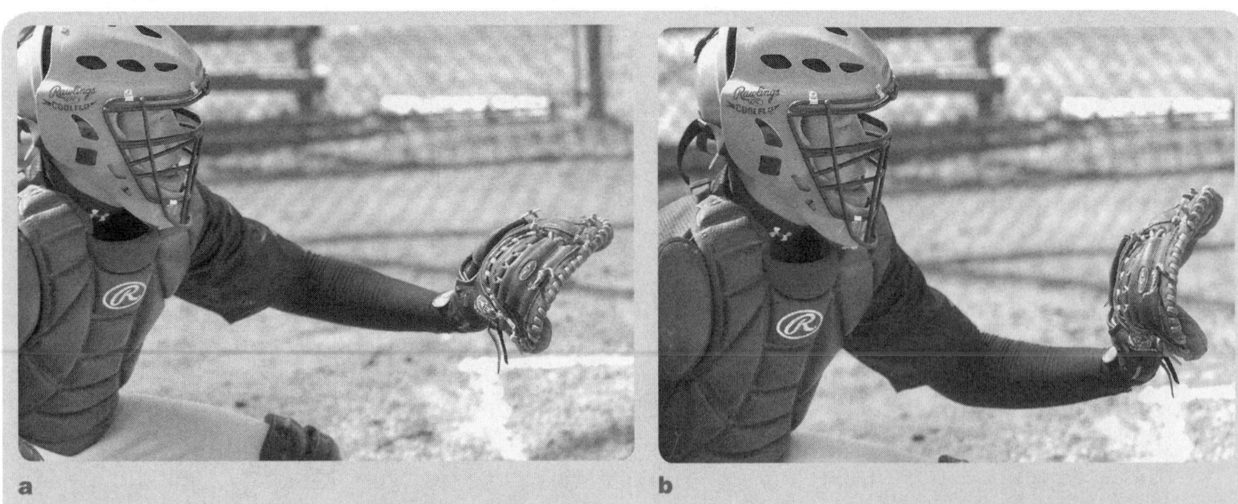

Figure 4.11 Positioning of the catcher's mitt: *(a)* correct and *(b)* incorrect.

Many catchers lock their wrists as shown in figure 4.11*b*, but this incorrect technique causes tension and makes it difficult to move the mitt smoothly and swiftly on inside or outside pitches. A locked wrist also prevents soft catching because when the wrist is locked, the catcher is more apt to stab at the ball than to catch and give, which he can accomplish with a loose wrist as the ball enters the mitt.

GIVING SIGNS

When a catcher assumes his sign-giving stance, he should consider two things: First, he must conceal his signs from the coaches at first and third, and second, he must be certain that the pitcher can see the signs easily. Figure 4.12 shows the proper body position for a catcher when giving signs. His feet are balanced beneath his body, with his right foot slightly closer to the plate than his left. His mitt hand and arm are next to and outside his left leg, with the mitt extending past the knee closer to home to block the signs from the third-base coach. By placing the right foot slightly ahead of the left—left toe even with right instep—the right leg is in position to block the signs from the first-base coach. The right arm rests on the right thigh, and the hand hangs freely between the legs. The catcher's back is straight but not stiff. The thighs should not be too close together because the pitcher needs a good viewing area to see the signs. The catcher should make sure that the fingers of the right hand do not drop too low and become visible under the thighs.

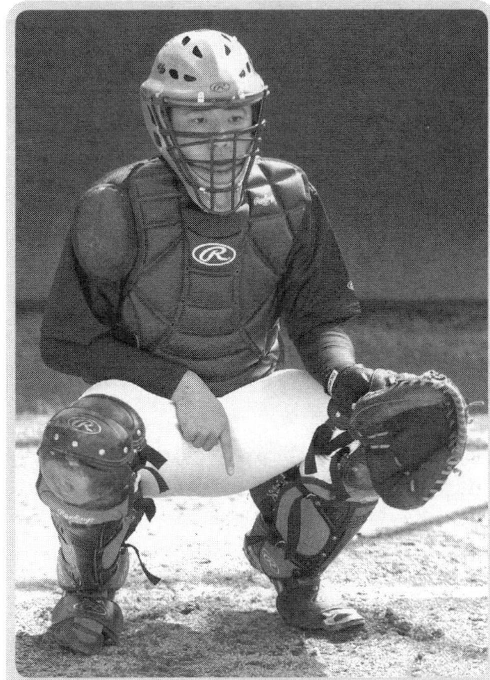

Figure 4.12 Proper body positioning for catcher when giving signs.

STANCE WITH NO RUNNERS ON BASE

After giving the pitcher the signal, the catcher needs to move into proper receiving stance when no runners are on base (see figure 4.13). To get into this position from the signal stance, the catcher should simply shift his feet and raise his buttocks. Note that the catcher tucks the throwing hand behind his back to protect it from injury from foul tips. He should do this, however, only when no one is on base. With runners on base, the glove should shield the throwing hand.

If the pitch will be outside to a right-handed batter or inside to a lefty, the catcher can take a step to the outside with the right foot and then position the left foot. On an inside pitch to a right-hander or an outside pitch to a left-hander, the catcher moves the left foot forward and then spreads the right foot comfortably.

In the receiving stance shown in figure 4.13, the catcher's feet are spread wider than the shoulders and his weight is centered on the inside of his feet. A stance that is too narrow inhibits balance and makes it harder for the catcher to move quickly into blocking position. The feet are angled toward the baselines, facilitating ease of getting into throwing and blocking position. The knees must be kept inside the feet, the

(continued)

Figure 4.13 Proper receiving stance with no runners on base.

mitt is relaxed and away from the body ready to receive the pitch and the shoulders are squared to the pitcher, creating a good five-point target—two knees, two shoulders and the mitt.

The catcher should not stand too far away from the plate. From his receiving stance, he should be able to reach up and touch the back elbow of a right-handed batter with his mitt. Moving closer to the plate enables a catcher to catch balls, especially breaking pitches, before they move out of the strike zone. When sitting in this position, however, the catcher should allow the ball to get to the mitt and resist the urge to reach the mitt out and get the ball.

Additionally, the head should be up and the eyes focused on the pitcher's release point. Seeing through a catcher's mask is not easy, and some catchers may need practice in the art. Have them take a mask home and wear it while watching TV. Doing so will help them acclimate to looking through the bars and help them focus better during games. They will also become comfortable wearing the mask and learn to resist the tendency to take the mask off on every play, which is a waste of time.

If a catcher's back is too straight, too much weight will be on his heels and he will not be able to move the mitt away from the body. A straight back also throws him off balance and makes it more difficult to get into blocking position. The catcher's weight should be on the balls of his feet with a little more weight on the left leg. This stance will make it easier to step with the right leg and block the ball on pitches to the outside.

Figure 4.14 Proper receiving stance with runners on base.

STANCE WITH RUNNERS ON BASE

With a runner or runners on base, the catcher should widen his stance slightly from the stance that he uses with no runners on base (see figure 4.14). He should also raise his buttocks slightly so that he is in a more ready position to throw should a runner attempt a steal. As mentioned earlier, he should not keep his right hand behind his back with runners on. Instead, he should hold it behind the glove as shown in figure 4.14. He should tuck the thumb under the fingers and place the hand behind the web of the glove to protect it from foul tips. A slight risk of injury is present here because the hand is exposed, but in this position a foul tip would hit the fleshy part of the fingers, not the knuckles.

Again, whenever the catcher is in the receiving stance—runners on base or not—his weight should be on the balls of his feet with a little more weight on the left leg.

FRAMING PITCHES

When a pitch is thrown, a catcher must move his glove around the strike zone to catch the pitch and frame it for the umpire. Framing refers to the technique of catching the ball by keeping the ball between the catcher's mitt and the strike zone using soft hands with as little body movement as possible. When receiving the ball, the catcher should always gently sway his body left or right so that his nose stays in line with the pitch. This movement assists in the framing technique.

Framing helps make the pitch look like a strike to the umpire and is especially useful on marginal pitches. There is nothing deceptive about catchers helping umpires "see" strikes. Umpires will call what they see and smooth framing techniques actually give umpires a better view of a pitch. Catchers should only "frame" pitches that are close to the strike zone. If the ball is more than 6 to 8 inches outside or is not an obvious strike, framing isn't necessary. Besides, most umpires dislike it when catchers try to frame balls that are obviously not strikes. Many feel in those cases that the catcher is attempting to show them up. When balls are far outside or inside the catcher must get his body in front of the ball to prevent wild pitches and should not be concerned with trying to steal a strike for his pitcher by framing. Also, with all pitches, if a runner is stealing a base, the catcher must be more concerned with making the throw than with framing the pitch.

Additionally, the catcher should receive low pitches closer to home plate and high pitches closer to his body. This tiny variation can help umpires see the pitch better and influence whether they call the pitch a ball or a strike.

In general, the catcher should try to frame four kinds of pitches within the strike zone:

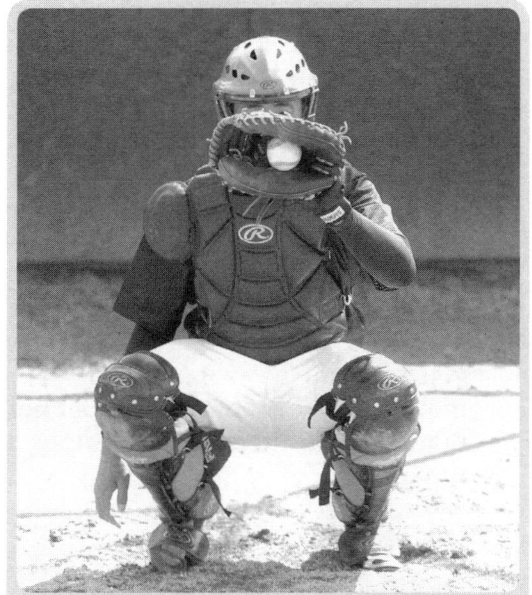

Figure 4.15 Catching a high pitch.

High Pitch

A high pitch includes all pitches from above the belt to the top of the strike zone. On these pitches, the catcher tries to catch the top half of the ball with his mitt by keeping the pocket above the ball (see figure 4.15). After catching the ball, the catcher should bend his wrist forward, which knocks the ball down and makes it appear lower. Catching the ball with the fingers up makes the pitch look higher because of the length of the glove. In addition, if the fingers are up, the catcher is catching the back of the ball, not the top.

(continued)

Figure 4.16 Catching a mitt-side pitch.

Mitt-Side Pitch

On this pitch, the catcher wants to catch the inside part of the ball if the batter is right-handed (see figure 4.16). He accomplishes this by turning the wrist counterclockwise and keeping the mitt between the batter and the ball.

Figure 4.17 Catching a backhand-side pitch.

Backhand-Side Pitch

On a pitch to the catcher's right side, the catcher wants to catch the outside part of the ball in the web of the mitt, rather than in the pocket (see figure 4.17). Again, the length of the glove will influence the umpire's call on this pitch. After catching the ball, the catcher should bend the wrist and the fingers should flip the web toward the strike zone. Also, it is extremely important that the catcher sway and keep his nose above the ball because if the arm gets separated too much from the body it makes it look as though the catcher had to reach for the pitch and the umpire will call a "ball."

Low Pitch

A low pitch is any pitch around the batter's knees. On this type of pitch, the catcher should keep his fingers slightly up while catching the top half of the ball (see figure 4.18). After catching the ball, the catcher should funnel it into the body by giving with the pitch and lifting slightly.

Figure 4.18 Catching a low pitch.

On close pitches, catchers should momentarily hold the ball in the spot where they caught it to give the umpire time to consider the pitch. In addition, they should not move too much when catching the ball so that the umpire doesn't have to move to see it. Some catchers rise up prematurely, making it difficult for the umpire to see the pitch well and giving him or her no alternative but to call the pitch a ball. Instruct catchers to sway in their movements, not jerk. Keeping their shoulders square and swaying to the pitch with their ankles is the smoothest way to accomplish this.

After catching the ball, the catcher should return it to the pitcher without making him move too much. Poor throws back to the mound aggravate pitchers and throw off their rhythm, especially if they have to jump or move too far to catch the ball.

At a Glance

The following parts of the text offer additional information on catcher mechanics.

Catcher Throwing	p. 82
Catcher Blocking	p. 86
Reacting As a Catcher	p. 90
Defending Bunt Situations	p. 186
Catcher Pickoffs	p. 194

Common Errors

You may run into several common errors when teaching catcher mechanics.

Error	Error correction
The catcher trips when chasing balls or making throws.	Check to make certain that the catcher's equipment fits properly and is not getting in the way of his running or throwing. Make certain that the clips on the shin guards, for example, are positioned on the outside of the catcher's calves.
The catcher has difficulty hanging on to pitches.	Make certain that the catcher's mitt is sufficiently broken in before letting him use it in a game. In addition, the glove should not be too tight or too loose.
Pitchers consistently ask the catcher to give the signs again.	The catcher's legs may be so close together that the pitcher cannot see the signs. Have the catcher open his knees to facilitate easier viewing.
The hitter's bat makes contact with the catcher's mitt.	The catcher is either too close to the plate or is reaching out for pitches. Emphasize allowing the ball to get to the mitt and not reaching for it.
The catcher drops many easy pitches.	The catcher might be blinking his eyes on swings. Have the catcher blink as the ball is being thrown.

Catcher Throwing

KEY POINTS

The most important components of throwing are

- getting into throwing position,
- throwing footwork and
- upper-body action.

While lamenting the sorry state of his catching corps when he was managing the New York Mets, Casey Stengel once quipped, "I got one that can throw but can't catch, and one that can catch but can't throw and one who can hit but can't do either!" The catcher has to be the most complete ballplayer on the team. He should be able to catch, field and throw, and throw well.

GETTING INTO THROWING POSITION

Because of the distance that the ball needs to travel and the time needed to get to its destination, the catcher's throw has to be hard. Infielders usually have between 4 and 4.5 seconds to make a throw between the time a ball is hit and when the runner reaches first base. The average time for a runner on first base with a lead to reach second base is 3.5 seconds. Because the runner usually takes off for the base on the pitcher's first move, the catcher has at most about 2.2 seconds to get the ball to second base after he receives it from the pitcher. That's half the time of anyone else. The catcher has to transform himself from receiver to thrower in less than a second.

Figure 4.19 Catcher bringing the mitt back past the vertical midline of his chest when receiving the ball.

To make this conversion easier, a catcher must always, as stated earlier, anticipate running situations and be in the runners-on-base receiving stance. He should not catch the ball as far away from the body as he normally does. By receiving it farther behind the plate and closer to the body, he can transfer it more quickly from the mitt to the throwing hand.

When the catcher receives the ball, he should bring the mitt back to a point past the vertical midline of his chest (see figure 4.19). The left arm then moves back, and he exchanges the ball from the mitt hand to the throwing hand. This process should occur in one smooth motion, almost a continuous motion in which he simply redirects the ball into the throwing hand. This technique takes constant practice to perfect, but when refined it can reduce the catcher's throwing time by precious 10ths of a second.

As in all throwing, the catcher should grip the ball across the seams when possible. When this is not possible, the key is to get the hand in the correct fingers-on-top, thumb-on-bottom position.

THROWING FOOTWORK

As the catcher's hands and arms are getting into throwing position, the feet should be shifting to make the throw. Catchers can shift to throw in several ways:

Jump Pivot Method

As he receives the ball, the catcher quickly shifts his feet into throwing position. The right foot opens up and moves to the spot where the left foot was, in effect replacing it. The catcher takes a short step with the left foot and throws (see figure 4.20, *a-c*). Sometimes catchers lift both feet simultaneously with this method. Either is acceptable, but you must make sure that the catcher does not step back with the right foot. The foot must move in the direction of the throw. In addition, the steps must be short. The longer the stride, the more time it takes to get rid of the ball.

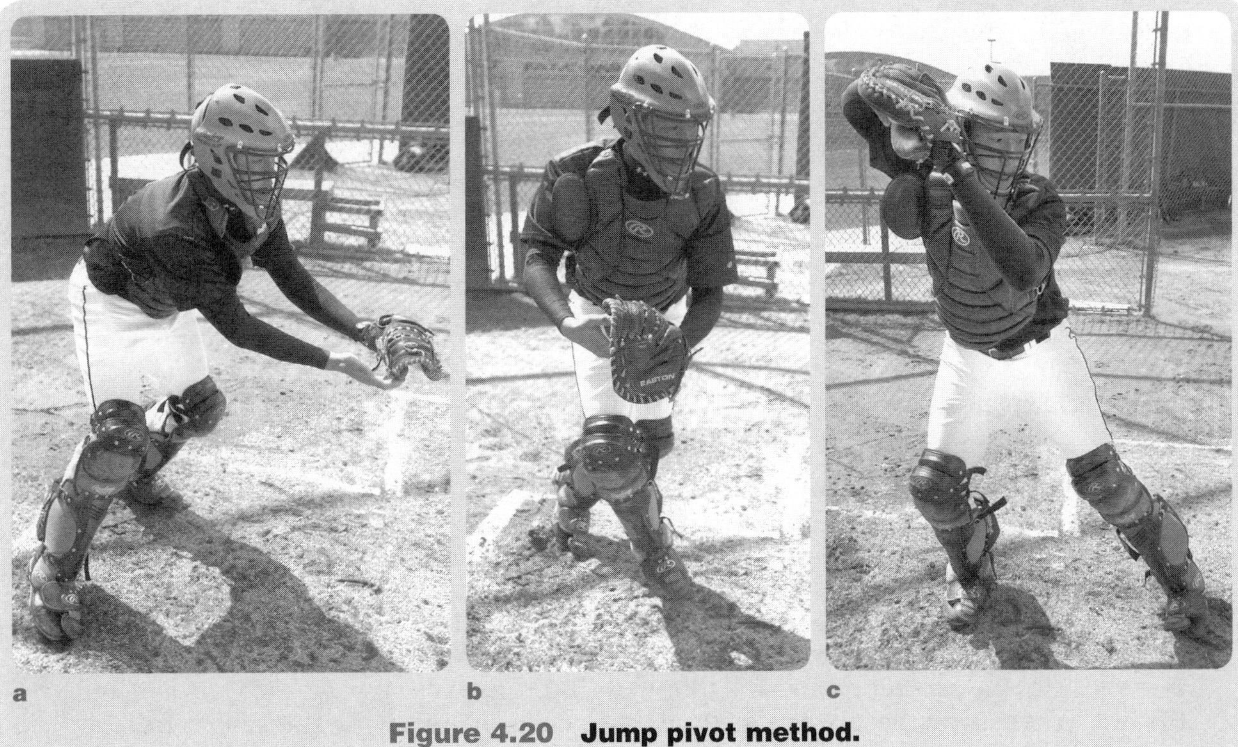

a b c

Figure 4.20 Jump pivot method.

Rock and Throw Method

Catchers with extremely strong arms can use the rock and throw method, but it is not recommended for catchers with average or below-average arm strength. As the ball hits the mitt, the catcher transfers his weight to his rear leg, literally rocking backward. At the same time he rotates his shoulders, bringing the mitt and bare hand up into throwing position. He then takes a step with his left foot and throws (see figure 4.21, *a-c*). Hall of Fame catcher Johnny Bench used this method.

(continued)

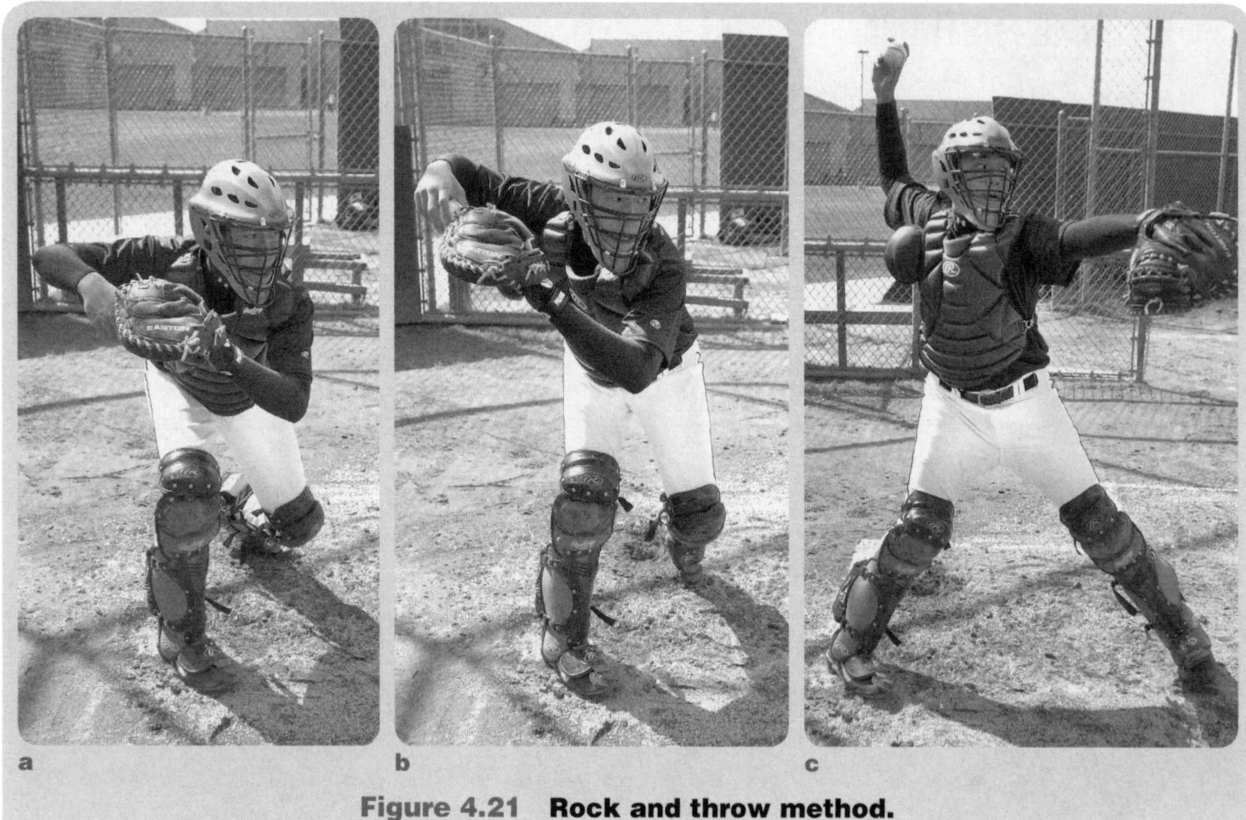

a b c

Figure 4.21 Rock and throw method.

Jab Step Method

If the catcher does not have a strong arm, this method gives him a head start on the throw. On pitches to the bare-hand side or down the middle, as the ball nears home plate the catcher takes a short jab step with his right foot toward the ball (see figure 4.22*a*). The foot must open up as he takes this step so that the instep points to second base. On pitches to the mitt side, the catcher takes a jab step with his left foot (see figure 4.22*b*). He should time the step so that it occurs when the ball hits the mitt. This technique enables the catcher to get some momentum toward the target. After the ball is in the mitt, the catcher rotates his shoulders, takes a quick step with the left foot and throws. When using the jab step method, balance in the receiving stance is extremely important. In order to jab the foot in the direction of the pitch, the catcher's weight must be evenly distributed. If too much weight is on the right or left side of the body, it will be difficult to get the weight moving in the opposite direction.

UPPER-BODY ACTION

The upper-body action must be correct during the catcher's throw. The front shoulder must always point at the target. The catcher accomplishes this by bringing the mitt arm back past the midline of the body. The catcher's arm action, as discussed in "Throwing Basics" on page 64, is shorter than the action of an infielder. The ball has to get up above the shoulder immediately. The head must remain level over the center

a

b

Figure 4.22 Jab step method for *(a)* pitches to the catcher's bare-hand side and *(b)* pitches to the catcher's mitt side.

of the body. Movement of the head out in front of the body destroys balance and weakens the throw. The catcher's weight should transfer from the back leg to the front leg. When the left foot hits, the catcher should execute a three-quarter to full overhand throw initiated by making a hard pivot on the ball of his right foot so that he turns the foot over, rotating the shoelaces to face the ground.

Forcing the right foot over in this fashion helps the right hip rotate toward the target so that the catcher can properly follow through on the throw. If this doesn't occur, the follow-through will be restricted and the catcher will have a whiplash type of throw.

At a Glance

The following parts of the text offer additional information on throwing.

Common Errors

You may run into several common errors when teaching your catchers how to throw.

Error	Error correction
The catcher seems to be throwing across his body when throwing to second.	Check to be certain that the catcher moves his left foot in the direction of the throw, not toward first base.
The catcher has too much loop in his throw.	A looping throw occurs when the player's head gets ahead of his body. Emphasize keeping the head over the body's center of gravity.

Catcher Blocking

KEY POINTS

The most important components of catcher blocking include

- moving into position,
- keeping the ball in front and
- recovering quickly.

Not every pitch thrown will be in the strike zone. Many pitches will hit the dirt before they hit the catcher's mitt. Other pitches will fly outside the catcher's range. In these instances, especially with runners on base, catchers must be able to get quickly into blocking position and stop the ball from getting by and runners scoring at home. Becoming skilled in blocking techniques helps the catcher keep pitchers relaxed. As mentioned earlier under "Catcher Attributes," the catcher should treat the area around the plate like his realm. Unlike medieval lords, however, who built castles to keep out invading knights and even dragons, the catcher's main goal is to keep the invading balls "in" his zone. The last thing a coach wants is a pitcher who has no confidence in his catcher's ability to stop a ball. That's when pitchers start to overthrow because they feel they have do everything because no one else is helping them. And all coaches know what happens when pitchers try to throw too hard.

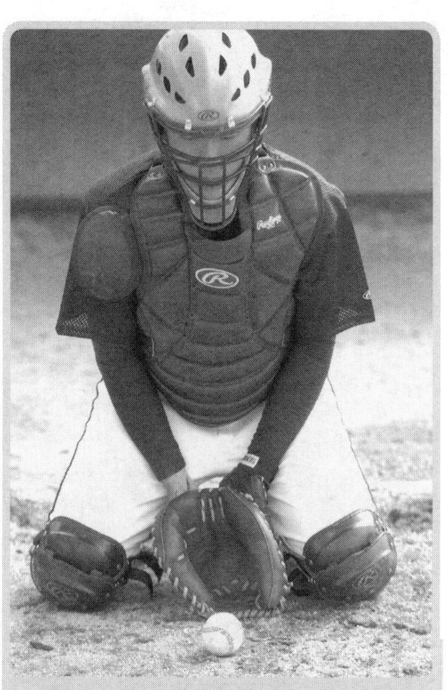

Figure 4.23 Catching a pitch straight at the catcher.

MOVING INTO POSITION

One of the problems with the large first-baseman-type catchers mitts of today is that they give catchers a false sense of security, leading them to believe that they can field balls in the dirt with their mitts. Any time a ball is thrown in the dirt, the catcher must lower his body and try to block the ball, not catch it.

When the catcher senses that the ball will be low, he should immediately lower his knees into the ground by rolling inward on his ankles. If the pitch is straight at the catcher, the knees will drop straight down and forward, as shown in figure 4.23. For pitches on either side of the catcher, the catcher must first sway or slide his body in the direction of the ball before the knees hit the ground, as shown in figure 4.24, *a* and *b*. In these cases, only the ankle farthest from the ball rolls inward. If the ball is thrown extremely wide of the body, the catcher must first take a quick jab step with the foot closer to the direction of the pitch before lowering his knees.

As the knees hit the ground, the catcher should push the fingers of his mitt hand and bare hand into the ground and lower his head so that his chin is tucked into his chest (see figure 4.25). His buttocks should be low and his shoulders rolled forward. The arms should be relaxed, not rigid, so that they can soak up the shock of the ball and keep it from bouncing too far from the blocking point. When the catcher assumes this position, the whole body acts as an absorbing agent, or a "big soft pillow," as Ron Davini, baseball coach at Corona del Sol High School in Arizona, likes to refer to it.

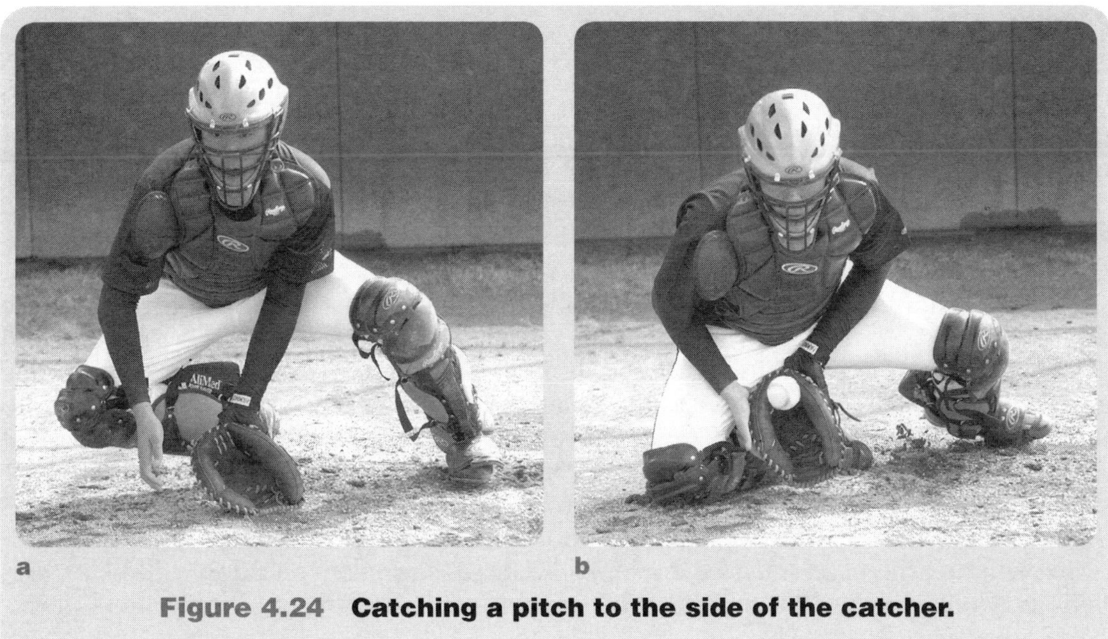

a b

Figure 4.24 Catching a pitch to the side of the catcher.

After blocking a ball, the catcher usually has to get up and make a throw. If the body is too rigid, the ball will bounce away and be difficult to retrieve. When trying to be soft, the catcher's body forms a C, as shown in figure 4.26. In a sense, he smothers the ball with his "big pillow," allowing the ball to bounce softly close to him so that he can quickly retrieve it and discourage any baserunners from advancing.

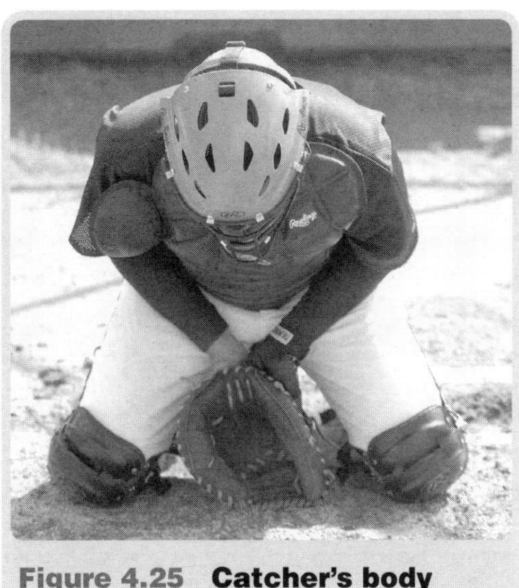

Figure 4.25 Catcher's body positioning as the knees hit the ground.

Figure 4.26 C position.

(continued)

KEEPING THE BALL IN FRONT

When the catcher gets into blocking position, he must always angle his body toward the plate. This position keeps the ball in front of him and makes it easier to collect and throw if a runner is stealing. For balls on the first-base side of the plate, the catcher must sway forward toward the angle created by the foul line. He turns the body so that, when blocked, the ball will bounce toward the area in front of the plate. He performs the opposite technique on balls to the third-base side.

Catchers should be alert to breaking balls to either side. A curveball thrown in the dirt will bounce in the opposite direction after it hits. For example, if a right-handed pitcher throws a curveball in the dirt to the outside part of the plate to a right-handed batter, the ball will bounce toward the batter after hitting the ground. A catcher who thinks that the ball is going to move more to the outside and reacts as such will be out of position and the ball will bounce over his left shoulder. Therefore, the catcher should not move too far left or right on breaking pitches. Because the catcher knows what type of pitch is being thrown, he should know whether to under- or overshift.

To reiterate, the head must be down. If the head is up, the shoulders will be up and balls may bounce over the shoulders because now the body is not in the C position.

RECOVERING QUICKLY

After the catcher blocks the ball, the play does not end. A good catcher has to pounce on the ball, retrieve it and get his body back up into throwing position. He must quickly move his feet back underneath his body and get the ball into position to throw. To do this, the catcher must push up quickly with his hands and feet and gather the ball with a scooping motion using both the mitt and the bare hand. Too often, when catchers use only the bare hand, they mishandle the ball and lose valuable time. Using both hands for this technique also helps them attain proper body position for the throw by forcing the left shoulder to point to the target.

As the hands are gathering the ball and bringing it up into throwing position, the catcher takes a quick right, left with his feet, as discussed in "Catcher Throwing" beginning on page 82, and is ready to unleash the ball to the base. A catcher who becomes adept in this technique will throw out most runners trying to steal because when runners see the ball going into the dirt, they subconsciously feel the catcher will give up on the steal attempt. Many high school catchers don't work hard on blocking balls and as a result, the balls bounce away from them with regularity. Runners know this and consequently don't run as hard as they normally would on the steal attempt, feeling that the ball is going to be out of the catcher's range. This gives the catcher with good blocking and recovery skills time to throw the runner out.

At a Glance

The following parts of the text offer additional information on blocking.

Catcher Basics	p. 74
Catcher Throwing	p. 82
Defending Bunt Situations	p. 186
Catcher Pickoffs	p. 194
Wild Pitches	p. 204

Common Errors

You may run into several common errors when teaching your catchers how to block.

Error	Error correction
Balls bounce regularly over the catcher when he attempts to block.	Emphasize tucking the chin and softening the shoulders to smother the ball.
Balls always bounce too far in front of the catcher.	Emphasize relaxing the body when blocking, turning it into a big, fat pillow. Balls may also bounce too far away if the catcher kicks his feet back instead of dropping to his knees. Kicking the feet in this manner thrusts the body toward the ball, pushing it farther away.

Reacting As a Catcher

KEY POINTS

The most important components of reacting as a catcher are:

- wild pitches,
- bunts,
- plays at the plate and
- backing up first base.

Catching is not only about receiving and blocking the baseball. Catchers also need catlike reflexes to react to other situations during a game.

WILD PITCHES

With no runners on base, a catcher doesn't have to worry about chasing down wild pitches—that's a job for the on-deck batter. But with a runner on, the catcher must react quickly to hold the runner to a one-base advance. With a runner on third base, the quicker the catcher can get to the ball, the better the chance he has of cutting down the runner at the plate.

Figure 4.27 Corralling a wild pitch.

When a ball gets by the catcher, he should turn his body in the direction of the ball and sprint to its location. Often, the catcher will need help from the pitcher. In these situations, the pitcher should sprint toward home and yell, "Left, left, left" or "Right, right, right" in case the catcher doesn't know where the ball is. If the ball has squirted toward the backstop, the best move a catcher can perform is to break into a bent-leg slide, scoop up the ball with both hands, turn and scramble to his knees while making a three-quarter-arm throw to the pitcher covering the plate (see figure 4.27). On balls that do not get as far as the backstop, the catcher should get his shoulders aimed at the plate when he is scooping the ball so that he can make a quick toss.

BUNTS

Catchers must also react quickly to the bunt. The way that a catcher goes after a bunted ball has a lot to do with the runner being safe or out, or, as in the case of the New York Mets in the 1973 World Series, can have a direct bearing on the outcome of the game. In that Series, on a ball bunted on the third-base side in front of home plate, the catcher fielded the ball incorrectly. As a result, he threw it past first base, allowing several runners to advance and contributing to the Mets' demise.

On all bunted balls, the catcher should scoop the ball by bringing his mitt and his hand together on the ball in much the same way that an earth-moving shovel used in construction scoops soil (see figure 4.28). As catchers develop this skill, they may then be able to flick the ball into the throwing hand with the mitt and quicken the process, but this technique is not recommended for beginning catchers. After scooping the ball, the catcher makes a quick right-left with his feet as discussed in "Catcher Throwing" on page 82 and throws to the base.

Figure 4.28 **Fielding a bunted ball.**

On balls bunted on the first-base side in front of the plate, the catcher should take his first few steps directly toward the pitcher's mound and then turn his shoulders to first base and field the ball (see figure 4.29). This path gets his body parallel to the foul line and in good position to make the throw. On balls directly in front of the plate, the catcher should move quickly to the ball and turn his body as he is scooping the ball. Then all he needs to do is the prescribed footwork and throw.

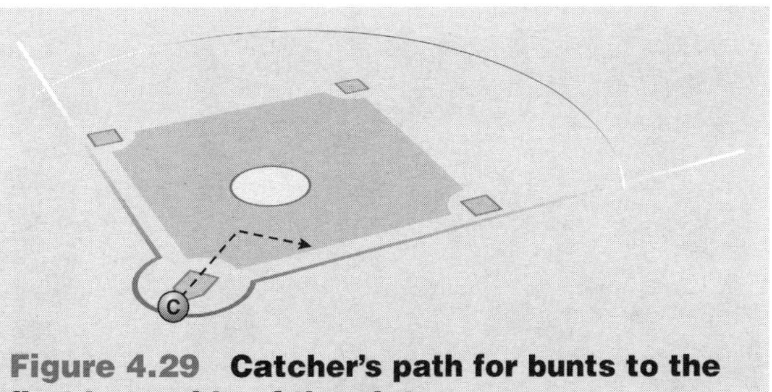

Figure 4.29 **Catcher's path for bunts to the first-base side of the plate.**

Balls to the third-base side require another technique. On these plays, the catcher should first move directly to the left of the plate in foul territory and take an arced route to the ball (see figure 4.30). This path gets the shoulders lined up with first base, allows the catcher to gather the ball, and makes an accurate throw possible. Some catchers like to take a direct route to the ball in this situation, but the problem with this path is that when the catcher scoops the ball, his back will be facing first base. He then has to spin around to his left side and pick up his target while doing so. On a "bang, bang" play, the catcher will have to hurry his throw, increasing the chances for an error.

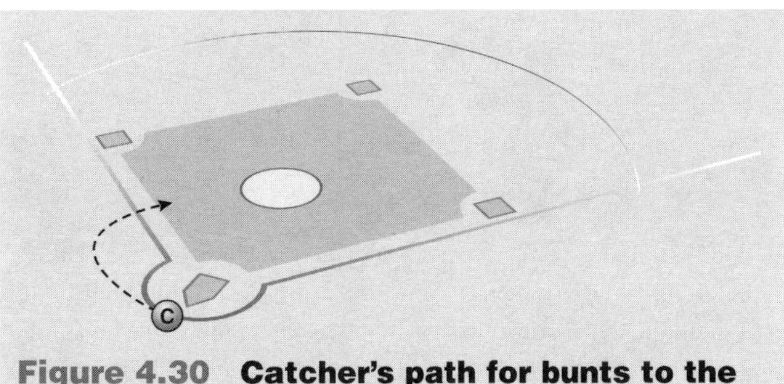

Figure 4.30 **Catcher's path for bunts to the third-base side of the plate.**

(continued)

PLAYS AT THE PLATE

On balls thrown to the plate from the left-field or center-field area of the diamond when the catcher will have to tag a sliding runner, the catcher should assume the basic athletic position, with his feet shoulder-width apart and his left foot parallel and close to the left-field foul line (see figure 4.31). He should be semicrouched, awaiting the ball much as an infielder does when covering second base on a steal. In this position, the catcher shows the runner a portion of the plate, giving him something at which to slide. When the ball arrives, the catcher should grasp it firmly in his bare hand within his mitt so that he's holding it with both hands. He then sweeps his mitt and hand straight down at the sliding runner while lowering his body and transferring most of his weight to his left side (see figure 4.32). In case of a hard collision on the play, having the ball gripped firmly in the hand will help the catcher retain possession. In addition, the catcher should allow the runner to push his left leg, which is protected by the shin guard, forward as shown in figure 4.32. When this occurs, the catcher will fall on the runner, stopping his progress and ensuring the out.

On force plays at the plate, the catcher should assume a position out in front of the plate, much like a first baseman, with his right foot positioned on the front edge of

Figure 4.31 Catcher positioning for balls thrown home from left or center field.

Figure 4.32 Catching a ball from left or center field.

the plate (see figure 4.33). He should square his body to the direction from which the throw will come and flex his knees. If the catcher has to make a throw after the force play, he shifts his feet like an infielder and makes the throw.

Figure 4.33 Catcher positioning for force plays at the plate.

BACKING UP FIRST BASE

A catcher also needs quick reactions when backing up infielders' throws to first base. When the bases are empty and a batter hits the ball into fair territory, the catcher should follow the runner to first base so that he can back up any overthrows. He should run hard here and actually try to beat the runner to the base, aligning himself with the infielder's throw. On base hits, if the catcher has hustled properly to a backup position, he will be able to cover the base in case the runner makes too big a turn toward second. This is especially true if the first baseman has been pulled far to his right and is out of position to get back to the base.

At a Glance

The following parts of the text offer additional information on reacting as a catcher.

Common Errors

You may run into several common errors when teaching your catchers how to react.

Error	Error correction
While grabbing for the ball on a bunt, the catcher fumbles it.	Reemphasize to the player that he should scoop the ball with his mitt and bare hand.
The catcher's throws to first base on bunts tail away from the fielder.	Most likely, the player is not lining up his shoulders to throw. Examine the route that the catcher takes to the ball and make certain that he lines up his shoulders and steps toward the base on the throw. A tailing throw can also occur when the catcher does not close his left side on the throw by bringing his mitt arm back.
The catcher drops many balls on tag plays at the plate.	Emphasize getting the ball into the bare hand first on all tag plays.

KEY POINTS

The most important components of pitching are

- the downward plane,
- strike zone knowledge,
- becoming the fifth infielder,
- achieving a solid base,
- setting the body in motion,
- balance position,
- approach position,
- release position and
- follow-through.

A good pitcher can frustrate even a great hitter because the hitter must continually try to outthink him. This task is not easy, especially if the pitcher has good mechanics and can put the ball where he wants to, when he wants to. Many coaches believe the old saying that defense wins ball games. And the bedrock of defense is pitching, because baseball is the only team sport in which the defense controls the ball.

The surest sign that winter is nearly over is TV coverage of spring training. Because pitchers need to get their legs in shape for the rigors of the long season, they report early. But strong legs are not the only physical attributes that a pitcher needs. Often, the tallest or biggest kids on the team, especially at the youth level, are chosen to be pitchers. Players who are not tall or strong, however, should not be discouraged from becoming pitchers. After all, Steve Dalkowski, the legendary Orioles pitcher who supposedly threw the hardest of them all, was only 5-foot-9, as was the Louisiana Lightning, Ron Guidry, who threw in the mid-90s. Bobby Shantz, a diminutive 5-foot-6, won 24 games one year for the A's, then playing in Philadelphia.

Pitching is not only physical; it is also mental and mechanical. Pitchers need stamina more than they need strength. They must have good reactions and be able to think several pitches ahead of the hitter. Above all, if they have control of their pitches they will be successful. Generally, a pitcher needs to do several things well to be successful. He must be able to throw the ball with control (location), make the ball move laterally or vertically (movement), hide the ball from the hitter as long as possible (deception) and throw with some speed (velocity). If a pitcher can do three of these, or perhaps even two, he will be effective.

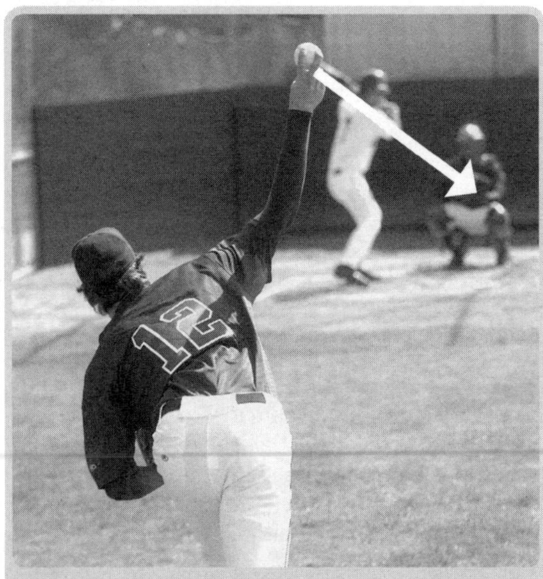

Figure 4.34 Pitching on a downward plane.

Pitchers also need to make the hitter aware that they are in charge because a good hitter will learn to exploit a pitcher who shows weakness. Pitchers can gain the aura of authority in several ways: they can stare down the hitter; they can work quickly between pitches; and they can alter their physical appearance a little to give themselves more presence. Tom Gordon, a successful major league pitcher, pulls the brim of his cap down right above his eyes. This may not make him pitch better, but it hides his face and makes the batter curious. All pitchers must do something to make themselves look like they are in charge. As Sandy Koufax said, "Pitching is the art of instilling fear."

THE DOWNWARD PLANE

The pitcher's mound is 10 inches higher than home plate. Pitchers can gain a great edge over hitters by throwing the ball on a downward angle to the hitter. For that reason, major league scouts place a premium on taller pitchers. Every motion of the pitcher should be predicated on throwing the ball on a downward plane. To do so, the pitcher should throw with his elbow above his shoulder toward the hitter's knees. This technique creates a steeper angle for the ball to follow to the plate, as shown in figure 4.34, and the steeper the angle, the harder it is for the hitter to make contact with the ball.

STRIKE ZONE KNOWLEDGE

Besides knowing the rule-book definition of what constitutes a strike, pitchers must be aware of the working definition of this zone as it varies from game to game. Because of where they stand, all umpires do not call strikes alike. Some favor lower pitches; others prefer higher ones. Most, however, can be influenced by how often the pitcher hits the target established by his catcher. If pitchers can prove that they can hit the mitt consistently, umpires will call strikes—witness the latitude that umpires give to great control pitchers like Greg Maddux and Tom Glavine.

Pitchers must acknowledge what the strike zone is on any given day and adapt to it. If the umpire is not calling the ball on the knees a strike, then pitchers must not continue to try to throw balls to that spot hoping that the umpire will suddenly start calling them strikes. They must modify their thinking and throw the ball into the area where the umpire is calling strikes! Pitchers must also know how to throw balls out of the strike zone when they need to. If the catcher signals for an outside breaking pitch on a 0-2 count, the pitcher should not throw the ball close enough to the strike zone that the hitter can make contact.

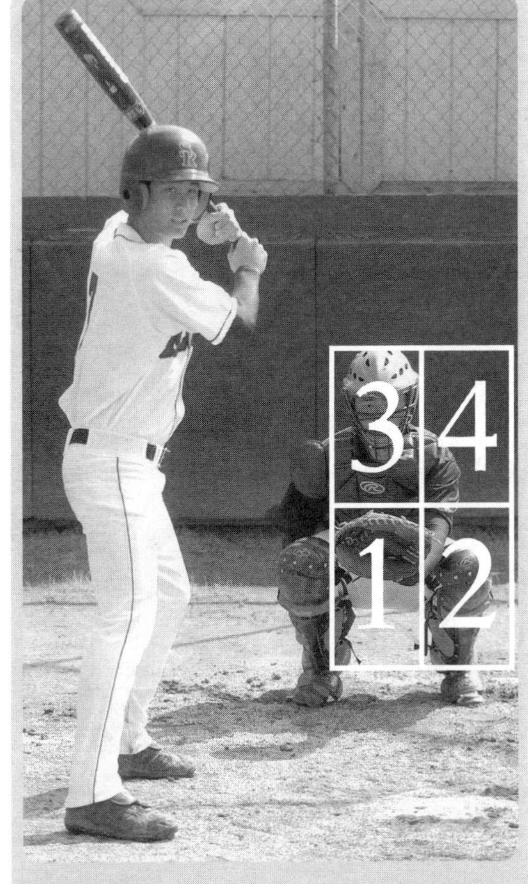

Figure 4.35 Areas of the strike zone.

Pitchers should think of the strike zone as a rectangle divided into four equal parts, as illustrated in figure 4.35. They should not throw the ball into the area out over the plate away from the hitter. This location allows the hitter to extend his arms and make good contact. Pitchers should avoid area 3 when throwing to a right-handed batter and area 4 when throwing to a left-handed batter. Instead, they should concentrate their pitches into the lower half of the strike zone—especially in the areas closest to the batter's knees, areas 1 and 2 in figure 4.35. Keeping the ball in these zones will make any pitcher effective over the long run because low balls are consistently more difficult to hit well than balls that are waist high. The reason for this is that batters don't like having to swing at low pitches. Also, when low pitches are hit, they are most likely going to be hit on the ground giving the infielders a chance to make a play and throw out the runners.

(continued)

BECOMING THE FIFTH INFIELDER

Pitchers are also infielders. When a pitcher finishes his follow-through, he should bring his glove hand forward so that he is in a position to field the ball if it is hit back to him. He must also be ready to go left or right for balls, or charge in to field bunts. The pitcher is the play caller in the infield on pop-ups. If the pitcher is unable to field the ball, he should point to it and help make the decision on who should field it by loudly calling out the player's name several times.

But pitchers should not be so concerned with fielding that they make it a priority over their throwing. As the old saying goes, "If a pitcher is worried about getting into fielding position, he'd *better* be!"

Figure 4.36 **Pitcher's starting position.**

ACHIEVING A SOLID BASE

Throughout the entire pitching motion, pitchers should think as good hitters do—begin slow and relaxed and then explode. They should attempt to use only the motion or actions necessary to deliver the ball. Unnecessary motions can cause loss of balance and rhythm, key elements of pitching. Hurried motions force the body out of sync and make achieving a downward angle impossible. These considerations require pitchers to start their motion with a solid base.

In the starting position for the windup, the feet should be shoulder-width apart and balanced on the pitching rubber (see figure 4.36). The pitcher's legs should be relaxed, and his arms should be hanging loosely at his sides or held in front of his chest. His pivot foot should be in contact with the rubber, and his stride foot should be even with the heel of the pivot foot. The pivot foot should be placed off center on the rubber to the throwing-arm side. The ball can either be in the pitcher's throwing hand or preset in the glove. If the pitcher keeps the ball in the hand, however, he must not hold the ball in the grip of the pitch that he is going to throw. The pitcher should distribute his weight evenly and hold his head up facing the catcher. He should not bend over because doing so creates unnecessary movement in the motion.

Figure 4.37 **Pitcher's foot positioning in the stretch position.**

In the stretch position, the pitcher should contact the rubber with the heel and little toe of his pivot foot, as shown in figure 4.37. The front, or stride, foot should be placed in a position so that it is slightly more than shoulder-width apart from the rear, or pivot, foot. The knees should be flexed, and the weight should be balanced. While in the stretch position, the pitcher should always keep the ball in the throwing hand to facilitate quick throws to first base.

When a pitcher assumes this setup properly, he will have a strong base from which to make his first movements.

SETTING THE BODY IN MOTION

This and the following sections address the five segments of the pitching motion: getting started; the balance, or power, position; the approach position; the release of the ball; and the follow-through.

To start the pitching motion, the pitcher first brings his hands together in front of his body (see figure 4.38). Some pitching coaches prefer that their pitchers lift the hands chest high; others want their pitchers to bring the hands above the head. Either method is acceptable. When the pitcher simply holds his hands in front of his body, this is often referred to as the "no wind-up" method. The pitcher should place the throwing hand in the glove in a way that does not reveal the pitch grip to either base coach. The pitcher can do this by grasping the wrist of the throwing hand with the thumb and little finger of the glove hand. To conceal the ball further, the back of the glove should face home plate.

Immediately after bringing the hands together, the pitcher should step back slightly with his stride foot. A step that is too long will throw off his balance. After shifting his weight, the pitcher slides the pivot foot forward and down to a position in front of the rubber with the little toe and heel in contact with the rubber (see figure 4.39).

Figure 4.38 Pitcher's hand positioning when starting the pitching motion.

Figure 4.39 Pitcher's foot positioning when the hands are brought together.

(continued)

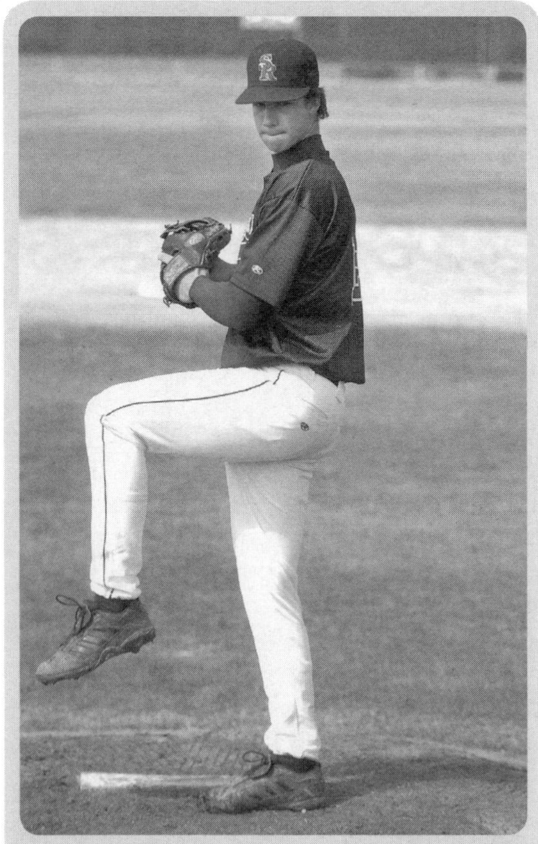

Figure 4.40 Pitcher's stride leg lifts and hips turn so that the body is perpendicular to the rubber.

travel on a level plane to the hitter. Hitters can hit balls on a level plane much easier than they can hit balls traveling on a downward plane.

After the initial movements with the pivot foot and hands, the stride leg should lift as the hips turn so that the pitcher's body is perpendicular to the rubber (see figure 4.40). The knee should be lifted so that it is approximately waist high, and the front foot should be positioned over the back foot. The pitcher should lift the leg by raising the knee, not by kicking the front foot out. Kicking the front foot out tends to force the pitcher to lean backward to compensate for the weight shift created by the kick. The back must remain straight throughout the balance position. The back leg should be flexed, but not too much.

The glove and hand should be held slightly past the vertical midline of the body, as shown in figure 4.41. This position helps the pitcher keep his weight over his back leg. As the stride leg lifts, the hands also lift. The shoulders remain level, and the head remains facing forward with the eyes on the target and the chin almost resting on the front shoulder. All these slow and deliberate motions cock the body like a spring and prepare it for the tremendous explosion of the pitch.

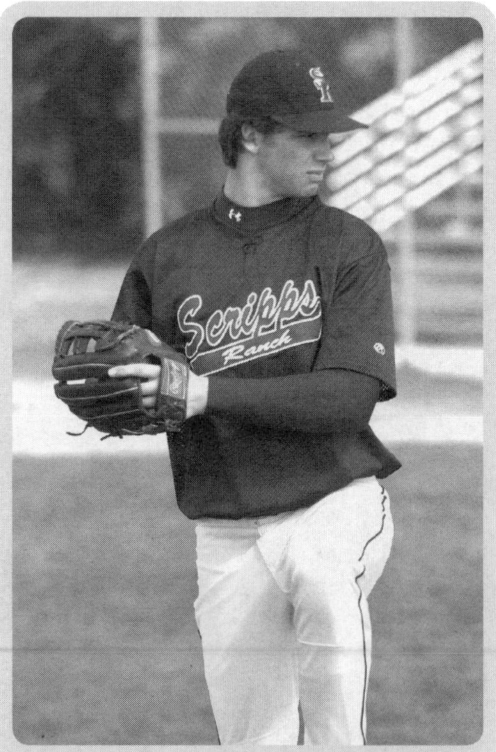

Figure 4.41 Pitcher's glove and hand held slightly past the vertical midline of the body.

APPROACH POSITION

After reaching the balance position, the pitcher begins the next phase—the movement of the body toward the plate and the movement of the arm into throwing position. When the knee reaches its highest point, which will vary from pitcher to pitcher, the hips begin to slide or glide toward home and the pitcher's stride begins. At the same time, the throwing hand breaks from the glove called the "break point" to begin the proper arm action—down, back, up and over (see figure 4.42, *a* and *b*).

The hands must not get too far from the body. Doing so destroys balance, which in turn spoils rhythm and can lead to serious mechanical problems.

Pitchers should avoid pushing off the rubber with the back leg. Some pitchers are successful with this method, but it requires adjustments to other pitching mechanics and is not recommended. Nolan Ryan, one of the greatest pitchers ever, said that when he was pitching he felt as if he were falling toward home plate with his body under control. Pushing, however, leads to rushing and loss of control.

a b

Figure 4.42 Pitcher's movement toward the plate when preparing to make the pitch.

The heel of the pitcher's stride foot should lead the foot toward the plate. This action helps keep the hips closed longer and enables the pitcher's body to stay coiled until the release point. The toes of the stride foot should point down. As the throwing arm travels back and down, the back of the glove hand should move toward the plate. This technique helps the pitcher hide the ball from the hitter, keep his front shoulder closed longer and maintain a good balance position. If the pitcher turns his glove palm toward the hitter, the front shoulder will open and create a weaker throw.

The stride foot should flip open just before landing, with the toes slightly closed to the hitter (see figure 4.43). The foot should land flat with the weight concentrated from the middle of the foot forward. Once the foot hits, the body should be in position to release the ball.

RELEASE POSITION

From the time that the hands break from the glove, all motions of the body should be in a direct line to the plate. This so-called power line helps keep the directional energy focused. Some pitching coaches like to have their pitchers think as if they are throwing in a narrow corridor. This visual metaphor

(continued)

Figure 4.43 Pitcher's stride foot opens just before it lands.

helps the pitcher stay focused on throwing the ball within a very confined area. It helps him understand that there should be very little deviation of the body from the straight power line to the plate.

Pitching, like hitting, is a rotational movement. After the stride foot hits, the coiled body is ready to unwind with terrific force. When the stride foot executes its little flip just before landing, the opening of the front hip begins. In turn, this action forces the hips to rotate explosively and moves the front shoulder out of the way, allowing the throwing shoulder to replace it.

As he is releasing the ball, the pitcher starts to bend at the waist, bringing his chest to a position over the thigh of his stride foot. The chin continues moving toward the plate. Where the chin goes, the head goes, and where the head goes, the ball goes. As the ball is released, the front arm is pulled toward the chest, enabling the throwing arm to finish its action. Do not allow pitchers to throw the glove hand behind them after they release the ball. This action may cause them to overrotate and prevent them from finishing in good fielding position.

The stride must not be too long. The pitcher must feel that he is throwing over his stride leg. When the stride is too long, the pitcher's torso cannot get into a position over the stride leg, causing loss of power and failure to use the downward plane. A long stride also forces the pitcher to land with his heel first. This in turn prevents the front leg from bending adequately and can lead to pitches that are high in the strike zone.

At a Glance

The following parts of the text offer additional information on pitching.

Throwing Basics	p. 64
Catching a Throw	p. 72
Defensive Positioning	p. 178
Defending Bunt Situations	p. 186
Pitcher Pickoffs	p. 190
Determining the Best Pitching Options	p. 198

FOLLOW-THROUGH

As he is releasing the ball, the pitcher moves from the release position into the follow-through position. The pivot foot should turn outward and then lift skyward. The shoelaces of the pivot foot should be facing down, and in many cases the foot will lift above the body. The throwing arm continues on its path and reaches toward home so that it finishes on the opposite side of the stride leg below the waist (see figure 4.44). If a pitcher throws from an overhead arm slot, the hand should finish opposite the stride leg below the knee. If a pitcher throws from a three-quarter arm slot, the throwing hand should finish opposite the stride leg between the knee and waist.

Coaches should not be too concerned with the height of the pivot leg in the follow-through. As long as they feel that the pitcher is adequately following through with his back shoulder and arm, the back leg is inconsequential. Some pitchers lift their pivot foot over their heads in this position while others simply bring their leg forward. What is important here, though, is that the foot pivots off of the rubber and initiates the pivoting of the hips and continues the unraveling of the throwing motion. Like the old song says, "the hip bone's connected to the . . ."

Figure 4.44 **Follow-through position.**

Common Errors

You may run into several common errors when teaching your athletes the techniques of the pithing motion.

Error	Error correction
The pitcher places his foot on top of the rubber in the balance position.	Pitchers who do this may have been taught to push off the rubber. Emphasize that pitchers don't push off the rubber and that placing the foot on top provides a poor and wobbly base for the balance position.
The opposing team seems to know what pitches are being thrown.	Emphasize turning the back of the glove to home plate and hiding the ball in the webbing. Another cause of tipping the opposition may be that the elbows are not relaxed in the setup position. Many pitchers give away breaking pitches by changing the angle of their elbow at setup.
Pitches are consistently high in the strike zone.	Make sure that the pitcher is not overstriding. A long stride makes it difficult to get the upper body over the stride leg at release and create a downward plane. The pitcher may be landing on the heel of the stride leg, resulting in a straight stride leg and erratic control.
The pitcher's stride foot consistently lands well to the closed side of his power line.	Emphasize making the first movement from a solid base with a short step straight back with the stride foot. Pitchers often step on an angle and then have problems getting the body back to the power line.

Pitcher Stretch Mechanics

KEY POINTS

The most important components of pitching from the stretch position are

- checking runners and
- shortening stride.

With runners on base, the pitcher must pitch from the stretch position. Because delivering the ball from the stretch, or set position, requires less time than making the delivery from the windup, the pitcher using the stretch can hold runners closer to the base, which helps thwart stolen base attempts. Because it involves less motion, many pitchers, especially in the major leagues, work exclusively out of the stretch position. Even many high school pitchers find it more comfortable to use only the stretch.

According to the rule book, a pitcher must come to a discernable stop after taking his sign from the catcher and bringing his hands together. He can't just bring his hands together and throw. That sort of motion would give the pitcher a distinct advantage because the runner would never know when the stretch ended and the pitch began.

CHECKING RUNNERS

When runners reach base, the pitcher has additional responsibility. Now he must not only play the cat and mouse game with the hitter but also try to hold, or check, the base runners so that they do not get big leads or good jumps on stolen base attempts.

Before a game begins, pitchers should become aware of who the players are on the opposing team that are the best base stealers. They can then focus their efforts on holding those runners close to the base and not waste throws on runners who are not likely to run. Where a player hits in the order, for example, is a cue to his speed and baserunning ability. Also, there are other indicators that coaches and pitchers can pick up which tip them off to the possibility of a steal. One such technique that a pitcher can use to identify a possible steal threat is to simply take his set position and hold it until the batter finally asks for "time." A runner who wants to steal will often give away his anxiousness in this situation with nervous movements of his hands or his legs. This is a clue that the pitcher should check this runner more often.

No matter how often a pitcher checks a runner, he should not get in the habit of throwing over to the base only when his hands come together in the stretch position. To keep runners close, the pitcher must try a variety of options, many of which are discussed in chapter 6, "Defensive Tactical Skills." When throwing to first base, for example, the pitcher must alter his rhythm so that the runner cannot always sense when he is going to throw over. The pitcher should vary the spot in his motion from which he throws to first in addition to varying the timing of the throw. The pitcher can vary his throw to first base in several ways:

- Throwing from the top of his stretch before his hands come together (see figure 4.45*a*)
- Turning and throwing while his hands are in the act of moving down toward, but have not yet reached, their final set position (see figure 4.45*b*)
- Coming to his set, waiting a few seconds and then throwing over
- Coming to the set position, waiting a few seconds and then quickly stepping back off the rubber with his pivot foot while raising his throwing hand as if to throw to the base (see figure 4.45*c*)

These techniques and others help keep the runners uncomfortable, and ultimately, closer to the base.

a b c

Figure 4.45 **Variations of a pitcher's throw to first base.**

SHORTENING STRIDE

Many right-handed pitchers prefer to take a very short stride when throwing from the stretch position. A short stride quickens the delivery to the plate and, in the event that a base runner is stealing, gives the catcher more time to get the ball to the base. Some pitchers, Greg Maddux, for example, forego this short stride and use a normal leg lift from the stretch because they feel that their main priority is to get the hitter out. These pitchers spend more time holding runners close by checking them often and don't worry too much if they try to steal.

Certainly, pitchers who use the short glide stride do not get as much of the body into a throw as those who do not. Some coaches feel that pitchers who use this technique lose too much velocity on their pitches and may become susceptible to arm stress because they use too much of their arm and not enough of their bodies. Coaches should watch pitchers carefully to make certain that the pitcher's arm action remains the same with the short stride as it does in the full windup. If there is a difference in the action, coaches must address and correct the mechanics. Left-handed pitchers do not have great concern with the short stride because they have the advantage of being able to face the base runner at first and hold him with deceptive leg kicks.

(continued)

a b

Figure 4.46 Pitcher shortening the stride by bringing the knees together first.

Pitchers can use several techniques to shorten the stride in the set position. Some pitchers choose to start the motion by bringing the front knee swiftly to the back knee and then striding toward home as the throwing arm begins its action (see figure 4.46, *a* and *b*). Other pitchers feel that keeping more weight on the back leg makes it easier to lift quickly and throw (see figure 4.47). Pitchers may even assume a closed stance with the stride leg closer to the third-base side of the mound (see figure 4.48). They feel that this stance presets their hips in a closed position and makes them quicker. The last two methods, however, as shown in figures 4.47 and 4.48, make it more difficult to throw to first base. In the first, with all the weight on the back foot, stepping off the rubber with the pivot foot is almost impossible. In the second, the body has to turn farther, increasing the time required to execute the pickoff.

Whatever method pitchers decide to use to quicken their motion in the stretch, they must be certain that

At a Glance

The following parts of the text offer additional information on the stretch.

Throwing Basics	p. 64
Catching a Throw	p. 72
Pitcher Basics	p. 94
Defensive Positioning	p. 178
Defending Bunt Situations	p. 186
Pitcher Pickoffs	p. 190
Determining the Best Pitching Options	p. 198

Figure 4.47 Pitcher shortening the stride by keeping the weight on the back leg.

Figure 4.48 Pitcher shortening the stride by assuming a closed stance.

they do not destroy proper arm action. If pitchers worry too much about runners by sacrificing their arm action and pitching mechanics, they will throw pitches that are easier to hit, creating more base runners and more problems.

Common Errors

You may run into several common errors when teaching your athletes how to throw from the stretch position.

Error	Error correction
The pitcher assumes his set position in an open stance.	Before the pitcher can throw home, he must bring his shoulder toward the plate. An open stance is easier to steal off. Emphasize a parallel or slightly closed stance in the set position.
Runners get a great jump off a right-handed pitcher even though he is quick to the plate.	The pitcher should do more to check the runner. Emphasize throwing the ball at different points in the stretch motion and throwing over to the base more often.

Throwing a Fastball

KEY POINTS

The most important components of throwing a fastball are

- the four-seam grip and
- the two-seam grip.

The term *fastball* is misnomer. The fastball isn't a ball thrown as hard as possible; it is merely the fastest pitch that a pitcher has in his repertoire. The fastball need not be thrown fast if it can be thrown with control and has some late movement. As explained in "Pitcher Basics," beginning on page 94, velocity is only one of the four components of pitching, and not necessarily the most important. The average high school pitcher throws somewhere between 75 and 82 miles per hour. Pitchers who throw in the mid-80s are considered fast, and anyone who can reach 90 draws scouts to his games by the dozens.

When throwing the fastball, the pitcher should adhere to the basic throwing-arm action—down, back, up and over. More emphasis should be placed on the wrist snap, however. The wrist should be relaxed to facilitate a quick snap. The fingers should pull straight down when releasing the ball, much like the way one would reach up and pull down the ring of a windowshade. The fingers should pull on the seams of the ball on the release and snap downward to give the ball spin. He must also learn to throw the pitch at different speeds—full speed, three-quarter speed, half speed and so on to keep hitters off balance. The idea is simply to throw the ball with less force than the time before or vice versa. Even if he doesn't throw hard, a pitcher who can alter the speed of his pitches can keep a hitter off balance. Pitchers who can make the ball move in the strike zone will also be successful. To do this, they have to learn to adjust their grip.

FOUR-SEAM GRIP

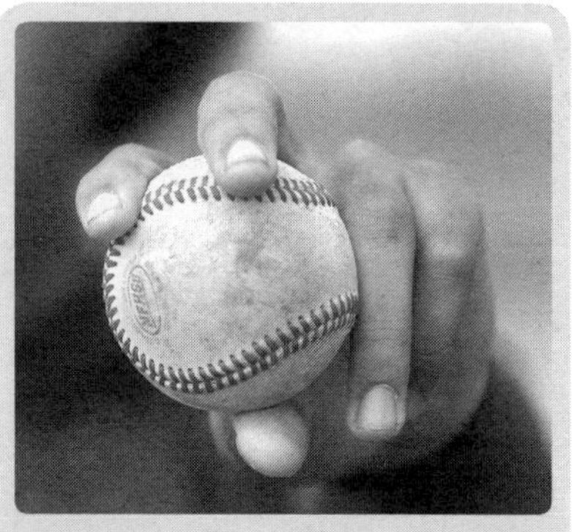

Figure 4.49 Four-seam grip.

The most common grip for a fastball is the four-seam grip, so called because as the ball moves through the air, drag is created on four of the seams. This type of fastball is also the straightest fastball. The ball should be held out in the hand with the pads of the first and second fingers resting on the seam as shown in figure 4.49. The horseshoe (round) end of the seams should face outside. The inside of the thumb should rest on the ball and bisect the two fingers as shown. The farther apart the fingers, the slower the pitch will travel but the more control the pitcher will have.

Pitchers should experiment with this grip and grips for other pitches by applying pressure to different parts of their fingers until they find a comfortable spot. For example, putting more pressure on the index finger may make the ball move differently. Putting pressure on the middle knuckles rather than the finger pads could do the same.

Pitchers should throw the fastball in situations when they desperately need to throw a strike, such as in 2-0 or 3-0 counts, or when they don't want the ball to move too much, such as a high and tight pitch.

TWO-SEAM GRIP

The two-seam fastball is often called the tailing fastball because it moves into a right-handed batter when thrown by a right-handed pitcher and away from the batter when thrown by a lefty. Again, the ball is held out in the fingers, but with this grip, the fingers are placed alongside the narrowest part of the seams, as shown in figure 4.50. The thumb bisects the two fingers as in the four-seam grip, but more pressure should be placed on the middle finger. This technique makes the ball leave the hand a little off center, creating more drag. A fastball thrown using the two-seam grip will not be as fast as the four seamer, but thrown correctly it will veer 4 to 6 inches off its flight line when it gets about three-quarters of the way to the plate.

Another fastball thrown with the two-seam grip is the sinker. This pitch will not only move laterally but also drop a few inches while veering. This is a great pitch to use when a pitcher needs a ground-ball out, such as in a double-play situation. To a hitter the sinker looks like a good pitch to hit, but the drop will force him to hit the top of the ball, creating a grounder. Throwing a sinker, however, is not easy and takes a lot of practice. A pitcher should modify the two-seam grip slightly by placing the ball a little farther back in the hand (see figure 4.51). The pitcher's thumb should be on the seam, holding the ball a little off center. The middle finger should not be on top of the seam, but inside it. This arrangement helps create more sidespin on the ball. When throwing this pitch, some pitchers like to think of pulling the arm across the body on a 45-degree angle on their follow-through.

At a Glance

The following parts of the text offer additional information on throwing the fastball.

Pitcher Basics	p. 94
Pitcher Stretch Mechanics	p. 102
Determining the Best Pitching Options	p. 198

Figure 4.50 Two-seam grip.

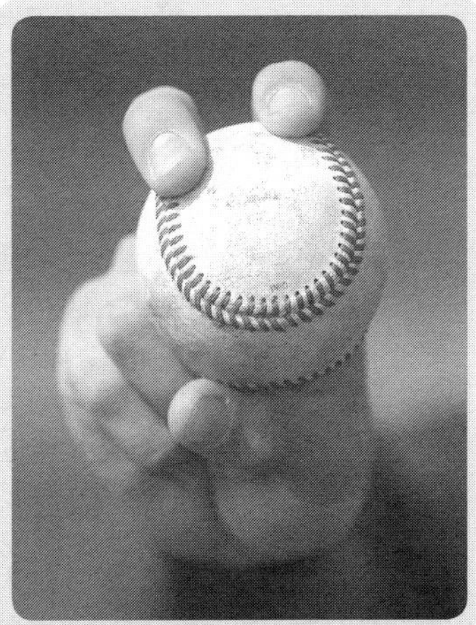

Figure 4.51 Modified two-seam grip for the sinker pitch.

Common Errors

You may run into several common errors when teaching your athletes how to throw a fastball.

Error	Error correction
The pitcher has good arm action but doesn't throw the ball fast.	Check to make sure that the pitcher is not gripping the ball too tightly. A tight grip stiffens the wrist and makes the arm slower.
The pitcher has good speed but has trouble controlling his fastball.	First, check the pitcher's grip. He may have his fingers too close together. Suggest that he move his fingers farther apart to get more control.

Throwing a Curveball

KEY POINTS

The most important components to consider about the curveball are

- grip,
- wrist action and
- arm action.

Before teaching pitchers to throw curveballs, you should first make certain that they have strong command of their fastballs. The curveball will not work well if the pitcher does not have a fastball. In addition, many pitchers have shortened their careers because they threw too many curveballs incorrectly when they were too young. Pitchers like to throw the pitch in youth leagues because hitters do not know how to approach hitting it, but as pitchers move up the ladder, they face intelligent hitters who are not fooled by a Little League curve. Therefore, pitchers must adhere rigidly to the correct mechanics of throwing a curveball.

Shortcuts in throwing a curveball can also lead to serious injury. The essence of a curveball is that it spins, and the more that a ball spins, the more it will break. The wrist and hand are essential in imparting spin. Therein lie the misconceptions about the curve that lead to injury. Some pitchers assume that they have to twist their wrists as if they were opening a doorknob to get a curve to break well. This is a great untruth. Instead, they need to use a motion with the wrist as if they were pounding in a nail with a hammer.

GRIP

As with teaching other pitches, the teaching of the curve begins with the grip. The pitcher can grip the curve in many ways, but the three most common grips are those shown in figure 4.52, *a* through *c*. The key is to grip the ball in a manner that creates the most spin. Pitchers should experiment with the different grips to find one that works best for them.

The pitcher should hold the ball loosely in the hand with the fingers close together. The ball should be held farther back in the hand than the fastball. The farther back the ball is held, the slower the pitch will be. Emphasize that the curveball is an off-speed pitch that should have a different look than the fastball. Held too far out in the fingers and thrown too quickly, the curve will not have the desired effect of destroying the

a

b

c

Figure 4.52 **Curveball grip *(a)* at the narrow point of the seams, *(b)* along the horseshoe and *(c)* reversed along the horseshoe.**

hitter's timing.

The only pressure on the ball should come from the middle finger and the thumb. The index finger merely rests on the ball and helps to guide it. The curveball leaves the hand off the middle knuckle of the middle finger, in contrast to the fastball, which leaves the hand off the fingertips.

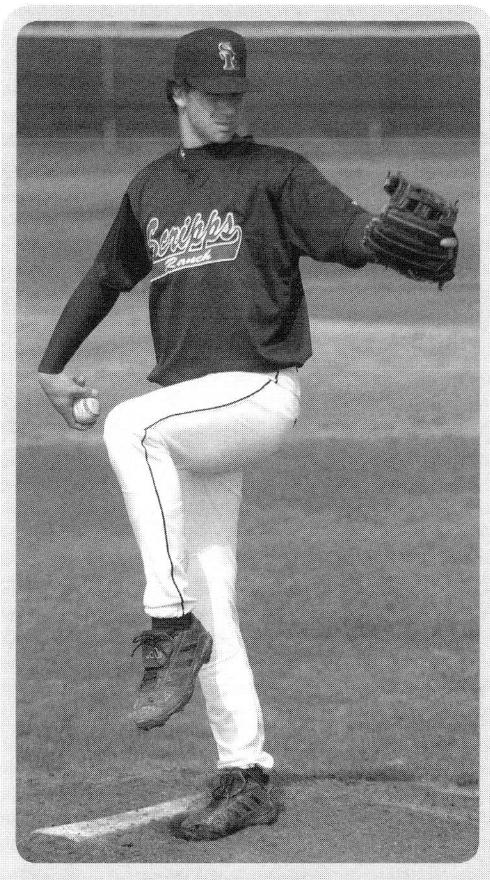
Figure 4.53 **Wrapping the ball.**

WRIST ACTION

Emphasize that the wrist should not wrap the ball too early. Wrapping is turning the wrist into the curveball release position as soon as the ball is taken out of the glove at the break point (see figure 4.53). Wrapping too early causes the wrist and forearm to tighten, which in turn slows the acceleration of the ball at the release point.

Instead, the pitcher releases the ball by snapping the wrist downward and flipping up with the thumb, imparting spin on the ball. The wrist should not supinate when throwing, as shown in figure 4.54. This action causes severe strain on the elbow tendons and can eventually lead to tendinitis, or Little League elbow. The correct downward wrist snap creates a downward movement of the ball. Supinating, similar to the motion used when screwing in a light bulb, creates a sideways movement that is much easier for the batter to distinguish. When thrown with proper downward wrist snap by an overhand pitcher, the spin will be from 12 o'clock to 6 o'clock, or as Charlie Greene, former coach at Miami Dade South Community College, says, "north to south." The ball will break sharply straight down. When thrown from a three-quarter arm slot, the spin is northeast to southwest, or 2 o'clock to 8 o'clock. With this motion, the ball breaks more across the strike zone than down.

Figure 4.54 **Incorrect wrist positioning when throwing.**

(continued)

A beneficial drill that a pitcher can do to learn the proper hand action is to practice snapping his fingers. This action produces the proper spin motion and when done with a downward wrist snap, it approximates the release of a curve ball. When a ball is placed in the hand and the fingers are snapped, the ball should spin upward with a backward rotation.

Figure 4.55 Pitcher's arm action when making the pitch.

ARM ACTION

When throwing a curve, the pitcher's arm should follow the same path out of the glove as it does with a fastball. This technique allows the arm to travel through its arc tension free. Emphasize keeping the elbow up above the shoulder. As the hand passes the ear near the release point, the wrist should turn so that the palm faces the pitcher's head (see figure 4.55). In essence, the pitcher should think fastball all the way until the ball gets to the ear. A good drill for this technique would be to have the pitcher think or even say the following throughout the arm action: "Fastball, fastball, fastball, curve!" When he hits "curve," the hand should be reaching the ear and should turn quickly.

Because the wrist breaks down in a hammerlike motion at the release point, the follow-through on the curve is somewhat different. Instead of finishing near the opposite knee, the hand should follow through so that it finishes near the pitcher's waist. Pitchers can imagine half a barrel growing out of their chests. After they release the ball, the hand and arm should follow the arc of the barrel to the waist as shown in figure 4.56.

Figure 4.56 Pitcher's arm action on the follow-through.

A key in the arm action of the curveball is that the arm must accelerate from the release point to the follow-through. Many pitchers tend to get lazy with their arms at this point and move too slowly, which leads to a slow break that the hitter can read easily. Pitchers can better visualize the arm action from release to follow-through by thinking about doing a karate chop with the throwing hand as they release the ball. Ask pitchers to give themselves a hard karate chop to the stride-leg thigh without actually touching the thigh. With this movement in mind—a quick, forceful downward chop—they will have proper arm acceleration on the pitch. If they follow this technique, the curveball will break sharply just as it reaches the plate.

At a Glance

The following parts of the text offer additional information on throwing the curveball.

Pitcher Basics	p. 94
Pitcher Stretch Mechanics	p. 102
Determining the Best Pitching Options	p. 198

Common Errors

You may run into several common errors when teaching your athletes how to throw a curveball.

Error	Error correction
The pitcher's fastball and curveball are almost the same speed.	Emphasize that the curve is an off-speed pitch. Make sure that the pitcher holds the ball far enough back in his hand.
The curveball breaks from side to side with little downward motion.	Emphasize a downward snap of the wrist. The pitcher may be supinating the wrist so that the palm faces upward at release point. Also, reemphasize keeping the fingers on top of the ball. When the wrist is supinated, the fingers are under the ball.
The curveball hangs, does not break sharply, over the plate.	The curveball hangs when the arm does not accelerate. Emphasize a karate chop motion.
The ball is thrown with a big, slow break.	Make certain that the pitcher does not hold the ball too deep in his hand. Doing so will inhibit thumb action and slow the release.
The pitcher consistently throws his curveball into the dirt—the classic 55-foot curve.	Emphasize a release point out in front of the bill of the cap. When the curve goes into the dirt, the pitcher is usually releasing the ball too late and getting his upper body in front of his hips.

Throwing a Changeup

KEY POINTS

The most important components of the changeup are

- the three-finger grip and
- the circle changeup (OK) grip.

Warren Spahn, the greatest left-handed pitcher in the history of the game, once said, "Hitting is timing, and pitching is upsetting timing." When a hitter times a pitcher's fastball, even the hardest throwing pitchers can get taken yard. But if a hitter thinks a fastball is coming and the pitcher throws a changeup, or a change-of-speed pitch, even the best hitter can be fooled.

Pitchers do not throw the changeup often enough generally because they do not have enough confidence in the pitch to throw it well. To be effective, the pitch needs to be thrown about 15 to 20 percent of the time. The changeup can be extremely effective against hitters who are anxious and want to hit the ball hard, and it is best used in situations in which the hitter is anticipating a fastball or after he has pulled a hard line drive foul. The arm action on the changeup pitch should be the same as that for the fastball—down, back, up and over. The identical action is what makes the pitch deceptive. The difference is that the objective of a fastball is to make a hitter miss the ball; the purpose of a changeup is to get the hitter to hit the ball, but hit it poorly.

Inexperienced pitchers sometimes make the mistake of slowing their body motion when throwing the changeup, making the pitch easier to spot and easier to hit. With enough practice they can become comfortable throwing the pitch with their fastball motion. Teach pitchers to grip the ball using the changeup grip and from that point on to think fastball. They should forget the fact that they're gripping a changeup, and instead let it rip! This method will produce a pitch that travels 8 or 10 miles per hour slower than the fastball but has the same spin and look. The hitter sees the pitcher's body throw a fastball, not a changeup, and he begins his swing too early.

To gain confidence with the pitch, however, pitchers must practice it often. Because the grip on the changeup is radically different from the grip on the fastball or curve, players should practice gripping the ball.

Another reason to practice the changeup grip is that it can help the pitcher conceal the pitch better. If the pitcher is not comfortable with the grip, he may take more time setting the grip in the glove, a dead giveaway to the hitter or coach that a change is coming. Many grips can be used to throw the changeup, and pitchers should experiment until they find one that gives them the results they need.

THREE-FINGER GRIP

The simplest changeup grip is the three-finger grip (see figure 4.57). The placement of the third finger on top of the ball has the same effect as widening the fingers on the fastball, but even more so. The three-finger grip automatically causes the ball to leave the hand more slowly. The difference between this pitch and the fastball is that with the fastball the pressure on the ball is with the fingertips; the three-finger changeup grip puts pressure on the ball with the middle knuckles. When pitchers are learning this pitch, they can even raise their fingertips off the ball so that they do not use them for pressure and involuntarily choke the ball. If pitchers choke the ball, the pitch will go in the dirt and will not be effective. With any changeup grip, pitchers must hold the ball firmly, but loosely, almost as if they were holding a raw egg in their fingers.

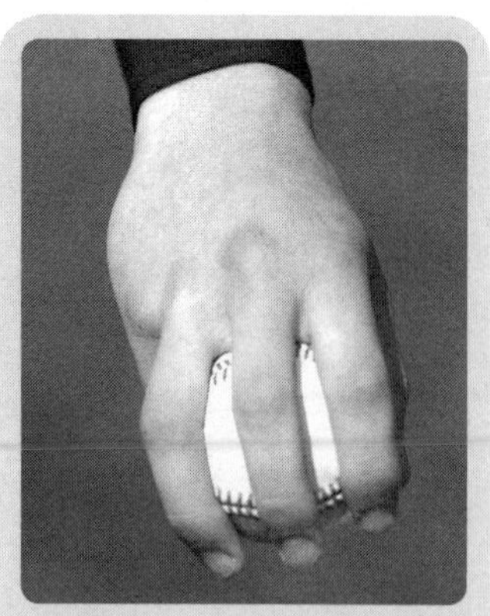

Figure 4.57 Three-finger changeup grip.

CIRCLE CHANGEUP (OK) GRIP

A grip that has recently gained popularity is the so-called circle changeup, or OK, grip. Throwing a changeup with this grip creates a pitch that not only is slower than a fastball but also has much more movement than a pitch thrown with the three-finger changeup grip. Invented by former Mets pitching coach Roger Craig, this grip is really a forkball for pitchers with small hands.

To grip the ball, the pitcher first forms the OK sign with the thumb and forefinger of his throwing hand (see figure 4.58*a*). He then places the ball in a two-seam fastball position back in his hand so that his middle and third finger are on top of the ball inside the seams (see figure 4.58*b*). He then finishes the grip by placing his little finger on the side of the ball opposite the thumb and forefinger. The key in this grip is that the little finger and the sides of the circle formed by the thumb and forefinger apply the pressure to the ball. The two fingers on top of the ball apply no pressure at all; they merely guide the ball out of the hand. This pitch will break down and away from the pitcher's throwing side, and the pitcher will feel the ball spinning out from underneath the two middle fingers.

Pitchers can hold the ball in different configurations in the circle grip—for example, across rather than with the seams—and they should experiment until they find the grip positioning that works best for them.

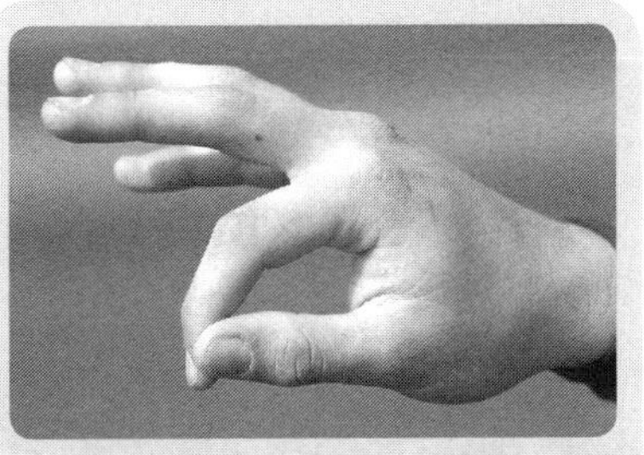

a

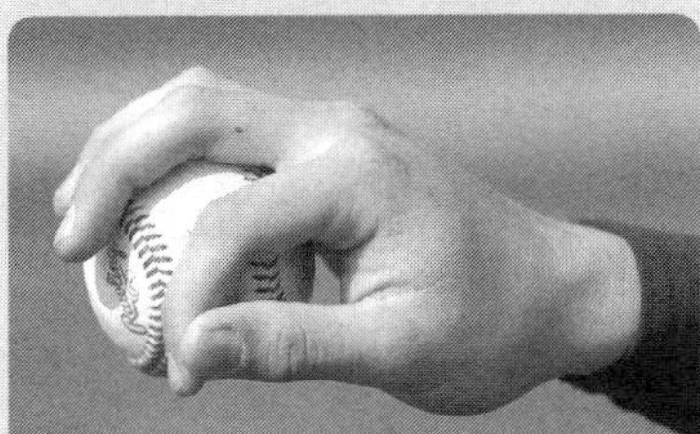

b

Figure 4.58 Circle changeup (OK) grip.

At a Glance

The following parts of the text offer additional information on throwing the changeup.

Common Errors

You may run into several common errors when teaching your athletes how to throw a changeup.

Error	Error correction
The pitcher's changeups usually end up in the dirt short of home plate.	Emphasize gripping the ball loosely, using the same pressure as that used for the fastball. Pitchers tighten their grips when they are not confident with the pitch. This, in turn, tightens the forearm, and they release the ball too late.
The pitcher's back leg drags rather than pivots when throwing the changeup.	Emphasize using the same body motion as that used with the fastball. Pitchers who have this problem have been taught to drag the pivot foot to slow their motion and thereby slow the pitch. The problem with this technique is that this motion exposes the pitch.

Outfield Basics

KEY POINTS

The most important components of outfield play are

- starting in the ready position,
- positioning based on the hitter,
- judging the flight of the ball,
- moving toward a batted ball,
- shading the eyes,
- knowing the environment and
- communicating with other outfielders.

When Babe Ruth first began playing in the outfield he complained that it was hard to stay awake with nothing to do. Outfielders may not get as much action as the other six fielders, but when a ball is hit to them, they need to be alert and know the techniques necessary to make the play successfully. A major theme of defensive baseball is that everybody backs up everybody else, but the outfielders are the last line of defense for a team. If they don't play balls properly, no one can cover for them!

STARTING IN THE READY POSITION

Like other players on the field, outfielders should not be tense before the ball is put in play. In the ready position, outfielders should be in a relaxed athletic position with the feet shoulder-width apart, knees slightly bent and hands together and relaxed in front of the body (see figure 4.59). Before the pitcher begins his motion, outfielders should scan the field making mental notes of the positions of the other fielders and the game situation, such as number of outs, men on base, score and so on. They should be preparing themselves for what they will do if the ball is hit to them. They should *want* the ball to be hit to them. This maxim of baseball is often cited to infielders, but it should be emphasized even more to outfielders. Tell them to say to themselves, "Hit it to me!"

Figure 4.59 Basic athletic position for outfielders.

When the pitcher's motion begins, outfielders should focus the eyes on the area in front of home plate where hitters make contact with the ball. Outfielders should not watch the pitcher because if they do, they lose precious milliseconds getting a jump on the ball. Focusing on the area at home can help outfielders get a good jump. For example, if the left fielder sees the bat of a right-hander out in front of the plate before contact occurs, the ball will be pulled to the left side, as discussed in "Swing and Follow-Through" beginning on page 26. This bit of knowledge might just be enough to get the outfielder moving to the pull, or strong, side. Conversely, if the fielder sees the ball getting closer to the plate and the bat has still not appeared in the focus area, most likely if the ball is hit, it will be hit up the middle of the diamond or to the batter's opposite field side. The closer the ball gets to the plate, the less likely it is that the batter will be able to pull it. This visual cue would get the outfield to subtly sway to the opposite field side.

POSITIONING BASED ON THE HITTER

You should help position outfielders in the field, but outfielders should be able to adjust to the situation on their own. Early in a game against an unfamiliar team, outfielders should play straight away or shaded slightly toward the hitter's pull side—toward left field for right-handers and toward right field for left-handers. They should not play too deep early in a game because most balls will probably be hit short of their positions. More on this topic appears in chapter 6, "Defensive Tactical Skills."

JUDGING THE FLIGHT OF THE BALL

Fielding a fly ball is partly a cultural phenomenon, a learned experience. The more fly balls one sees, the more acclimated one becomes to judging their flight path. Unfortunately, fewer people are playing baseball today, and this learned skill is disappearing. Coaches must teach the skills, and players must repeatedly practice fielding fly balls.

In general, outfielders should open up their shoulders slightly toward the foul line—left fielders to the right side, right fielders to the left side. Because these outfielders have help from the center fielder on balls hit to the other side, positioning themselves toward the foul line helps them get a jump on a ball hit in their direction. When the ball is hit, the outfielder should use the brim of his cap as an orientation point. If the ball ascends above the brim, the player should execute the movement to go back on the ball because, without factoring wind into the equation, the ball will likely go over his head. If the ball is hit below the brim, the fielder should momentarily hold his position before running toward the infield.

In judging the flight of the ball, the outfielder must also consider whether the hitter is right- or left-handed. Line drives hit to left field by left-handed batters always curve toward the left-field line. The left fielder will really have to hustle on a ball hit to his right by a left-hander because it will be curving away from him. On a ball hit by a left-hander to his left side, however, the left fielder will not have to run as hard because the ball will be curving back toward him. Of course, the opposite principle holds for right-handed hitters. Line drives hit to right field by right-handed hitters will curve to the right-field foul line. Also, the higher and deeper the ball is hit, the more it will curve. Balls hit right at a fielder are difficult to judge, so the fielder must hold his position on these balls before charging to make sure that they aren't going over his head.

MOVING TOWARD A BATTED BALL

A cardinal sin of outfield play is to drift on a ball hit over the head. Drifting occurs when the outfielder feels he has an easy play to make and has a bead on the ball. He moves slowly to the point where he thinks that he will be easily able to catch the ball on the fly. Drifting—jogging toward the landing point of a fly ball—is a lazy approach to fielding fly balls and often when this occurs the outfielder will have to speed up his steps at the last moment as the ball is descending because he finds he has misjudged its flight or that the wind increased while the ball was in flight and changed its path. This is why an outfielder must always accelerate quickly toward the point at which he feels the catch will be made. Remind outfielders that it is much easier to slow down just before a catch than it is to speed up.

(continued)

An outfielder's initial movements toward the ball should get him going to a good position to field it. The most basic step to learn is the drop step. On a ball hit to the outfielder's right side, his first movement is to drop his right foot behind his body (see figure 4.60*a*). As he does this, the foot should be pointed outward slightly. This step opens the fielder's right shoulder toward the flight of the ball and starts moving him backward immediately. The next step is to cross over the right foot with the left foot (see figure 4.60*b*). If the crossover step occurs without the drop step, the player's first step will take him only to the right, not back. On balls hit over the outfielder's head to the left side, he executes a drop step with the left foot and then a crossover with the right. Besides getting the outfielder moving quickly, the drop step puts him on a direct route to the ball instead of the L-shaped route that often occurs when the outfielder crosses over to either side without first using the drop step. The crossover step initiates a sideways movement that gets the body's momentum going to the side rather than directly to the ball.

If the ball is hit over either shoulder, the fielder should run directly toward the spot where he assumes that the ball will land. The outfielder's first three steps, after the drop step, should be hard and quick. After three hard steps, if the fielder sees that he will be able to meet the ball without much effort, he should slow down and get his body under control.

Figure 4.60 Outfielder making a *(a)* drop step and *(b)* crossover step.

Of course, some fly balls may only stand a chance of being caught by the fielder if he races after them at full speed and reaches out or leaps with the glove at the last second. If an outfielder finds himself in a situation where he must race toward a ball, he should run with his weight focused on the balls of his feet. If he runs in a flatfooted fashion, the ball will appear to move up and down with each step, making its path more difficult for the outfielder to follow. Whenever possible, if there is a runner on, the outfielder should position his body so that he fields the ball on his throwing side. Sometimes the fielder may have to circle around under the ball to accomplish this type of positioning. Even on balls hit to the throwing side, fielding is easier when the outfielder approaches the ball with his momentum taking him toward the infield.

If the fielder reaches the point where the ball will land before the ball arrives there, he should try to position himself a few steps back from that point so that he can get into the habit of moving into the ball when making the catch. When possible, he should try to catch the ball above the eyes and between the middle of his body and his throwing side, as shown in figure 4.61. Catching the ball in this manner puts the outfielder in a position to make a throw with a minimum number of steps, which will be extremely important if a base runner is advancing on the play.

Figure 4.61 Outfielder in proper position to field a fly ball.

There are also additional factors that could cause a fielder to misjudge a fly ball. Some high school fields do not have good backdrops behind home plate to block out distractions that could hamper a fielder's focus on the ball. In some cases, the shirts or jackets of the spectators showing through the cyclone fencing might make it that much more difficult to accurately track the ball into the hitting zone. Some surfaces behind backstops might give off a glare, which also affects concentration. There are even times when the color of the sky is such that the ball could get literally lost in the clouds. These are just a few reasons why it is so important for an outfielder to have exceptional concentration and focusing skills.

(continued)

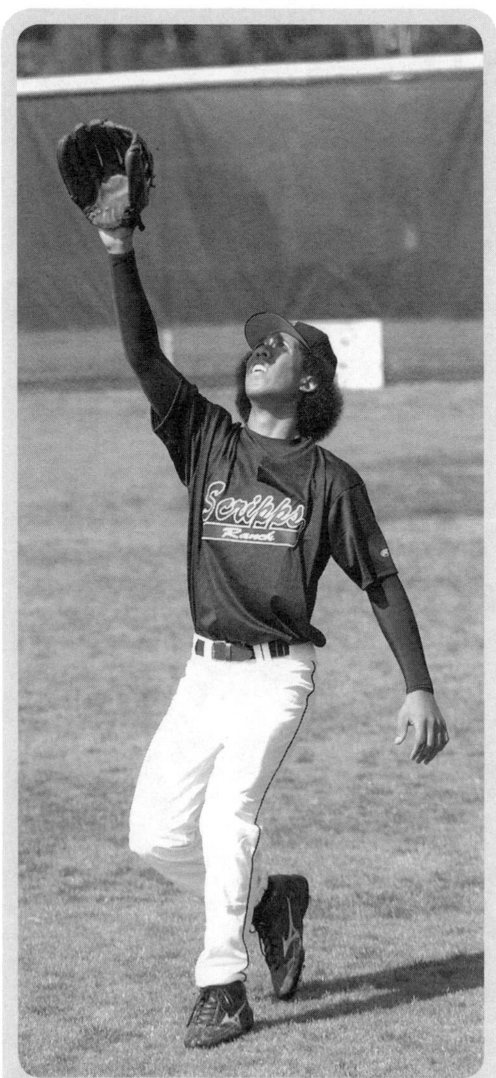

Figure 4.62 Outfielder properly shading the sun from his eyes.

SHADING THE EYES

An outfielder is not properly equipped unless he has a pair of sunglasses with him for day games. Several manufacturers make flip-down models that players can wear under their cap brims. When the sun may possibly obscure the flight of a fly ball, the player should have his glasses down. If the ball is hit directly into the sun, the outfielder should extend his glove hand to block the sun so that he can get a clear view of the ball (see figure 4.62). If a right-handed outfielder is running to his left and the sun is over his right shoulder, he should use his bare hand to shield his eyes from the sun.

KNOWING THE ENVIRONMENT

The outfielder should examine his turf as soon as he arrives at a field for a game. Chinese philosopher Sun-Tzu, who wrote the groundbreaking treatise *The Art of War,* devotes more discussion to knowledge of the battlefield terrain than he does to any other subject. Just as the environment where a battle occurs should never surprise a general, depressions in the surface of the outfield or wet spots should never surprise an outfielder. He should know about these things beforehand and consider them when fielding his position. Likewise, he should be aware of the wind or wind shifts during a game. The simple act of pulling out a few blades of grass and tossing them in the air reveals wonders about wind. Outfielders should also pay attention to the length and thickness of the grass on the field, which can affect the speed at which a batted ball travels.

COMMUNICATING WITH OTHER OUTFIELDERS

Communication is extremely important on balls hit between outfielders. They must talk with each other and call the ball to avoid collisions and nasty injuries. They should also be aware of fielding priorities and remember that the center fielder always has priority over the other outfielders. Practicing these kinds of plays produces confidence and reduces the number of botched plays.

Outfielders should talk to each other constantly, about the wind, what the batter did his last time up, the situation and so on. The center fielder, the quarterback of the outfield, should be the most vocal of the three and should keep the others alert. Any time a ball is hit to an outfielder, the outfielder nearest him should help him make the play. The nearest outfielder should orally cue the outfielder making the play on the location of the ball or on the movements that he should make, repeating each command three times to avoid misinterpretation. He should be shouting, "Back, back, back" or "Run, run, run" on balls hit over the head of the outfielder making the play. When he thinks that the outfielder should turn and catch the ball, he should yell, "Look, look, look" or "Now, now, now" or other such phrases. The same is true on balls hit in front of outfielders. Often, the outfielder not making the play, because of his angle on the ball, will be able to judge the flight path of the ball easier and can give needed assistance by yelling, "In, in, in" or "Hurry, hurry, hurry." In addition, a good rule for balls that fall in the gap between fielders is to have them observe high-low rules. The center fielder should always try to catch the ball low, and the other outfielders should try to catch it high. The center fielder thus takes a route that gets him to the ball just before it hits the ground. This guideline will help players avoid collisions.

At a Glance

The following parts of the text offer additional information on the basics of playing the outfield.

Remind outfielders not to call for the ball too soon. If an outfielder calls early on a ball that is between himself and a teammate, the fielder who has not called for the ball will subconsciously give up on it and the ball may land uncaught. Fielders should clearly yell, "Mine, mine, mine" or "Ball, ball, ball" when they have made the decision to catch it. The outfielder who has not called for the ball should peel off and get to a backup position so that he does not interfere with the catch. Outfielders should let each other know when a ball is definitely going for extra bases. They should yell, "Triple, triple, triple" to let the fielder know that the throw should go to third base. That way, the outfielder who retrieves the ball will not be confused about where to throw it.

Outfielders should also help each other when they come near fences. Yelling a code word like "Red" when a player is within 10 feet of a fence or wall provides valuable information. Further information about playing the fences can be found in "Challenging Outfield Plays" beginning on page 120.

Common Errors

You may run into several common errors when teaching your athletes how to play the outfield.

Error	Error correction
After catching an easy fly ball, the outfielder allows his momentum to carry him away from the infield.	Emphasize that the fielder should round the ball before catching it to place his body in a position facing the infield.
The player is often fooled on line drives, running in and then having the ball go over his head.	Tell the player to pause momentarily on balls below the brim of the cap before charging in.
Balls hit between outfielders routinely fall uncaught.	Emphasize communication among the outfielders. Make sure that the outfielders are not calling for the ball too soon. An outfielder should not call for a ball until it has reached the highest point of its arc.

Challenging Outfield Plays

KEY POINTS

The most difficult plays for outfielders are

- fielding balls overhead,
- fielding balls in the gaps,
- fielding line drives,
- making the shoestring or diving catch,
- playing the fences,
- fielding ground balls and
- throwing to home plate.

Not all balls hit to the outfield will be easy to handle. Some, because of the spin imparted on the ball by the bat, will sink or rise rapidly. Others will curve away or curve toward the approaching outfielder. Even ground balls hit to the outfield can take crazy bounces, depending on the condition of the playing turf. Consider that a line drive curving away from a hitter might hit the ground and then spin faster and farther in the direction of the spin, causing an even more demanding situation for the outfielder.

FIELDING BALLS OVERHEAD

One of the greatest outfielders ever, Joe DiMaggio, once wrote a how-to manual. In it he told young players that "No outfielder is a real workman unless he can turn his back on the ball, run his legs off and take the catch over his shoulder. Backpedaling outfielders get nowhere."

First, then, an outfielder should never run backward. On balls hit far over their heads, outfielders should execute the drop step and crossover to the side on which the ball is hit, as shown in figure 4.60 on page 116. Once running, they must observe good running form. They do not run with the glove extended, but instead with the arms pumping. Because they must run hard on these plays, they should guess where the ball will come down, turn their heads and run to that spot without looking toward the ball. When they get to the spot, or near it, they can turn, pick up the ball and then extend the glove to make the catch.

FIELDING BALLS IN THE GAPS

The important thing to remember on balls hit between outfielders is that they must take a straight route to the ball. The outfielder should not run an L route, as discussed on page 116 in "Outfield Basics." Mentally, he should establish where the ball will land and then run a straight route to that point. Good outfielders play as shallow as they can because more balls are hit in front of them than are hit over their heads. On balls hit past them, however, they must drop step and execute proper running form.

a b

Figure 4.63 Outfielder properly fielding a ball (*a*) above his waist and (*b*) below his waist.

FIELDING LINE DRIVES

Balls hit directly at outfielders and below the brim of their caps can be extremely tricky to catch. After the fielder has determined that the ball will land short of his position in the outfield, he should sprint toward it. Again, he should use good form and not reach out with his glove until the ball arrives. If the flight of the ball is above the fielder's waist, he should catch the ball with the fingers of his glove pointed upward (see figure 4.63*a*). If the ball is below the waist, the fingers should point down and the palm of the glove should be facing up (see figure 4.63*b*).

MAKING THE SHOESTRING OR DIVING CATCH

If an outfielder determines that he will not be able to catch the low sinking line drive while staying on his feet but still feels he has a chance to catch it, he may decide to dive for the ball. In making this decision, however, he must consider the score and inning. In a close ball game, an outfielder may not want to risk a diving catch because the ball might get past him and allow runners to advance several bases instead of just one if he were simply to play the ball on the bounce. The outfielder can use either of two techniques in these situations if he chooses to dive for the ball:

Regular Forward Dive

This technique is similar to that used for a runner's headfirst slide, with one modification. The outfielder dives for the ball with his arms stretched out in front of him. After catching the ball, he slides on his chest and forearms just as if he were sliding into a base. The sole difference is that the backs of his hands are facing the ground instead of the palms being down as they would be on a slide into a base. See figure 4.64 for an example of the regular forward dive.

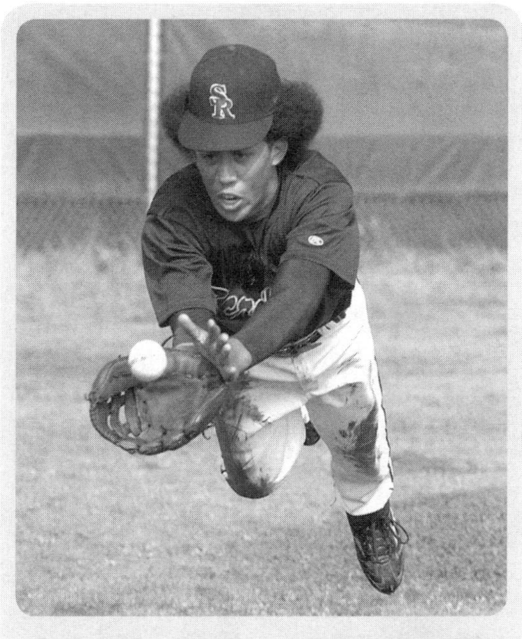

Figure 4.64 **Regular forward dive.**

Bent-Leg Sliding Catch

This technique has recently gained popularity and is similar to the bent-leg slide for a base runner. As the player approaches the sinking liner, he executes the slide, tucking one leg under the other while holding the other leg in the air so that the spikes do not catch on the turf. While he is sliding, he extends both arms outward, catches the ball and cradles it to his chest (see figure 4.65). As soon as he makes the catch, the outfielder takes the ball out of his glove with his throwing hand so that the umpire can see that he made the catch. Some coaches feel that this technique is safer than the straightforward dive because it eliminates the possibility of injuring the arms if they roll underneath the body.

(continued)

Figure 4.65 Bent-leg sliding catch.

PLAYING THE FENCES

When a ball is hit close to the fence, the outfielder must execute caution to avoid running headlong into it. In these cases, a little knowledge of the area is not a dangerous thing. Before the game begins, the outfielder should measure the width of the warning track by running from the grass onto the track. During the game then, when he feels the track beneath his feet, he will know how much room he has without looking at the fence. Physically looking for the track takes the outfielder's eyes off the ball and may cause him to lose the ball. The other outfielders can provide help in playing the fence by orally cueing the one fielding the ball, as suggested in "Outfield Basics" on page 118.

After he feels the warning track under him, the outfielder should reach out his throwing arm without looking to feel for the fence so that he knows when to stop. He can also use the hand as a brace to push off of to jump and make a catch over the wall. If a hit is over the wall, outfielders should be sure to jump straight up so that they don't injure themselves.

If the ball is hit so hard that the outfielder will not be able to catch it before it hits the wall, he should stop advancing and try to gauge the angle that the ball will take after it hits the wall. He should then move to the spot where he thinks the ball will rebound off the wall. If an outfielder senses that a deep fly ball has a chance to get to the fence, he should get there as soon as he can.

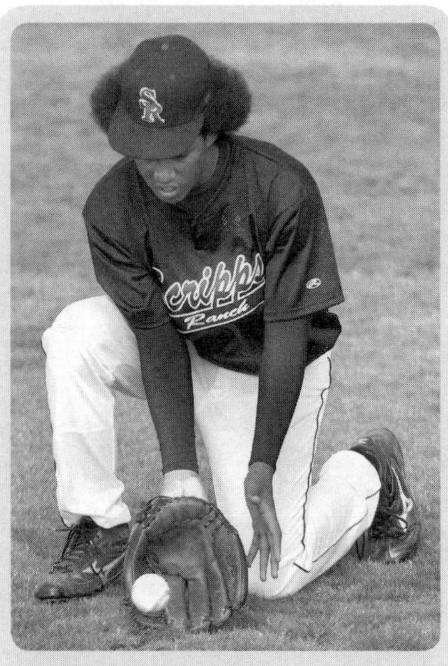

Figure 4.66 Outfielder properly blocking a ground ball.

FIELDING GROUND BALLS

Most balls hit to the outfield are hit on the ground. Outfielders must therefore be as adept at making plays on ground balls as their infield counterparts are. The technique they employ, however, is slightly different.

On a ball hit directly to an outfielder with no one on base, the outfielder should make sure that he blocks the ball so that the runner cannot take an extra base. As the outfielder approaches a ball that is taking short bounces, he should lower his throwing-side leg to the ground and drop both hands into the gap between his legs (see figure 4.66). On balls that take only one or two long bounces before reaching the outfielder, going down on the knee is sometimes not possible, so he should field those balls standing up.

When runners are on base, however, the technique changes. Now the outfielder must field the ball and return it quickly to one of the bases to stop runners from advancing. This type of play is often called the do-or-die play because if the player fields the ball cleanly, the play works, the ball is returned to the infield and the runner doesn't advance or is thrown out if he tries to advance.

To execute the do-or-die play correctly, the outfielder must approach the ball so that he fields it outside his glove-side leg. If the ball is to the left or right, he must take an appropriate route to get his body in position. As the ball nears, the outfielder should take short steps, trying to time catching the ball with his glove just as his glove-side foot hits the ground. The fielder should scoop the ball with his palm facing forward, and then bring the ball and the glove over to his throwing side to execute the throw.

As he shifts the ball to the throwing side, the outfielder executes a jumping step with his throwing-side foot. This extremely important movement, called the crow hop, helps the outfielder get his body into the throw. Stated simply, the outfielder pushes up with his glove-side foot after fielding, which allows the throwing-side foot to hop upward and forward as well to gain momentum in the direction of the throw.

At a Glance

The following parts of the text offer additional information on challenging outfield plays.

Throwing Basics	p. 64
Catching a Throw	p. 72
Outfield Basics	p. 114
Defensive Positioning	p. 178

THROWING TO HOME PLATE

When outfielders make a do-or-die play in a crucial game situation, they have to know their limitations beforehand, especially when they are throwing home. To develop outfielders' awareness so that they don't make futile throws home, give them something concrete to use as a benchmark. First, during practice, find out from how far away each outfielder can make a hard, one-hop throw to the plate. Then give them something visual to use as a guide. For example, if the left fielder can make a strong, one-hop throw from only 230 feet away from home plate, mark a line with chalk or place cones in left field 230 feet away from home plate. This will serve as a cue to the fielder of his limitations on a throw home.

Common Errors

You may run into several common errors when teaching your athletes about challenging outfield plays.

Error	Error correction
The player has difficulty handling line drives hit below his waist.	Remind the player to field low line drives with his palm facing the ball. Often, improper glove positioning is the cause of this mistake. The player should be able to pivot the wrist quickly from a fingers-up to a fingers-down position if the ball suddenly dips.
When executing the do-or-die play, the player often kicks the ball out of his glove with his foot.	Emphasize keeping the glove outside the glove-side leg so that the feet do not get in the way.

Infield Basics

KEY POINTS

The most important components of infield play are

- the four Rs of fielding,
- ready position,
- footwork,
- fielding position,
- fielding the short hop,
- switching from fielding to throwing position,
- covering bases on steals,
- positioning for cutoff and relay throws, and
- backing up the bases.

During an average game, half of the balls that are hit fair are ground balls, and even more when pitchers like future Hall of Famers Greg Maddux and Tom Glavine are throwing. Because ground balls are common, infielders have to be coached repeatedly on basic infielding skills. A significant portion of practice time should be devoted to the honing and polishing of these proficiencies. Never can a team have too much fielding practice.

THE FOUR RS OF FIELDING

In school, teachers stress the three Rs of reading, 'riting and 'rithmetic. No one can be successful without mastering those subjects. In baseball, no infielder can master playing the infield without paying attention to the four Rs of fielding: relax, ready, receive and release. These four words signify the four phases that an infielder must perform in sequence on each play.

Between pitches, while the pitcher is getting his sign, infielders must *relax*. During this phase, fielders should scan the infield, review the situation, take deep breaths and adjust their position on the dirt. In this set position, fielders can place their hands on their knees and take a breather. After the pitcher toes the rubber to get his sign for the next pitch, infielders should assume their *ready* position. This phase, discussed in detail later in this section, prepares the infielder to focus on the ball and react. If the ball is hit to the infielder, he must get himself in a position to *receive* the ball with the glove, transfer his weight and then *release* the ball with a strong, accurate throw. Going through these four stages on each pitch or batted ball is essential to being a successful infielder.

Figure 4.67 Infielder in ready position.

READY POSITION

The ready position is the basic athletic position assumed in all sports—the position that a tennis player adopts while awaiting a serve, the stance taken by a goalie in soccer or hockey when there is a threat on the goal, the setup of a basketball player defending an opponent. In baseball, from this position the infielder is ready to move in any direction.

As the pitcher begins his pitching motion, the fielder should assume the ready position, an upright position with his feet a little more that shoulder-width apart (see figure 4.67). The knees should be flexed and the weight positioned on the front part of the feet. The infielder should bend only slightly at the waist and hold his glove in front of his body. He should face his head and focus his eyes on the area in front of the plate where the hitter will make contact with the ball. The infielder should be able to see the hitter and his glove at the same time, which means that he must extend the glove hand somewhat from his body.

To get from the relaxed position to the ready position, most fielders rise from their relaxed position and make a subtle movement toward the plate (see figure 4.68, *a* and *b*). Usually, this movement is two steps toward the home plate area—right-left for a right-handed infielder, left-right for a left-handed first baseman. As infielders take these two small steps forward, they widen their stance slightly and finish in the ready position as shown previously in figure 4.67.

One of the basic rules of physics is that bodies in motion tend to stay in motion. Considering this, most infielders feel that they get a better jump on the ball when their bodies are moving as the ball enters the hitting zone. Some infielders, however, prefer just to lean their weight forward somewhat as the ball is delivered rather than take a few steps. Fielders and coaches should find which of these methods is most comfortable and adopt it.

Figure 4.68 Infielder *(a)* in relaxed position and *(b)* moving to get into the ready position.

(continued)

FOOTWORK

If the ball is not hit, the infielder rises up, relaxes and returns to his original position for the next pitch, but if a ground ball is hit toward him, fielding becomes mostly a matter of good footwork. As he approaches the ball, a right-handed fielder should keep his glove shoulder to the right of the ball. A lefty would do the opposite. When the ball is about 15 feet from the fielder, he should break down into fielding position. To do this, the right-handed fielder takes a step with his right foot toward the ball (see figure 4.69*a*). As he takes this step, the fielder begins to lower his body into fielding position so that when he takes the next step with the left foot, the ball is centered on the body (see figure 4.69*b*). This breaking-down movement puts the fielder in rhythm to field the ball and shift into throwing position. This technique is extremely important to good fielding. Many fielders break down too late and never give their bodies a chance to get into perfect fielding position. Some never break down at all and try to field the ball on the run.

Notice also that the word *charge* is not used here. People often use this term to describe what an infielder should do, as in "charge the ball." Charging connotes recklessness. Fielders should glide to the ball with finesse, not charge it as a runaway rhinoceros might. They must approach the ball aggressively, but under control. A common fielding

a b

Figure 4.69 Infielder *(a)* breaking down and *(b)* centering on the ball.

problem occurs when infielders do not properly "break down" into a wide base fielding position before getting to the ball. These fielders try to field the ball on the run, often with only one hand, never getting into good fielding position as explained below. They fail to center their bodies in line with the ball and often wind up overrunning it or fielding it off to the side.

FIELDING POSITION

As the infielder's left foot widens the stance, the arms should extend toward the ball with the back of the glove turned to the ground and the throwing hand situated above the glove, ready to close on the ball once it has been caught (see figure 4.70). The feet are twice the width of the shoulders, the toe of the right foot is even with the instep of the left foot, the knees are bent and the buttocks are down, the back is flat, the head is looking at the ball and the hands extend in front of the body. As the ball enters the glove, the fielder's head and eyes should follow the ball into the glove. When fielders perform this correctly, coaches will note the brim of the cap pointing downward, as shown in figure 4.71. Coaches should note that the term breaking down does not imply that the fielder stops at any time during this action. When the ball is fielded, the player is still moving forward, preparing to switch from fielding to throwing.

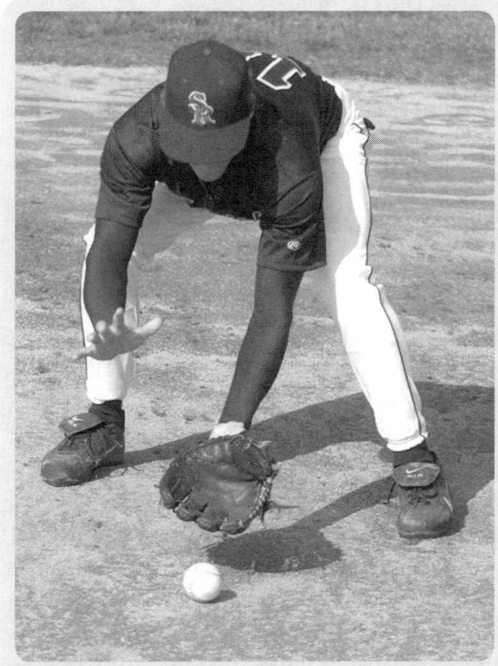

Figure 4.70 Infielder in fielding position.

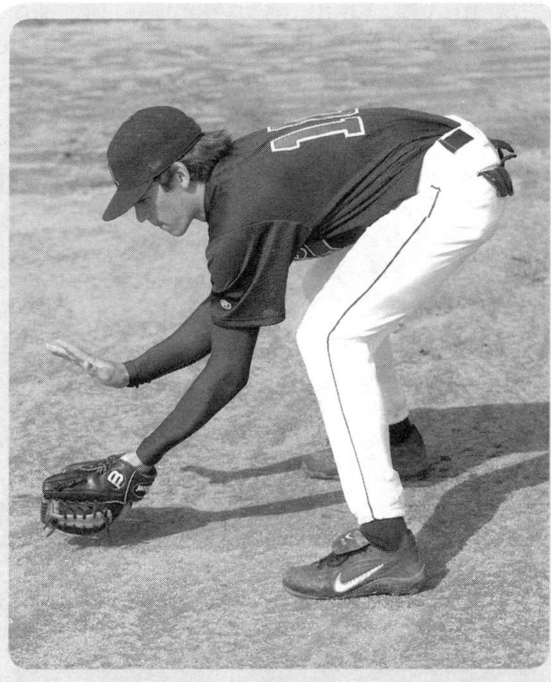

Figure 4.71 Infielder following the ball into the glove.

(continued)

Figure 4.72 **Infielder fielding the ball on the short hop.**

FIELDING THE SHORT HOP

Whenever possible, infielders should time their arrival to the ball so that they field it on the short hop (see figure 4.72). This means that they should strive to catch the ball either just before or just after it has bounced. If fielders allow the ball to bounce higher than this, the play becomes more difficult. The ball will handcuff the fielder because he will not be able to extend his arms as far from his body, and he will have to shift his weight to the balls of his feet, taking his momentum away from the throw. In addition, he will be unable to follow the ball into the glove with the eyes.

Depending on the spin put on the ball by the hitter and the condition of the infield, a ball may take very big, slow hops. When a fielder sees a ball taking a big hop, he should quicken his pace to field the ball. In this situation, the fielder can catch the ball with his body already standing in throwing position.

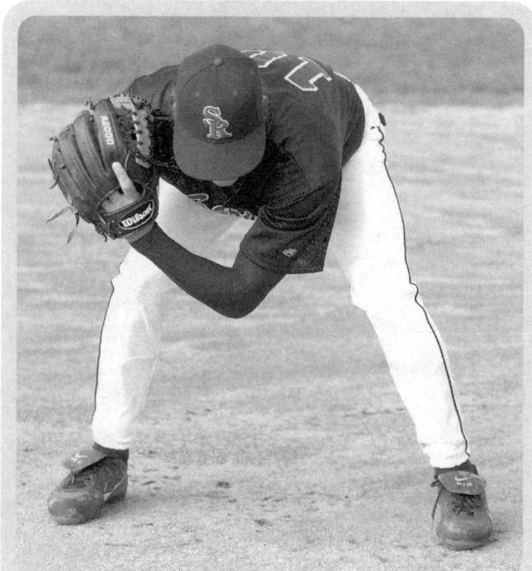

Figure 4.73 **Infielder hinges the ball and glove toward his throwing shoulder after fielding.**

SWITCHING FROM FIELDING TO THROWING POSITION

Just as fielding the ball is a simple matter of footwork, switching from fielding position to throwing position takes just a few steps. After taking the right-left steps that get the body into perfect fielding position, a right-handed fielder should execute another set of right-left steps to throw.

After securing the ball, the player should smoothly bring the ball and glove into the center of the body in an action called funneling the ball, or bringing the ball and glove into the center of the body. An alternative called "hinging" is to bring the ball up toward the throwing-side shoulder (see figure 4.73). Either way, the fielder must bring the ball up and back to begin the conversion into the throwing position. As he brings the glove inward or upward, the fielder should be searching for the right grip on the ball and beginning his footwork for the throw. After gripping the ball securely, the fielder should draw the hand back and begin the throwing motion. He does this in conjunction with planting the glove-side foot. So the sequence of fielding, funneling and throwing can be condensed into a simple mantra—right-left, field; right-left, throw!

COVERING BASES ON STEALS

As you know, the difference between being out and safe is a matter of a small fraction of a second. If the catcher cannot grip the ball across the seams, his throw may be slower. A pitcher's leg kick might be too slow. Likewise, the position of the infielder on the base can have great bearing on a safe or out call.

When a runner breaks for second or third, the fielder covering the base should move toward the base, but after a few steps, he should hesitate and glance at home to see what the batter is doing. If the hit and run is on, this slight hesitation might allow him to stop and get back in position to field the ball. If the batter is not swinging, the infielder should get to the front of the base and place his foot against it, with his body turned perpendicular to the field (see figure 4.74). He should assume the basic athletic position with knees bent, waist bent and feet apart. If the throw is on line, he can move his feet into a straddling position on the base. If not, he can easily go either way to catch the ball from this position. He should wait for the ball to get to him instead of reaching out for it and bringing it back. The ball travels faster than the glove.

Figure 4.74 Infielder covering his base when a runner breaks for the next base.

When making the tag on the sliding runner, the fielder should bring his glove straight down into the runner and then lift it back up in a V fashion. Holding the ball on the sliding runner too long could cause the ball to be dislodged from the glove. At first and third, infielders can use the same technique on throws from the catcher if they can get to base early enough. On most plays at these bases, however, infielders will have to sweep a tag on the runner while on the run.

POSITIONING FOR CUTOFF AND RELAY THROWS

When the ball is hit to the outfield and a throw will come to one of the bases, the infielder responsible for the cut play should hustle to his position holding his hands up and waving them back and forth so that the outfielder sees him well. When the throw leaves the outfielder's hand, the infielder should turn his back to the first-base foul line, assume a basic athletic stance with knees bent and be ready to move in any direction

(continued)

for the throw (see figure 4.75). In this stance, he can catch the ball and throw it immediately without turning his body to make the throw. If the infielder covering the base to which the ball has been thrown has lined up the cutoff man properly and the ball is not on line, the cutoff man should immediately move to catch the ball without being told to cut it.

If the ball is on line and the fielder covering the base does not call for a cut, the infielder should fake a cut by slapping his bare hand into his glove and then quickly turning to fake a throw at the player on the trailing base. This impedes the progress of the batter or the trailing runner and often stops him from advancing an extra base.

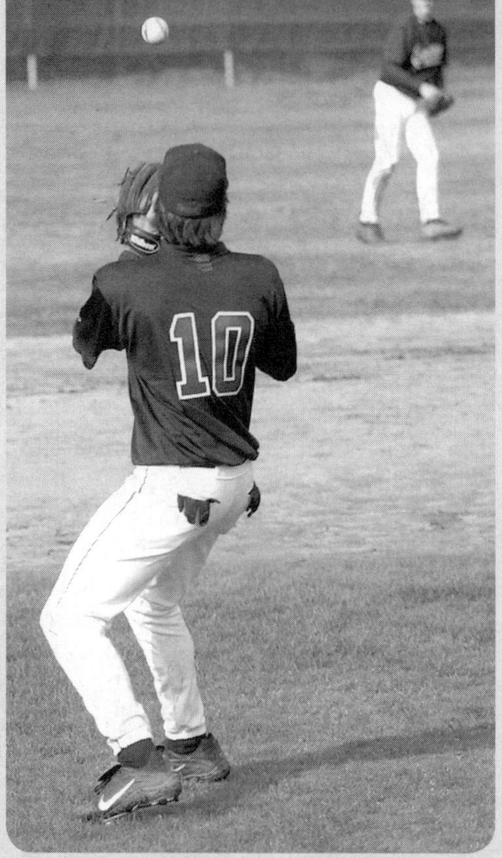

Figure 4.75 Infielder positioning when cutting off a throw from an outfielder.

BACKING UP THE BASES

If runners are on base, every throw made between the catcher and pitcher or between the first baseman or third baseman and the pitcher must be backed up by the fielder immediately behind the play. For example, when the first baseman returns the ball to the pitcher after an attempted pickoff at first, the third baseman should move into a position directly in line with the throw in case of an overthrow or misplay. This precaution stops runners from taking extra bases.

Also, whenever a runner is on first base, the second baseman or the shortstop should move in the direction of second base after every pitch in case the opposing team tries a delayed steal.

Additionally, all infielders should watch base runners as they round the bases to make sure that they tag the bases. If a runner misses a base, the infielder can call for the ball and make an appeal play at the base.

Another often overlooked backup skill occurs when the batter hits a pop fly between the second baseman, shortstop and centerfielder with no one on base or with a runner on first. In this situation the third baseman must hustle to cover second base in case the ball falls in for a hit. The aggressive hitter will run full speed from the batter's box and continue past first. If the ball falls in and the base is not covered, he will have an easy double. With a runner on first, if no one covers second, the runner can

At a Glance

The following parts of the text offer additional information on infield basics.

advance easily, but if the third baseman covers the bag, the fielder who picks up the ball can throw to second base for a force out.

In every game situation, the pitcher must back up bases in case an outfielder throws to one. A good way to teach pitchers this responsibility is to have them on the field when outfielders are doing their warm-up throws during a pregame routine. When throws are going to third base, for example, the pitchers could take turns backing up the base and reacting to the thrown balls. Teach pitchers to be at least 15 to 20 feet from the base when backing up so that they can react efficiently to balls that get past the infielder.

Common Errors

You may run into several common errors when teaching your athletes how to play the infield.

Error	Error correction
The player seems to have trouble getting the glove under the ball.	Emphasize moving toward the ball with the glove between the ball and the eyes. When the fielder breaks down into fielding position, the glove drops straight down and will automatically be in front of the fielder. When the fielder is slow getting the glove in play, he is probably approaching the ball with the glove held too close to the body.
The player seems to be rushed, fielding many balls while on the run.	Emphasize breaking down into fielding position when the ball is 15 feet away. This method gives the fielder the opportunity to set the body in fielding position.
Too many balls seem to go through the infielder's legs.	When the ball goes under or through the infielder, he is usually bending his back rather than his knees to get to the ball. Tall players often have difficulty fielding because they want to bend their backs to get the glove to the ball. Emphasize bending at the knees.
The player fields the ball with the knees too close together.	Keeping the knees together does not allow the buttocks to get low enough and stops the back from flattening. Show how a wider base helps get the hands farther in front of the body.
The player stands behind the base waiting for the throw on a steal.	Emphasize that the fielder will save a split second by getting the ball and the tag on the runner in front of the base.
The player reaches for the ball with the glove and then brings the glove back to tag the runner.	Reiterate that the ball can travel faster than the hand can. The player should position his glove close to the spot where he will make the tag and wait for the ball to get there rather than reach for it. Of course, if the ball is off line, the player will have to move his glove or his body.

Fielding Ground Balls

KEY POINTS

The four types of ground balls infielders must handle are

- "at 'em" balls,
- balls on the forehand side,
- balls on the backhand side and
- slow rollers.

Depending on the angle and force of the bat on the swing, the ball can do funny things on its way to the fielder. Balls beaten into the ground at a steep angle tend to take big bounces as they move depending on the condition of the turf. Wet grass can make the ball skip or skim, much like what happens when a person skips a stone on a lake. Generally, though, an infielder will have to react to only four types of ground balls.

"AT 'EM" BALLS

Sometimes the most difficult balls to handle are those hit directly to the infielder on which he will not have to move left or right, just in. Infielders often commit errors on these so-called routine plays because they fail to focus intently. They tend to relax on these "at 'em" balls because they resemble the kind they so often get during infield practice.

When the ball is hit at the fielder, he should approach it under control and concentrate on keeping his glove under the ball. Often the fielder will freeze—stand and wait for the ball—in the spot on the field where his ready position took him. Instead, the fielder should keep his body in motion because he can more easily break down into fielding position if he is moving rather than standing still.

BALLS ON THE FOREHAND SIDE

On most batted balls the infielder will have to move to the left or the right to make the play. Usually, he will take a "banana" route to the ball. As figure 4.76 illustrates, the fielder should take an arced route so that he will be moving toward first base after he reaches the ball. If the fielder does not take a banana route, his momentum will take him away from first base and make the throw more difficult.

The first steps the fielder makes are similar to the first steps of the base stealer discussed in "Stealing Second Base" beginning on page 50. The fielder makes a jab step in the direction of the ball and then crosses over using a crossover step. This movement is much like the outfielder's drop step except that the infielder makes it toward the ball path instead of away from it. The distance that he takes in the first step is dictated by how hard the ball is hit. If it is not hit hard, the jab step will be only far enough to allow the fielder to time his arrival to the ball so that he can be in front of it. On hard-hit balls, the fielder will execute the jab step and crossover deeper. In these cases, the fielder will take a 45-degree angle route directly to the ball and not worry about getting in front of it as he does in the arcing

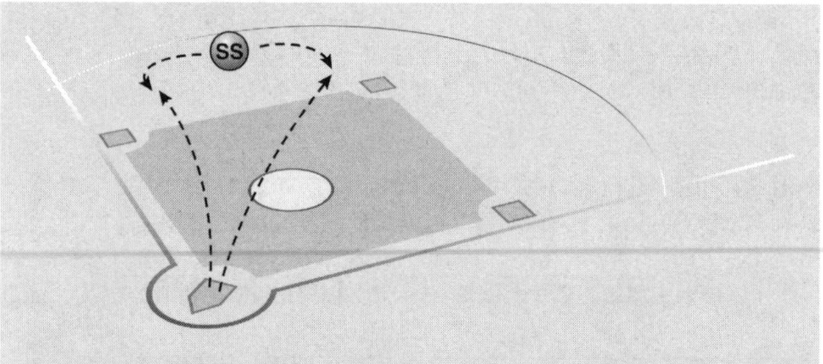

Figure 4.76 **Infielder taking an arced, or banana, route to the ball.**

banana route. The objective with hard-hit balls is just to get to the ball and not worry about how it's done because the fielder might have to reach or dive anyway.

The infielder, like the outfielder, should not run to this spot with his glove extended. He should wait until he gets to the point where he will field the ball before extending the glove. On balls hit to the forehand side, the fielder should take his final step at the ball with his throwing-side foot rather than his glove foot so that he can reach a little farther at the end, as shown in figure 4.77.

Figure 4.77 Infielder fielding a ball on his forehand side.

After catching the ball, the fielder should give with the glove hand and then try to get his feet centered back under his body to make the throw. Because the momentum of the forehand play carries the infielder away from first base, this skill is difficult to master. On some balls, the fielder will be better off pivoting to his glove side after catching the ball. This technique stops the momentum and helps get the feet under the body for the throw. To do this, the right-handed fielder hops onto his right foot, pivots his body around to the direction of the throw, gets the ball into throwing position and then steps toward the base with the left foot (see figure 4.78, *a-e*).

a

b

(continued)

Figure 4.78 Fielder pivoting to his glove side after catching the ball.

(continued)

c d e

Figure 4.78 **(continued)**

BALLS ON THE BACKHAND SIDE

Balls hit to the backhand side require a slightly different technique. Again, the decision to take a banana route or a 45-degree angle to the ball depends on how hard the ball has been hit. The nature of the backhand play, however, usually dictates that the infielder will be sprinting hard to cut off the ball and won't be able to get in front of it.

Figure 4.79 **Infielder fielding a ball on his backhand side.**

If the player can get to the ball without extending too much, he should field the ball with his right leg extended. From this position, he can dig the foot into the ground and bring the ball up into throwing position without turning his back to first base. He should bend the right leg so that he can get the glove under the ball. His chest should be over his lead thigh (see figure 4.79).

If the ball is hit so hard that the fielder cannot get the right leg forward, then he must field it off the left leg (see figure 4.80). When this happens, the fielder will usually have to take several small steps after capturing the ball to get his body into throwing position (see figure 4.80). Taking these extra steps will delay the throw a little bit, but it is unavoidable in these situations. The first rule for infielders is to get to the ball and stop it from going through.

Figure 4.80 Infielder making a backhand play on a hard-hit ball.

SLOW ROLLERS

Because this is one of the most difficult plays for an infield to execute, the fielding technique for slow rollers is radically different from the technique that infielders use on other balls. On slow rollers the fielder charges the ball using correct running technique by pumping his arms hard, but even so, he must be under control before making the play. As the infielder approaches the slowly hit ball, he should try to circle his body a little so that after fielding he will be angled toward the direction of the throw (see figure 4.81*a*). As he nears the ball, he should also start to take small,

a b c

Figure 4.81 Infielder fielding a slowly hit ball.

(continued)

choppy steps and get his body under control and to the right of the ball if it is moving fast enough (see figure 4.81*b*). He fields the ball with his glove hand only, and then, while still running, in one continuous motion, transfers it to his throwing hand for the toss to the base (see figure 4.81*c*). The fielder should keep his body moving and continue to run after fielding the ball. If he stops and tries to gather his balance, he will have no chance to get the runner at the base for the out. If possible, the fielder should take the ball straight up in the air from his glove to make the throw and not worry about the normal arm action (down, back, up and over).

It is preferable here for the fielder to throw the ball from above his shoulder rather than from the side. A ball thrown over the top does not sink or move as much as one thrown from the side and is much easier for the first baseman to handle. One of the exceptions to the above, however, is the slow roller fielded by the second baseman. Since most of the time on this play the second baseman will be moving toward home plate and away from first base, the only way he can make a quick, strong throw will be to throw from the side of his body. In order to enable the first baseman to track the ball better on this type of throw, the second baseman must work to clear his glove out of the way by thrusting his glove arm and hand backward on his left side. At the same time the glove hand is moved out of the way, the waist must be swiveled around so that the player's belly button faces first base as much as possible. The ball is then thrown with a strong side arm motion with the arm path as much as possible parallel to the ground.

a b

Figure 4.82 Infielder fielding a ball that is barely moving or has stopped.

To become proficient at this difficult play, infielders must practice it often. Also, in the process of practicing and executing this play the infielder should also consider whether or not a throw will be successful. Much of this depends upon where the ball is hit, how fast the runner is and the location of other runners on base.

If the ball is barely moving or has stopped, the fielder should stay to the left of the ball and grab it with his throwing hand by pushing down on the top (see figure 4.82*a*). He will then quickly bring his right elbow back and throw the ball from underneath his chest to make the play (see figure 4.82*b*). When throwing, the fielder should get his left side out of the way and aim about 4 or 5 feet inside first base because a ball thrown in this manner will tail sharply to the right.

At a Glance

The following parts of the text offer additional information on fielding ground balls.

Common Errors

You may run into several common errors when teaching your athletes how to field ground balls.

Error	Error correction
The player has trouble getting control of the ball when trying to barehand slow rollers.	Make certain that the player is not trying to scoop the ball with the bare hand. Emphasize pushing down on the ball and grabbing it from the top.
The player tries to get in front of every batted ball, often not getting in good fielding position.	Fielding a ball on the forehand or backhand side is often easier than fielding it out in front. Emphasize that sometimes when fielders try to get in front of the ball, the ball may handcuff them and create a difficult play. Players must learn by repetition which balls they should field on the forehand or backhand side.
The player often seems to be caught with in-between hops on balls hit directly toward him.	Emphasize breaking down into fielding position when the ball is 15 feet away.

Double Plays

KEY POINTS

The most important components of turning the double play are

- positioning and getting to the base,
- feeding the ball,
- making the pivot,
- completing the throw and
- considerations by position.

Although not completed as often in high school as in higher levels of ball, the double play can still be accomplished with some regularity if you teach the basic mechanics and convince players that sufficient practice will enable them to turn two on many occasions.

With each day of practice on double-play techniques, infielders become more of a unit. The more they work in unison, the more double plays they will be able to complete. Infielders should always keep in mind that the first throw, the throw to second, should emphasize accuracy, and the second throw should emphasizes quickness. Finally, when the team practices the double play, you should use a stopwatch so that infielders know whether they are performing quickly enough. They'll need to turn the play in less than 4.1 seconds (average left-handed batter's time running to first base) or 4.3 seconds (right-handed batter's time).

For the elements of the double play listed, the following definitions apply: The feeder is the person who fields the ground ball and makes the initial throw to a teammate covering second base; the pivot, or pivot man, is the player who receives the initial throw, steps on the base and throws the ball to first.

POSITIONING AND GETTING TO THE BASE

To execute the double play, the middle infielders have to play at what is called double-play depth. They move from their normal starting positions with no runners on base to two steps closer to second base and two steps closer to the grass. Many baseball studies have concluded that most batted balls, up to 80 percent, are hit up the middle of the diamond. Therefore, playing closer to the base does not greatly diminish the ability of the infielders to field the ball. When the ball is hit, the pivot man has to get to the base quickly! He should not try to time his arrival at the base with the throw from the feeder. He should always be thinking, "Get to the base early."

The pivot must also get to the base in time to assume the basic athletic position. His knees should be bent slightly, his shoulders square to the flight of the ball and his hands in front of his chest in position to receive the ball. When he gets close to the base, the pivot should take short, hard steps to bring his body under control, putting it in position to move in either direction in case of an errant throw. A good rule for players to follow is fast, slow, fast. They run fast to the base; when they get there, they slow down; and after they get the ball, they move their feet fast to make the throw.

Figure 4.83 Pivot's hand positioning when catching a ball.

The pivot's hands should be in position to catch the ball—both hands together, fingers up—as referenced in "Catching a Throw" beginning on page 72 and shown in figure 4.83. This position facilitates not only catching the toss from the feeder but also transferring the ball quickly from the glove into the throwing hand and throwing to first.

One final thought about positioning deals with communication. As the pivot moves into position, he should yell, "Inside, inside, inside" or "Outside, outside, outside," depending on his position on second base. This call helps the feeder know where he needs to throw the ball.

Figure 4.84 Fielder's form when using an underhand feed to the pivot.

FEEDING THE BALL

Players can make several kinds of feeds in the double-play situation. The type of feed used depends on the direction in which the ball is hit in relation to the fielder and second base.

Balls Hit to Second

When the ball is hit in the direction of second base, the fielder, or feeder, should field the ball correctly and then throw a firm, underhand toss to the pivot. When doing this, the feeder should take care to separate his glove hand and throwing hand as shown in figure 4.84 so as not to hide the ball from the pivot man's view. The feeder should also make certain that he continues moving in the direction of the throw even after the ball has left his hand.

On balls hit directly at the shortstop or a few feet to either side, he should field the ball properly and pivot his right foot toward second, while at the same time lowering his right knee toward the ground and pivoting his hips (see figure 4.85). While performing this action with his lower body, he should raise his arm into throwing position and make a strong three-quarter-arm toss to the base. The second baseman should use the same technique on balls hit directly at him. The only difference is that the second baseman pivots his left foot and lowers his left knee, as shown in figure 4.86. In both cases, the feeder should always follow through and "paint" the ball across the body on the throw, much like the stroke used by a painter making a diagonal brush stroke on a fence. This procedure allows the middle infielder to keep the

Figure 4.85 Shortstop lowering his right side to get into position to feed the ball to second.

(continued)

Figure 4.86 Second baseman getting into proper feeding position on a ball hit directly at him.

throw straight and level with the pivot's chest. Infielders tend to throw the ball down instead of level if they stand up after fielding these "at 'em" balls.

Balls Hit to the Gaps

Balls hit into the holes, between first and second or between second and third, call for other techniques. On a ball hit to his right, the shortstop should get to the ball as quickly as possible, field it properly, plant his right foot to stop his momentum (see figure 4.87*a*), gather the ball into throwing position and make a strong throw to second base (see figure 4.87*b*). The shortstop will often have to field these balls backhanded, so he must stop his motion toward the foul line quickly. Jabbing the right foot into the ground enables him to do this.

a b

Figure 4.87 Shortstop planting hard on the right foot and transferring into throwing position on a ball hit in the gap to his right.

Because balls hit to the second baseman's left mean that he will be fielding the ball on his forehand side, he must use different footwork. The second baseman has two options on this play, depending on the speed of the runners and the velocity at which the ball is traveling. One option is to field the ball, drop his right foot back while rotating his hips and upper body clockwise toward second base, take a step with his left foot and then throw. When a quicker throw is needed, another technique is to field the ball to the forearm side, take an additional step into the hole with the right foot, plant the foot, pivot counterclockwise to the glove-hand side and make a strong overhand throw to second base similar to the shortstop's throw as illustrated earlier in figure 4.77 on page 133. This method can be quicker even though it has the disadvantage of having the fielder turn his back to second base momentarily.

Balls Hit to the Middle

On balls hit hard up the middle, the fielder must get to the ball and, after fielding it, decide what type of throw to make. "Double-Play Defenses" on page 196 in chapter 6 will cover more about this decision-making process. Sometimes in these situations, the infielder will have to perform a backhand flip. This throw, which must be practiced often to develop proficiency, is executed by turning the wrist of the throwing hand counterclockwise and flipping the ball with the wrist and fingers toward the base (see figure 4.88). When making this throw, the feeder, normally the shortstop, is moving away from second base, so he must throw backward. When the second baseman fields hard-hit balls behind second, he can usually perform a regular underhand toss, but because his momentum often carries him away from the base, he should first turn his hips perpendicular to the base before tossing to ensure accuracy.

The second baseman can execute the same kind of backhand flip on slowly hit balls that he fields on the infield grass in front of the base. Because the fielder's momentum is carrying him toward the pitcher's mound in this case, the only way that he can make a throw is backward with the backhand flip.

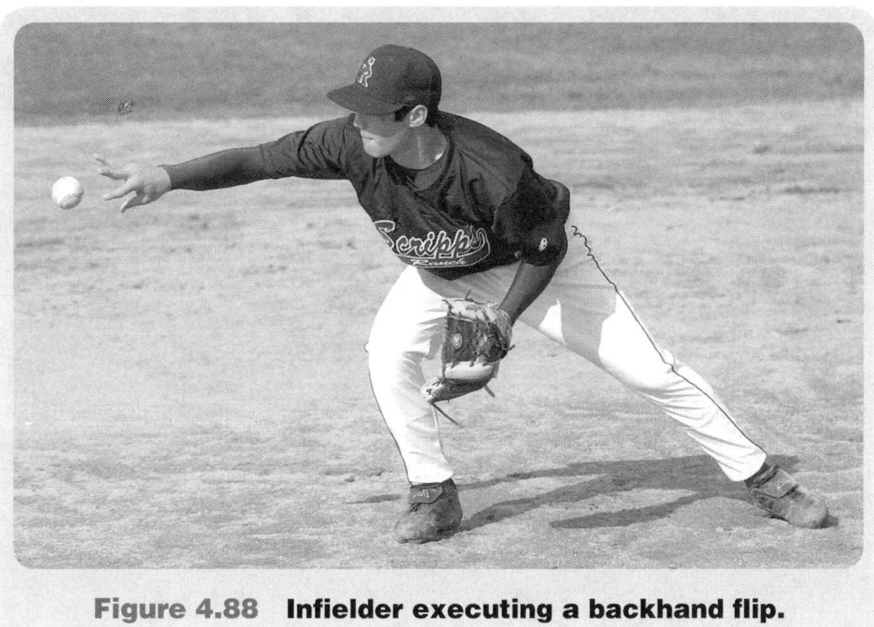

Figure 4.88 Infielder executing a backhand flip.

(continued)

MAKING THE PIVOT

There are probably as many ways of making the pivot at second base as there are infielders playing the game. The important concept in the pivot is to get the job done—tag the base, get into position to throw to first and then make an accurate, strong throw. Although infielders may sometimes be creative in their approach to the pivot, several methods are basic and easier to perform.

Shortstop

When the shortstop is the pivot man, the pivot is usually a little easier to perform because he has fewer options and his momentum always takes him toward first base. The most common pivot for the shortstop is to plant the left foot on the right-field side of second (see figure 4.89*a*), catch the ball from the feeder and then drag the right toe along the left-field side of the base while getting the ball into throwing position (see figure 4.89*b*). This motion normally gets the shortstop out of the way of a sliding runner. If the shortstop gets to the base early in the play, he can set his right toe against the left-field side of the base, catch the ball, crow hop and throw to first.

When the ball is thrown to the infield side of second, as might be the case on a throw from the first baseman or a ball fielded by the second baseman on the grass, the shortstop should place his left foot on the inside of the base, catch the ball from the feeder and then step and throw.

a b

Figure 4.89 Shortstop executing the pivot.

Second Baseman

The second baseman needs to practice more options to become adept with the double-play pivot. One option is to get to the base early, place the ball of the left foot on the base (see figure 4.90*a*), receive the feed, push off the base with the foot while transferring the weight to the right foot (see figure 4.90*b*), step to first with the left and throw (see figure 4.90*c*). If the ball is thrown far to the pivot's right in this setup, he merely steps to the ball with his right foot, drags his left foot across the base, plants and throws to first.

Another option for the second baseman is to straddle the base with both feet while awaiting the feed. This setup allows the pivot man to use either foot to contact the base for the force out, depending on where the ball is thrown.

If the second baseman cannot get to the base early and must field the ball on the run, he should time stepping on the bag with his left foot just as he is receiving the ball. He then steps across the base with his right foot, planting and throwing. When this type of pivot is necessary, the second baseman should round the base a little so that his momentum takes him more toward the pitcher's mound as he steps over the base rather than toward third base. Otherwise, he will be making the throw across his body, diminishing the chances of a successful double play.

a b c

Figure 4.90 Second baseman executing the double-play pivot.

(continued)

Two additional considerations are important here. First, any time one of the middle infielders is close to the base, he should step on the base himself and make the throw rather than slow things down by feeding the ball. Through practice, players will learn when to make the play themselves. Second, and maybe most important, catching the ball is more important than having the pivot foot on the base. If the throw is wide of the base, the fielder must forget the base and get the ball.

COMPLETING THE THROW

Both the shortstop and second baseman need to practice getting out of the way of the sliding runner after making the throw to first. The best way to teach this is to have them jump over an imaginary wire strung across their path about a foot off the ground. After making the throw, the pivot should jump over the wire to get out of the way of the sliding runner. To do this, he hops up in the air with his left foot, jumps over the wire and lands on his right foot. Although rules are in place to prevent takeout slides by runners, high school middle infielders should learn the technique of hopping over the wire to help avoid needless injuries. Infielders must learn not to do this before releasing the ball because jumping too early takes power away from the throw.

CONSIDERATIONS BY POSITION

The second baseman or shortstop does not always make the initial throw on a double play. Other infielders should be aware of a few techniques to make certain that their feeds to the bases are accurate and timely.

Third Baseman

When the third baseman fields a ball hit directly at him with plenty of time to make the feed, he should use proper throwing footwork and make a strong, level throw to the first-base side of second. On balls hit to his left, the third baseman may have to throw on the run. The important technique for these hits is to stay low and throw the ball from a lower arm slot rather than try to bring the ball up high, which will likely cause a throw into the dirt.

Pitcher

On balls hit back to the mound, the pitcher should field properly, turn his body into throwing position and make a strong throw toward the first-base side of second. The pitcher should not wait for the pivot man to get to the base on this play because doing so hurts the chances of making the double play. If the infielders have done their jobs and have let the pitcher know before the pitch who is going to be covering the base, then the pitcher should trust that the infielder will be there and get the ball to the base. An important aside here is that the middle infielder who is not covering the base should not back up the play. He should stay away from the base because moving toward it only confuses the pitcher.

First Baseman

If the first baseman has been holding the runner at first and the ball is hit toward him, he will field it on the inside of the diamond and make a strong throw to the inside of second base. If he fields the ball even with the baseline, the runner and second base, he must first take a step to the inside of the field before making the throw. His main concern is being far enough inside the baseline that his throw does not hit the runner advancing to second.

At a Glance

The following parts of the text offer additional information on double plays.

Common Errors

You may run into several common errors when teaching your athletes how to complete the double play.

Error	Error correction
Middle infielders have problems handling underhand flips from feeders.	Emphasize that the feeder must separate his tossing hand from the glove so that the throw is easily visible to the fielder waiting to make the pivot.
The feeder must wait before throwing because the pivot is not in position at the base.	Make certain that the middle infielders are positioned at double-play depth when a runner is on first base with less than two outs. If the fielder is too far from the base, he will be unable to get into pivot position soon enough, destroying the timing of the play.
On easy feeds to second, the feeder consistently throws low to the pivot.	Emphasize that on balls hit directly to him, the feeder must lower his body and give a strong, controlled three-quarter-arm flip to the pivot. Standing up while throwing often leads to throws that move downward.
The second baseman's momentum carries him away from first base after his pivot at second base.	Stress to the fielders that they must approach second base from the center-field side so that after they catch the feed and make the pivot, their momentum takes them closer to first base. This action shortens the throw so that it gets to first base faster.

Fielding Pop-Ups in the Infield

KEY POINTS

The most important components of fielding pop-ups are

- getting behind the ball,
- establishing priority and
- communicating.

No play is more likely to get airtime on *Sports Center* than the botched pop fly. Many of the misplays that appear are of two or three players surrounding an easy pop-up and watching it drop harmlessly to the ground between them while they all wait for the other guy to make the play. Most of the time, this happens because players get away from sound fundamentals and lose focus.

The skills necessary to field pop-ups in or around the infield are basically the same as those used by outfielders to field fly balls (refer to "Outfield Basics" on page 114 and "Challenging Outfield Plays" on page 120). The biggest difference is that the ball is hit much higher and will be coming back to earth on a much steeper angle than a regular fly ball will.

GETTING BEHIND THE BALL

The biggest problem for an infielder is waiting underneath the ball. Again, as with an outfielder, an infielder will have a better chance of making the play on a pop-up if he can get behind the ball and then move into it as it descends. The infielder should catch a pop-up, if possible, above his eyes on the throwing side of the body. He must avoid backpedaling on a pop-up, especially if the field is not in good condition and has lips on the edge of the infield. On a pop-up hit into foul territory, the second baseman and shortstop should hustle to get into position to make a play because they will have a better angle on the ball than will the first or third baseman.

At a Glance

The following parts of the text offer additional information on fielding pop-ups.

ESTABLISHING PRIORITY

Catching a pop-up can become difficult in breezy conditions. Wind currents can move the ball several feet in a split second, requiring quick movement of the glove just before the catch. For this reason, players must follow a priority system when fielding fly balls in the infield. If two players call for a ball in the air, the one with the highest priority has the responsibility of catching the ball. Other players need to get out of the way. As in the outfield, where the center fielder has priority over the other outfielders (see "Outfield Basics" on page 114), the infield has a pecking order. Shortstops have priority over any other infielder. Second basemen have priority over everyone except the shortstop. Corner infielders have priority over the catcher and pitcher, and the pitcher has priority over no one.

COMMUNICATING

Communication on pop-ups is extremely important. When the ball is in the air in the infield, all fielders should move in the direction of the pop-up. When it reaches its highest point, the infielder who feels that he can catch it should call, "Mine, mine, mine" and begin to settle under the ball. If, however, this infielder hears a teammate who has priority calling for the ball, he should move away from the ball to reduce confusion and avoid a collision.

Infielders who are not close enough to the ball to make the catch, especially the pitcher, should also communicate by yelling the name of the fielder who should catch the ball. When the wind is madly carrying the ball, a third fielder may have to make a call at the last second. When this occurs, other fielders should quickly peel away to avoid a collision.

When a pop-up carries into the outfield, communication between outfielder and infielder is crucial because the outfielder will often be running fast toward the fly while the infielder is slowly drifting with his back to the outfielder. In case of doubt, the outfielder always has priority over any infielder. The infielder should not call for the ball. If he thinks that he can field the ball easily, he should simply wave his hands vehemently while extending both arms above his head (see figure 4.91). If the outfielder calls for the ball, however, the infielder should rapidly vacate the area where the ball will land to avoid colliding with the outfielder.

Figure 4.91 Infielder signaling to others that he can field the ball.

On plays that are truly between the outfield and the infield in which no one makes a clear-cut call for the ball, infielders should catch the ball high and outfielders should try to catch the ball low, just before it hits the ground. Again, on these plays other fielders who have a better angle on the ball can determine who has a better chance of making the catch. They can help by yelling the player's name.

Common Errors

You may run into several common errors when teaching your athletes how to field pop-ups.

Error	Error correction
The player calls for the ball too soon on infield fly balls.	Emphasize that players should wait until the ball reaches the peak of its arc before they call for it.
Balls often fall between fielders on pop-ups.	Emphasize the priority system for catching fly balls. Go over this frequently in practice sessions.

PART III

Teaching Tactical Skills

Tactical skills get at the heart of baseball. Without proper understanding and execution of this type of skill, your players will often commit basic errors in game situations. You can empower your athletes by teaching them how to read situations, apply the appropriate knowledge and make the correct decisions.

This part focuses on the basic and intermediate tactical skills in baseball, showing you how to teach your athletes to make good decisions on the field. These skills include offensive tactical skills such as the first-and-third play, hit and run, stealing second and getting out of a rundown and defensive skills such as defending the first-and-third double steal, defending against the bunt and double-play defenses. Like the technical skills chapters, these chapters have been designed so that you can immediately incorporate the information into your teaching.

THINKING TACTICALLY

Throughout the presentation of tactical skills, you will see references to the need for athletes to know what is called the game situation. As described in Rainer Martens' *Successful Coaching, Third Edition*, the game situation includes "the count on the batter, the number of outs, the inning and the score." In other words, your players need to know specific information when your team faces a specific situation. For example, when you need to get a runner to second base in position to score, you may ask yourself, "How important is the run at second? Is it the tying or winning run? Is it an insurance run?"

You and your team must know what key information you need to make the best decision. Following are a few questions that you and your team must keep in mind when facing tactical situations during a game:

- What is your strategy?
- How does your game plan affect your strategy?
- How does the game situation (the score, the strengths and weaknesses of the players involved, the physical playing conditions and so on) affect your game plan?

In the skills that follow, you will first be presented with an overview that puts you and your athletes into a specific scenario in which you would be likely to use that particular tactical skill. The "Watch Out!" element highlights the distractions that may affect your athletes' ability to make appropriate decisions and provides insight on what to look for. The "Reading the Situation" element offers important cues that your athletes need to be able to read so that they can make appropriate decisions. Next, you will find a section called "Acquiring the Appropriate Knowledge," which provides the information that your athletes need to understand in order to make the proper decision and successfully execute the skill, as presented in the overview. Finally, as in the technical skill chapters, the "At a Glance" section refers you to the other important tools in this book that will help you teach the skill.

chapter 5

Offensive Tactical Skills

This chapter will cover the offensive tactical skills that you and your players must know in order to be successful. In this chapter, you will find:

Aggressive Baserunning

Aggressive baserunning challenges the opposition and forces them into mistakes. Teams that use aggressive baserunning keep the pitcher, catcher and middle infielders on edge and disrupt the pitcher's concentration on the batter, because he is too concerned with runners. Aggressiveness on the bases exploits a team's weaknesses. This section looks at aggressive baserunning by the batter and by the runner at first base in a nonstealing situation. To learn more about how to use aggressive baserunning after your players are on base, read other tactical skills in this chapter. You will find "Knowing When to Steal Second" on page 162 and "Knowing When to Steal Third" on page 166 particularly helpful.

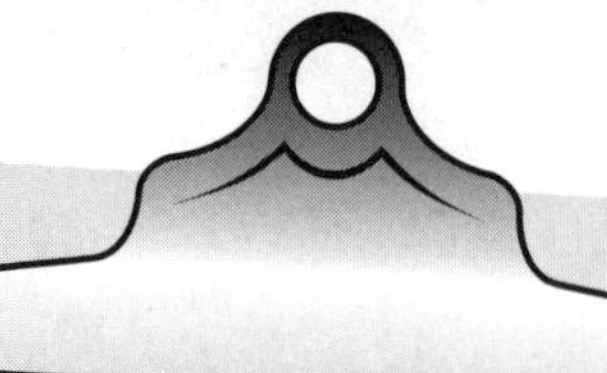

READING THE SITUATION

How do you teach your players to be aggressive and to keep the defense on edge? Teach your players to do the following:

- Know the game situation.
- Watch the base coach for the sign.
- Make good contact with the ball consistent with the sign that the coach has given.
- Sprint toward first and watch the first-base coach for signals to run straight through the base or to make the question mark turn.
- Know when and when not to tag up on fly balls after reaching first base.

WATCH OUT!

The following circumstances may distract your athletes:

- Head fakes by the pitcher
- Pitchers who frequently throw over to check the runners on base
- Pitchers who continually step off the rubber with their pivot foot and stare at the runner after coming set
- The ball itself because sometimes the batter watches the ball rather than running toward first

REMINDER!

When making the decision to use aggressive baserunning, you and your team must understand the team strategy and game plan. Don't forget to consider the questions on page 150.

ACQUIRING THE APPROPRIATE KNOWLEDGE

To use aggressive base running, you and your athletes must know about the following:

Rules

You and your athletes need to know several main rules when you are using aggressive baserunning:

- Rules pertaining to touching all the bases
- Rules about force plays
- Rules about a dropped third strike with two outs

Physical Playing Conditions

The physical playing conditions will significantly affect the game. Thus, you should teach your players to pay attention to the following physical conditions when contemplating aggressive baserunning:

- The surface quality of the infield. For example, if the field is wet, players need to know where in the base path they can get the best footing.

- The condition of the bases. For example, wet bases become slippery, thus increasing the chance of injury. Players must take more care when rounding the bases.

Strengths and Weaknesses of Opponents

You and your players must account for your opponent's strengths and weaknesses to know how to gain the best advantage when using aggressive baserunning. Teach your players to consider the following about your opponents:

- Do the outfielders have strong, accurate arms? If the runner is rounding first and a weak-armed outfielder has not yet fielded the ball, the runner may gamble and go to second.
- Do the infielders adjust to the correct defensive position after the ball is hit? Infielders who are slow to cover the bases provide a greater opportunity to go to second.

Self-Knowledge

In addition to being aware of your opponent's strengths and weaknesses, you and your players need to have knowledge about your own team's ability. When using aggressive baserunning, teach your players to be aware of the following:

- How fast is the batter? If you have a fast runner hitting the ball, you have more chance to make the aggressive turn and go after the additional base or bases.
- How good is the batter at recognizing opportunities to take additional bases? Work with the batter to improve his ability to recognize opportunities on his own.
- What is the strength and reputation of the on-deck batter? With two outs and a good hitter on deck, be more conservative with your baserunning.

At a Glance

The following parts of the text offer additional information on aggressive baserunning.

Decision-Making Guidelines

When deciding whether or not to use aggressive baserunning, you and your players should be sure to consider the previous information. Also consider the following guidelines:

- Batters must protect runners by calling time if the pitcher is taking too much time from the set position.
- Batters should swing through pitches on steal attempts to distract the catcher, unless the ball is outside the strike zone.
- Runners at first should go halfway (four or five steps toward second) on fly balls hit to left field, shallow center field or toward the gaps. On deep left-field hits that look as if they will be caught, the runner should tag up at first and then decide whether to advance.
- The first runner to reach base in any game should take an overaggressive one-way lead to draw throws from the pitcher.
- Use aggressive baserunning more often when your team is ahead but do not necessarily abandon it when you are behind.
- Use aggressive baserunning more often against outfielders who have weak or inaccurate arms or infielders who have slow reaction times.

Baserunning From Second

In any situation, scoring from second base involves not only speed but also the ability to make split-second decisions. Players must realize that they should not try to score on every base hit. Imagine a close ball game with the runner on second representing the tying or winning run. With two outs, the batter hits a ground ball or line drive into the outfield. Should the runner automatically try to advance home on the hit and risk being thrown out? Or should he hold at third and wait for the next batter to drive him home? Statistics show that the chance of scoring from second with two outs is 26 percent; the chance from third is 32 percent. Of course, if a runner doesn't make an effort to score, the chance will always be 0 percent! Therefore, properly executed strategy becomes crucial.

READING THE SITUATION

How do you and your players gain the best advantage when you have a runner at second? Teach your players to do the following:

- Know the game situation.
- Watch the third-base coach for any signs that he may be giving.
- Know how deep the outfielders are playing and what their respective arm strengths are.
- Know how big a lead the runner is able to get.
- Know what kind of move the pitcher has to second base if he has thrown there previously.
- Know whether the batter is a pull or spray hitter.
- Track the ball after it is hit and look and listen to the base coaches for additional guidance.

WATCH OUT!

The following circumstances may distract your athletes:

- The second baseman and shortstop hold the runner close to the bag with various decoy moves.
- The catcher likes to throw behind the runner after a pitch that is taken or swung through by the hitter.

ACQUIRING THE APPROPRIATE KNOWLEDGE

When a runner is at second base, you and your athletes must understand the following:

Rules

You and your athletes need to know several main rules when you have a runner on second base:

- Rules about force plays
- Rules about tagging up after fly balls
- Rules giving fielders the right to field the ball over the runner's right to the baseline

REMINDER!

When a runner is on second base, you and your team must understand the team strategy and game plan. Don't forget to consider the questions on page 150.

Physical Playing Conditions

The physical playing conditions will significantly affect the game. Thus, you and your players must pay attention to the following physical conditions when contemplating the best way to gain an advantage when a runner is at second base:

- The length and condition of the grass in the outfield. For example, the longer the grass, the slower the ball will move on ground balls. If the grass is wet, the ball will move quicker on ground balls. Likewise, outfielders may slip on wet grass when making a quick turn toward a deep fly ball.

- The strength and direction of the wind. Wind may affect the flight of the ball and the ability of the outfielders to catch the ball. On extremely windy days, runners may not be able to reach top speed.

Strengths and Weaknesses of Opponents

You and your players must account for your opponent's strengths and weaknesses to know how to gain the best advantage when a runner is at second base. Teach your players to consider the following about your opponents:

- Do the outfielders have strong, accurate arms? Do they charge the ball, ready to throw? These tendencies will influence whether or not you will gamble when trying to score from second.
- How good is the opposing team at using deceptive timed pickoff plays? How good are the middle infielders at holding the runner close to the base? Their skills in these areas may affect the base runner's ability to get a good lead.

At a Glance

The following parts of the text offer additional information on baserunning from second.

Rounding the Bases	p. 48
Stealing Third Base	p. 54
Bent-Leg Slide	p. 56
Headfirst Slide	p. 60
Aggressive Baserunning	p. 152
Knowing When to Steal Third	p. 166
Pitcher Pickoffs	p. 190
Catcher Pickoffs	p. 194

Self-Knowledge

In addition to being aware of your opponent's strengths and weaknesses, you and your players need to have knowledge about your own team's ability. When baserunning from second, teach your players to be aware of the following:

- What is the ability of the hitter on deck? Has he been able to put the ball in play or make contact against the pitcher? If so, perhaps it's better to stop at third and try to score in one of the nine ways explained on page 156.
- How fast is the runner on second? How are his legs feeling on that particular day? If you have a slow runner on second, you will take less of a gamble.
- How big a lead does the runner on second take so that he can get a good jump on the play?
- How good is the runner at reading the pitcher? This will affect his ability to get a good jump.

Decision-Making Guidelines

When deciding the best way to gain an advantage when your team has a runner on second, you and your players should be sure to consider the previous information. Also consider the following guidelines:

- Take less risk when your team is behind than when you are ahead. But if it is late in the game, you have two outs and you are down by one run, you may want to try to score on the play.
- Take less risk when your team is facing an outfield with strong, accurate arms.
- Take less risk when the on-deck hitter is hitting well.
- Be more aggressive when the runner on base is fast and his legs are fresh.
- Be more cautious when the batter has a full count with two outs in a force situation. In this situation, the runner must make sure that the pitcher is going home with the ball. Runners often fail to concentrate and, in their anxiety to score, become ripe targets for pickoff moves.
- Always have the runner tag on fly balls hit to the right-field side of second. Have the runner watch the ball and be ready to advance if it is caught or travels over the head of the outfielder.
- Always have the runner take a few steps in the direction of third on fly balls hit to the left-field side. The closer the ball is to second, the less the runner should stray.

Scoring From Third

When asked why he became a base stealer, Lou Brock once said, "First base is nowhere!" He meant that it was hard to score runs from first base, but once he got to second he was much more valuable to his team. Based on this logic, if first base is nowhere, then third base must be everywhere! If you really want to score runs, third base is the base from which to do it. A runner can score from third base in nine ways: hit, error, passed ball, wild pitch, balk, sacrifice fly, infield ground ball, squeeze bunt or stolen base. The ability to score from third base involves having the expertise to be able to recognize scoring opportunities and be prepared for any contingency. When a runner reaches third, a team will not want to waste that golden scoring opportunity.

READING THE SITUATION

How do you and your players gain the best advantage when you have a runner at third base? Teach your players to do the following:

- Know the game situation.
- Watch and listen to the base coach for any signs.
- Know where the infielders are positioned: grass, normal or deep.
- Track the ball after it is hit and look and listen to the base coach for additional guidance.

WATCH OUT!

The following circumstances may distract your athletes:

- The third baseman may move to the base for a possible pickoff throw.
- The pitcher's delivery. Some pitchers pause at their balance point or use head fakes to try to hold runners closer.
- Outfielders may move toward a fly ball as if they were going to catch it, knowing that they cannot reach the ball but forcing the runner to stay close to the base and delay his jump home.

ACQUIRING THE APPROPRIATE KNOWLEDGE

To score from third, you and your athletes must understand the following:

Rules

You and your athletes need to know several main rules when you are trying to score from third:

- Rules about tagging up before running home on a fly ball
- Rules about interference and obstruction
- Rules about what a pitcher may or may not do from the windup or stretch positions
- Rules about leading off the base in foul territory to avoid bring struck by a live batted ball

REMINDER!

When attempting to score from third, you and your team must understand the team strategy and game plan. Don't forget to consider the questions on page 150.

Physical Playing Conditions

The physical playing conditions will significantly affect the game. Thus, you and your players must pay attention to the following physical conditions when contemplating the best way to gain an advantage when a runner is at third base:

- The surface quality between third and home. For example, if the dirt is soft (if it has a lot of diamond mix on it), runners will have more difficulty getting their footing.

- The condition of the infield surface. Various conditions will affect the time that it takes a batted ground ball to reach the fielder.

At a Glance

The following parts of the text offer additional information on scoring from third.

Strengths and Weaknesses of Opponents

You and your players must account for your opponent's strengths and weaknesses to know how to gain the best advantage when you have a runner at third. Teach your players to consider the following about their opponents:

- Do the outfielders have strong, accurate arms? Do the outfielders charge the ball and come up ready to throw?
- How quick is the pitcher's delivery to home plate? How good is his pickoff move to third base? How good is the third baseman at holding the runner on the bag? Does the catcher watch the runner at third? These considerations will affect your runner's ability to get a good lead.
- How good is the pitcher's control? Is he able to locate his pitches? His control will affect the batter's ability to hit the ball where he wants to hit it.
- Where are the infielders positioned? Are they on the grass, normal or deep?

Self-Knowledge

In addition to being aware of your opponent's strengths and weaknesses, you and your players need to have knowledge about your own team's ability. When a runner on your team is on third, teach your players to be aware of the following:

- What are the strengths and weaknesses of the batter?
- How fast is the runner at third?
- How long a lead can the runner at third take?
- How is the communication between the runner, the base coach and the batter?

Decision-Making Guidelines

When deciding the best way to gain an advantage when your team has a runner on third, you and your players should be sure to consider the previous information. Also consider the following guidelines:

- Take more risk in your baserunning from third when your team is ahead. In doing so, however, be sure that you show respect to your opponents and the game.
- Use the first-and-third play when applicable. For example, if you have runners on first and third and only one out, have your runner on first try to steal second. This play can create an error that can allow your runner on third to score (see "First-and-Third Play" on page 158).
- Have your runner take a bigger lead when the defense has weak pickoff abilities.
- Always have your runner tag up on medium to long fly balls. The runner should assume a sprinters' stance when tagging up, making him ready to run on the catch.
- Have your runner take a secondary lead on shallow fly balls hit to center or right field. If the ball is caught, the runner can retreat easily. If the ball falls in front of the fielder, the runner can score easily.
- Have your runner hesitate on line drives before running home. Runners should practice reading the angle of the flight of the ball off the bat until it becomes second nature.
- On a passed ball or wild pitch, have your runner break for home when his momentum is already going toward home, rather than when he has begun his retreat to third. Be sure that the batter helps the runner decide whether to come home.

First-and-Third Play

The first-and-third play is an aggressive strategy designed to eliminate the possibility of the double play and, perhaps, to score a run. Its main purpose is to put pressure on the defense by causing confusion. In high school, because of the lack of arm strength, this play is relatively easy to run. The main reason that a team should try this play is that, if executed well, it places two runners in scoring position. Most coaches mistakenly see this play only as a way of scoring a run without the batter's help.

READING THE SITUATION

How do you and your players gain the best advantage when runners are at first and third? Teach your players to do the following:

- Know the game situation.
- Watch the coach for signs.
- Know how closely the runner at first is being held.
- Know whether the second baseman or shortstop moves to cover second after every pitch.
- Know whether the opposing team uses pitchouts.
- Recognize that when the ball beats the runner to second, the runner should get into a rundown to allow the runner at third an attempt to score.

WATCH OUT!

The following circumstances may distract your athletes:

- The pitcher may fake a pickoff throw to third base and then wheel and throw to first.
- The pitcher may step off the rubber to try to disrupt the timing of the play.
- The pitcher may fake a cut on the catcher's throw to second.

ACQUIRING THE APPROPRIATE KNOWLEDGE

To be successful in a first-and-third situation, you and your athletes should understand the following:

Rules

You and your athletes need to know several main rules when you are in a first-and-third situation:

- Rules about interference and obstruction and what a player can and cannot do when caught in a rundown.
- Rules about establishing and leaving a baseline. Players need to know that each time they run, they establish a personal baseline, which may be different from the line as stated in the rules.
- Rules about what a pitcher can and cannot do while standing on the pitching rubber.
- Rules about when a pitcher becomes an infielder.

Physical Playing Conditions

The physical playing conditions will significantly affect the game. Thus, you and your players must pay attention to the following physical conditions when in a first-and-third situation:

- The surface quality between first and second, and between third and home. For example, if the field is wet, players need to know where in the base path they can get their best footing. Likewise, they will need to know where to start the slide so that they can make it to the base they are trying to reach.
- The strength of the wind.

REMINDER!

When in a first-and-third situation, you and your team must understand the team strategy and game plan. Don't forget to consider the questions on page 150.

Strengths and Weaknesses of Opponents

You and your players must account for your opponent's strengths and weaknesses to know the best way to gain an advantage during a first-and-third situation. Teach your players to consider the following about your opponents:

- Do the infielders have strong arms? Especially important is knowing the arm strength of the infielder covering second to determine whether he can get the runner going for home.
- Are the infielders level headed or easily flustered? Are they alert for trick plays? Do they cover second after every pitch?
- Do the pitcher and catcher watch the runner closely on a base on balls to see if the runner continues directly to second base? If not, you might be able to take advantage of their inattention and go for the double steal.
- How quick is the pitcher's delivery to home plate? Does the defense pay attention to the runners' leads? If not, your runners will be able to take good leads.

At a Glance

The following parts of the text offer additional information on scoring from third.

Self-Knowledge

In addition to being aware of your opponent's strengths and weaknesses, you and your players need to have knowledge about your own team's ability. When in a first-and-third situation, teach your players to be aware of the following:

- Is the batter a strong hitter? Can he bunt? Can he put the ball in play to allow the run to score the conventional way?
- How effective are the players in rundown situations?
- How good is the runner at third at recognizing when the ball is in the optimum position for his break to home plate?
- How good is the communication between the third-base coach and the lead runner?

Decision-Making Guidelines

When deciding how to gain the best advantage during a first-and-third situation, you and your players should be sure to consider the previous information. Also consider the following guidelines:

- When a batter is walked and a runner is on third, the batter should be alert to the possibility of continuing to second for a first-and-third play. Another option, the early break play, is for the batter to break for second as the pitcher is coming into his set position or taking his sign.
- A runner about to be tagged should try to get into a rundown so that the other runner has a chance to advance.
- The responsibilities of the runner at first on a steal include getting a good lead and breaking for second on the pitch; looking to the plate after a few steps to see what happens on the pitch; allowing himself to get caught in a rundown only when the catcher has held the runner at third and has a chance to get him at second; and sliding to the outside of the base to avoid a tag or, if about to be tagged, to fall to the ground and lie flat or to run to the right-field side of the baseline. If caught in a rundown, the back runner tries to force more than one throw and make sure that any attempted play occurs nearer to first than to second. This tactic buys the runner at third some time.
- The runner at third should hold his lead and not try to run home until the defense has made a commitment to the runner going to second. The lead runner can bluff toward home, forcing a cut or gradually extending his lead during a rundown involving the back runner. A good time to break is when the second baseman has the ball and the back runner is in a rundown. As soon as the second baseman releases the ball to first, the lead runner should go.
- Make sure that hitters are patient when runners are on the corners. They should not swing at the first pitch in the event that the play is on.

Using the Bunt

The bunt is a batted ball that is not hit hard but is strategically placed on the diamond so that the defense must make a play on the batter rather than the runner. A well-placed bunt can help you and your team gain an advantage, but the defense can field a poor bunt and force the lead runner out.

 **WATCH OUT!**

The following circumstances may distract your athletes:

- A pitchout in a bunt situation
- In a squeeze situation, a ball thrown up and tight in the strike zone
- A special bunt defense, that is, using five infielders or having the third baseman play 45 feet from home plate
- The first baseman and third baseman charging as soon as the batter shows bunt

READING THE SITUATION

Players must be aware of situations that call for a bunt, and they must bunt according to the way the defense reacts when they show bunt. Except in squeeze bunt situations, they must try to place the ball away from charging infielders or to spots on the field from which it would be difficult to make a play on the advancing base runner. You and your players should understand the following:

- In late innings of close, low-scoring games, the bunt may be used more frequently. A tight game puts more pressure on the defense.
- If the pitcher is getting batters out, the need to bunt to get runners on is greater.
- If both sides of the infield charge when the hitter shows bunt, a steal or a fake bunt may be a better option.

ACQUIRING THE APPROPRIATE KNOWLEDGE

To know when to use the bunt, you and your athletes must understand the following:

Rules

You and your athletes need to know several main rules when you are in a situation that could call for either a bunt or a steal:

- Rules about placement of feet in the batter's box
- Rules about running outside the 45-foot line on the way to first base
- Rules about what is a swing and what is not when trying to pull back out of the bunt position

REMINDER!

When deciding whether to bunt or steal, you and your players should know your team strategy and game plan. Don't forget to consider the questions on page 150.

Physical Playing Conditions

The physical playing conditions will significantly affect the game. Thus, you and your players must pay attention to the following physical conditions when contemplating whether to bunt or steal:

- The surface quality of the infield grass. Bunts will roll more slowly in long grass.
- The foul-line dirt. Is it level, or does it slope toward or away from fair territory?
- The surface quality between bases. On a poor-quality surface, runners on base cannot get a good jump, so the bunt may be safer than the steal.

Strengths and Weaknesses of Opponents

You and your players must account for your opponent's strengths and weaknesses to know whether it makes the most sense to bunt or to steal. Teach your players to consider the following about your opponents:

- How fast and agile is the pitcher? A quick, good-fielding pitcher may reduce the chance of success.
- Is the first baseman right-handed or left-handed? An athletic left-handed first baseman who is fast enough to field the bunt and get the runner at second base may make you think twice about using the bunt.
- How quick is the pitcher's delivery to home plate? A slow delivery may increase your chances to bunt successfully.
- How fast are the infielders? Slow-footed fielders will increase the chances of a successful bunt.
- How good is the pitcher at controlling pitches? A pitcher who usually throws strikes will actually help you in a bunt situation because you know that you're going to be getting good pitches.
- How strong and accurate are the catcher's throws? Catchers who have weak or inaccurate arms will improve your chances at bunting.

At a Glance

The following parts of the text offer additional information on deciding whether to bunt or steal.

Self-Knowledge

In addition to being aware of your opponent's strengths and weaknesses, you and your players need to have knowledge about your own team's ability. When deciding whether to bunt or to steal, teach your players to be aware of the following:

- What is the speed of the base runner and the bunter? Even with a well-placed bunt, is the runner fast enough to advance to the next base? Do you have a quick runner on first base who is adept at stealing? Perhaps stealing is a better option when that player is on base.
- How good is the batter at placing the bunt?
- How good is the on-deck hitter? Sometimes a team may successfully bunt a runner to second to eliminate a double-play possibility only to have the team walk the next hitter intentionally, thus creating the same scenario.

Decision-Making Guidelines

When deciding when to use the bunt, you and your players should be sure to consider the previous information. While the decision is ultimately yours, you should strive to empower your players to make this decision on their own when the opportunity presents itself, as players need to be ready for this task. Also consider the following guidelines:

- Bunt more when the corner infielders are slow in reacting to the ball.
- Bunt more when the pitcher's follow-through carries him far to either side of the mound.
- Bunt more when you have not had success with the steal.
- Bunt more when you are in the late innings and need an insurance run.
- Bunt less when you hold an extremely large lead, because you do not want to run up the score.
- Bunt less when your strong (3, 4 and 5) hitters are at bat (unless you want to bunt as a surprise).

Knowing When to Steal Second

Speaking at a coaching clinic, Lou Brock, the great St. Louis outfielder, told a story about how he decided to become a base stealer. He said he just got tired of diving back into first base on pickoff attempts from the pitcher, and then getting punished with ferocious tags—with the ball in the glove—from burly first basemen, especially big Willie McCovey of the Giants. Brock went on to say that rather than be bruised and battered, he'd take his chances getting to second base! Stealing a base is always a strategic gamble, even when there isn't a 6-4, 250-pound first baseman playing for your opponent, but if it helps your team maintain an aggressive mindset, then it is definitely worthwhile. And besides, as Brock went on to say that day, "First base is nowhere!"

Stealing second is the act of taking an additional base without aid of a hit or bunt. The runner takes a calculated risk that, on the pitch, he will be able to get to second base safely by beating the catcher's throw or avoiding a tag by a middle infielder. If you coach an aggressive offensive philosophy, your players should assume that any time they reach first base, they should be thinking about stealing second. As mentioned earlier, the threat of a steal puts the defense, especially the pitcher, on edge. Although always a strategic gamble, if the attempted steal helps your team maintain an aggressive mind-set, then it is worthwhile.

READING THE SITUATION

How do you and your players decide to steal second? Teach your players to do the following:

- Watch the coach for the steal sign, or steal if they see a great chance to steal successfully.
- Study the pitcher throughout the game to determine how far they can get off base before the pitcher throws over.
- Study the first baseman throughout the game to learn where he plays in various situations.
- Look at home after the initial break to see whether they should continue running, pause and watch the ball, or retreat to first base.
- Watch the infielder covering second while running to determine whether to slide to the inside or outside of the bag.

WATCH OUT!

The following circumstances may distract your athletes:

- A pitcher who continually changes his rhythm in the stretch position by sometimes coming to a set and throwing immediately, or by coming to a set, holding and then stepping off and staring at the runner
- Successive pickoff attempts by the pitcher, which subconsciously convince the runner to take a shorter primary lead
- A pitcher who intermittently steps off the rubber after coming to a stretch, making the runner lose focus
- Early movement by a first baseman who breaks off the base as if going into fielding position but then spins back to the base to get a pickoff throw from the pitcher
- Hard tags put on the runner by the first baseman on pickoff attempts
- A first baseman who plays behind the runner and kicks dirt, trying to divert the runner's attention

REMINDER!

When deciding whether to steal second base, you and your players should know your team strategy and game plan. Don't forget to consider the questions on page 150.

CUES FROM THE PITCHER

When playing against right-handed pitchers, your players should attend to the following cues:

- Front foot. As soon as the pitcher lifts his front foot, the runner can begin to steal. Lifting the front foot before moving the back foot commits a pitcher to throwing home.
- Back foot. If this foot moves, the runner better hustle back to first base. Lifting this foot means that the pitcher is not throwing a pitch.
- Front shoulder. Some right-handed pitchers begin their stretch position with the front shoulders slightly open to first base. If the shoulder begins to turn to first, the pitcher is committed to throwing there. After that shoulder begins to close and turn toward home, the pitcher has committed to throwing a pitch. The runner can steal second.
- Front elbow. Some right-handers pull the elbow toward the body when they are going to throw to first and move it up when throwing home.

The cues for left-handed pitchers are much different. Although left-handers have the advantage of having their eyes facing the runner in the stretch position, they can be just as easy to steal off. Most left-handers give away their move to first base in some way, and good base runners will try to identify the telltale sign. Following are the main keys for left-handed pitchers:

- Head. Most pitchers become creatures of habit and tip off their moves with their heads. The typical lefty tip-off is this: When the head is looking at the runner, the pitcher will throw home; when the head is looking home and the foot lifts, the pitcher will throw to first. Although not always true, this rule usually holds form. Players should study the head movements of left-handed pitchers every time a runner reaches first base.
- Front foot. Watch the angle of the toes here. Some lefties point them up when going to first and down when going home.
- Front knee. Some lefties bring their leg back toward second base when throwing home and lift it straighter when they are throwing to first. Remember that if any part of the left-handed pitcher's front foot passes the front of the pitching rubber, according to the rules, the pitcher is committed to throwing home. The runner should steal second!
- Front leg lift. Some lefties lift the leg high when going to first, hoping to hold the runner at his primary lead longer with the high leg kick. When they are going home, the kick is not as high.

ACQUIRING THE APPROPRIATE KNOWLEDGE

To steal second successfully, you and your athletes must understand the following:

Rules

You and your athletes need to know several main rules when they are stealing second:

- Rules about tagging up after fly balls
- Rules about balks
- Rules about overrunning the base
- Rules about interference and obstruction

(continued)

Physical Playing Conditions

The physical playing conditions will significantly affect the game. Thus, you and your players must pay attention to the following physical conditions when contemplating whether they should steal second:

- The surface quality between first and second. For example, if the field is wet, players need to know where in the base path they can get their best footing. Likewise, they will need to know where the slide has to start so that they can make it to second.
- The strength of the wind. Extremely high wind may reduce the runner's ability to reach top speed or, to your advantage, may cause fielders' throws to be ineffective.

Strengths and Weaknesses of Opponents

You and your players must account for your opponent's strengths and weaknesses to know whether you can pull off the steal. Teach your players to consider the following about your opponents:

- Does the pitcher have quick moves to first? Is it easy to predict when he is going to first? Against pitchers with outstanding moves that are difficult to read, a bunt or delay steal may be a better approach.
- How fast is the pitcher's delivery to home plate? How strong and accurate is the catcher at throwing? The average runner can reach second base in 3.5 seconds (from a 10-foot lead). If a catcher can make a throw to second in 2.2 seconds, then the pitcher must be able to throw glove to catcher's mitt in 1.3 seconds or better to have a chance of making the play.
- Does the pitcher use high or slow leg kicks from the stretch position? These kicks lengthen the time that it takes the pitcher to deliver the ball home.
- Do the middle infielders quickly cover second base after each pitch in case of a steal? This defensive action would affect the runner's ability to get a good lead.

Self-Knowledge

In addition to being aware of your opponent's strengths and weaknesses, you and your players need to have knowledge about your own team's ability. When stealing second, teach your players to be aware of the following:

- Is the runner experiencing any physical limitations that may affect his normal ability to steal? For example, if his legs are particularly fatigued, he may not be as quick as he is normally.
- How adept is the runner at reading the pitcher's throw to first or home? If he does this well, he may be able to get a quicker jump toward second.
- How quickly can the runner retreat to first?
- How comfortable and successful is the runner at sliding into second?
- How good is the runner at disguising the intent to run? Runners should be able to do this by sometimes taking long primary leads to draw pickoff throws and then taking shorter leads when the steal sign is given. This approach fakes the pitcher into thinking that he has forced the runner into becoming conservative.
- How good is the runner at using the bluff run, that is, the fake steal? Done often enough, the bluff run can lull the defense into a false sense of security.
- How good is the batter at swinging through pitches to protect the runner?
- What is the strength and reputation of the batter? If you have a good batter at the plate and the runner at first steals second, some teams may choose to walk the batter intentionally rather than let him drive in the runner. In this case, deciding not to steal may be better.

Decision-Making Guidelines

When deciding whether or not to steal second, you and your players should be sure to consider the previous information. While the decision is ultimately yours, you should strive to empower your players to make this decision on their own when the opportunity presents itself, as players need to be ready for this task. Also consider the following guidelines:

- Take more risk in stealing when your team is ahead.
- Steal more often when facing a right-handed pitcher. Getting a good lead on left-handed pitchers may be more difficult because they are facing the runner on first.
- Steal more often when the pitcher is likely to throw a breaking pitch or a changeup, on counts such as 0-1 or 1-2.
- Steal less often on pitchers who have a quick delivery home because your players will have to shorten their leads and will be unable to take off quickly to second.
- Steal less often on catchers with strong, accurate arms.
- Steal more often when you have a runner on third because an error may allow him to score.
- Steal more often when your team is struggling to get a hit. A successful steal may give you the break that you need.
- Always have your players return to first base on the outfield side on pickoff attempts because the tag is more difficult.
- Always have your players lead off slightly inside the baseline to reduce the angle between the runner and first base from the pitcher's viewpoint and make the lead look shorter than it really is.

At a Glance

The following parts of the text offer additional information on stealing second.

Swing and Follow-Through	p. 26
Rounding the Bases	p. 48
Bent-Leg Slide	p. 56
Headfirst Slide	p. 60
Aggressive Baserunning	p. 152
Situational Hitting	p. 172
Defensive Positioning	p. 178
Pitcher Pickoffs	p. 190
Catcher Pickoffs	p. 194

Knowing When to Steal Third

Just like the steal of second, the steal of third is a way to advance the runner on base without benefit of a hit ball or sacrifice. However, one of baseball's unwritten commandments, "don't make the first or third out at third base," causes many conservative baseball coaches to look with disdain on the steal of third base. Many coaches feel that once a runner has reached second base, he is in good enough scoring position because the chances of scoring a run, according to major league baseball statistics, do not increase dramatically between being on second base with less than two outs or being on third in the same situation. Why, in these coaches' minds, should they risk getting the runner to third on a steal? But coaches who believe in taking the aggressive approach to baserunning feel that getting a runner to third base, especially against a lazy defense, adds greatly to their ability to put pressure on the opponent. And, although there has been no definitive study on the matter, the chances of scoring from third base are significantly greater in youth baseball than they are in professional ball. Coaches previously learned that there are nine ways to score from third base. Why wouldn't a coach want to get as many runners as possible there when doing so greatly increases scoring chances and puts additional stress on the defense?

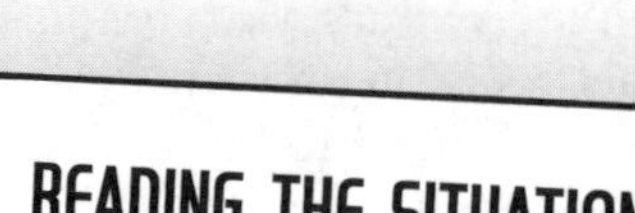

READING THE SITUATION

How do you and your players decide to steal third? Teach your players to do the following:

- Know the game situation.
- Watch for the sign from the coach or react to a good opportunity to steal.
- Know the number of looks the pitcher gives to second.
- Know the pitcher's time to the plate.
- Determine the predictability of the pitcher.
- Be aware of a change in the pitcher's timing.
- Watch the position of the third baseman.

WATCH OUT!

The following circumstances may distract your athletes:

- Bluff moves toward the base by the second baseman or by the shortstop as if a pickoff throw were coming
- The shortstop makes noise or kicks dirt behind the runner to trick him into thinking that he is breaking for the bag
- The shortstop or second baseman hitting his glove with his bare hands as if he were signaling for a pickoff
- The pitcher using numerous quick head fakes to hold the runner
- Oral distractions from the second baseman and shortstop
- The pitcher who has a deceptive inside move on pickoff attempts
- Timed plays between pitcher and middle infielders that work on a count system with no prior movement by the middle infielders to tip the play

REMINDER!

When deciding whether to steal third, you and your players must understand the team strategy and game plan. Don't forget to consider the questions on page 150.

BEING READY FOR PITCHER PICKOFFS

If the runner has been observant throughout the game and has been paying attention to a pitcher's normal motion with a runner on second, he will not be taken by surprise on attempted pickoffs at second.

Generally, pitchers use two moves to pick a runner at second. The first is similar to the pick at first base in which the pitcher steps off the rubber with his right foot and then wheels and throws to second base. The second type is sneakier but usually easier to spot by an observant runner. In this move, as the pitcher lifts his front foot to the balance position, instead of stopping and moving the foot toward home for the pitch, he continues moving the lead foot toward second base and then throws to a covering infielder for a pickoff attempt. If the pitcher has been using a glide stride (see "Pitcher Stretch Mechanics" in chapter 4 beginning on page 102 for more information on this technique), in which he uses little lift with the front leg from the stretch position, then a higher leg lift should be a signal to the runner to watch for a pickoff attempt. Also, pitchers who use this type of move tend to move their upper bodies toward second before the foot begins moving in that direction. As soon as a runner sees this upper-body movement, he should use it as a clue to return to the base. Note here that the pitcher, after he turns to second base, does not have to throw to the base as he does at first base.

Another key to watch is the movement of the pitcher's head. Sometimes the pitcher will hint at a throw to second by doing something different with his head or eyes. Runners should also be aware of any telling movements by the second baseman or the shortstop. The shortstop may move in front of the runner to try to distract him while the second baseman sprints to the bag for a pickoff attempt. The shortstop may even talk to the runner in an attempt to distract him. If any of these occur, the runner should be prepared for a pickoff.

ACQUIRING THE APPROPRIATE KNOWLEDGE

To steal third successfully, you and your athletes must understand the following:

Rules

You and your athletes need to know several main rules when you are deciding whether to steal third:

- Rules about leading off without interfering with the shortstop's ability to get to a batted ball
- Rules about running in the baseline
- Rules about overrunning the base

Physical Playing Conditions

The physical playing conditions will significantly affect the game. Thus, you and your players must pay attention to the following physical conditions when contemplating whether to steal third:

- The surface quality between second and third. For example, if the field is wet, players need to know where in the base path they can get their best footing. Likewise, they need to know where the slide has to start so that they can make it to third.
- The strength of the wind.

(continued)

Strengths and Weaknesses of Opponents

You and your players must account for your opponent's strengths and weaknesses when deciding whether or not you can steal third. Teach your players to consider the following about your opponents:

- Are the middle infielders quick, and do they work at holding the runner close to the bag? For example, middle infielders who coordinate and disguise their movements will affect the runner's ability to get a good lead.
- Does the catcher have a strong arm and like to throw behind runners? If the opposing catcher has a rifle arm and the base runner is not adept at getting a jump or is not quick, you may want to reconsider stealing third.
- Does the pitcher use a variety of methods to hold the runner close to the base, or does he tend to forget about the runner once he's on base? Pitchers who use a variety of methods to hold runners on base are often difficult to read. Against these pitchers, a bunt or delay steal may be a better approach.
- Does the catcher have a habit of dropping to his knees each time he returns a pitch to the pitcher? Catchers can get into the habit of doing this and forget that there are runners on base. Most high school catchers cannot throw strongly from their knees.

Self-Knowledge

In addition to being aware of your opponent's strengths and weaknesses, you and your players need to have knowledge about your own team's ability. When trying to steal third, teach your players to be aware of the following:

- How good is the runner at getting primary and secondary leads? Runners need to be able to disguise their intent to run by sometimes taking long primary leads to draw pickoff throws and then take shorter leads when the steal sign is given. This pattern may fake the pitcher into thinking that he has forced the runner to be conservative.
- How good is the runner at using the bluff run, a move that is also commonly referred to as the fake steal? If this is done too frequently, the bluff run can lull the defense into a false sense of security.
- How good is the runner at getting a quick jump with good running form?
- How good is the runner at sensing and timing the pitcher's delivery to the plate?
- How good is the runner at executing the headfirst slide?
- How good is the batter at swinging through pitches and protecting runners?

Decision-Making Guidelines

When deciding whether or not to steal third, you and your players should be sure to consider the previous information. While the decision is ultimately yours, you should strive to empower your players to make this decision on their own when the opportunity presents itself, as players need to be ready for this task. Also consider the following guidelines:

- Steal third more often when you have one out and when your team is ahead, tied or no more than one run behind.
- Steal third more often on the first pitch after reaching the base, especially immediately after a steal of second.

- Steal third more often when the pitcher does not do a good job of holding the runner.
- Steal third more often when you have a base runner at second who is good at using the angled lead at second base to get a better jump (for more information about the angled lead, see pages 54-55 in "Stealing Third Base").
- Steal third more often when your batter is late in the count, when he will get a better pitch to hit.
- Steal less often when you are protecting a lead late in the game.
- Rarely steal third when you have two outs.

At a Glance

The following parts of the text offer additional information on stealing third base.

Hit and Run

The hit-and-run play is misnamed. It should be called a run-and-hit play because on the pitch, the runner or runners break for the next base as if stealing. The batter tries to hit the pitch, if it is a strike, on the ground to the right side of the field. The purpose of this play is twofold: to get defensive players to move out of position and to eliminate the possibility of a double play. Imagine that you're playing a team with quick-reacting infielders, a pitcher who has a good move to first base and a catcher with a quick release and a cannon arm. In this scenario you will have difficulty implementing an aggressive game plan. Stealing on a team with all those defensive weapons is tough, and in such a situation, a hit-and-run play may be just what you need to get your offense going and move the defense out of position.

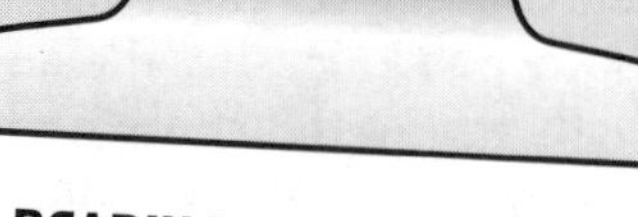

READING THE SITUATION

When deciding whether to use the hit and run, players should do the following:

- Know the game situation.
- Watch for the sign from the coach.
- Study the pitch count because if it favors a fastball (such as a 1-0, 2-0 or 1-1 count), the hit and run may be used.
- Watch the second baseman. If he has been overreacting and moving quickly to the base on every pitch, anticipating the steal, the hit and run is more likely to be successful.

WATCH OUT!

The following circumstances may distract your athletes:

- A pitcher who throws frequently to first base, causing the runner to become defensive and not get a good jump
- A pitcher using a glide stride and then throwing a pitchout

ACQUIRING THE APPROPRIATE KNOWLEDGE

To use the hit and run, your athletes must understand the following:

Rules

Your athletes need to know several main rules when they are in a hit-and-run situation:

- Rules that pertain to the strike zone
- Rules about interference and obstruction
- Rules about tagging up after fly balls
- Rules giving fielders the right to field the ball over the runner's right to the baseline

REMINDER!

When deciding whether to use the hit and run, you and your players must know your team strategy and game plan. Don't forget to consider the questions on page 150.

Physical Playing Conditions

The physical playing conditions will significantly affect the game. Thus, you and your players must pay attention to the following physical conditions when contemplating whether to use the hit and run:

- The surface quality between first and second
- The condition of the infield and its effect on the speed of the ball

Strengths and Weaknesses of Opponents

Players must account for opponent's strengths and weaknesses to know whether to use the hit and run. Players should consider the following about their opponents:

- How quick is the pitcher's delivery to home plate? Does the catcher have a strong, accurate arm?
- Is the defense alert, paying close attention to the runner's leads? Do they react quickly and cover the bases on steal attempts? These factors will affect your runner's ability to get a good lead.
- Is the pitcher consistently ahead of the hitters? If he is, the batter may not get a good hit-and-run count.
- Do the middle infielders overreact on steal attempts by covering early? If they do, they often leave big gaps in the defense.
- Is the pitcher predictable, making it easier to guess when he will throw a fastball? When the pitcher throws a fastball, the batter is more likely to put the ball in play, which is critical for the hit and run.

At a Glance

The following parts of the text offer additional information on the hit and run.

Self-Knowledge

In addition to being aware of your opponent's strengths and weaknesses, you and your players need to have knowledge about your own team's ability. When considering the hit and run, teach your players to be aware of the following:

- How good is the batter's knowledge of the strike zone? Batters need to know that they must swing at balls, too, to distract the catcher and make the throw to second more difficult.
- How fast is the batter, relative to how good he is at controlling the bat and placing the ball in play on the right side? For example, if the batter hits more fly balls than ground balls, you may be better off using a steal instead of a hit and run.
- Is the batter right-handed or left-handed? A left-handed hitter can more easily hit behind the runner.
- How good is the base runner at breaking for second and then reading the situation to see where the ball is and how he should react to it? If the base runner is not adept at reading the pitcher, making the hit and run work will be difficult, especially in a pitchout situation.
- How good is the base runner at making the defense move to create infield holes?

Decision-Making Guidelines

When deciding whether or not to use the hit and run, you and your players should be sure to consider the previous information. Also consider the following guidelines:

- Use the hit and run more often when you are facing a pitcher who has been throwing outside consistently, feeding into the strength of a right-handed batter.
- Use the hit and run more often when you are facing a pitch count that favors a fastball, such as a 1-0, 2-0 or 1-1 count.
- Use the hit and run more often when the game is close and you have had few runners on base.
- Use the hit and run more often when your team has had difficulty stealing bases.
- Use the hit and run more often when your batter has been in a slump. The hit and run is a good way to help him make contact at the plate.

Situational Hitting

Situational hitting is the ability to assess changing game situations and hit accordingly. As you know, game situations vary enormously, so each time a batter comes to the plate, he must take into account the game conditions before he decides what he should try to do with the bat. Your hitters should never come up to the plate and just swing at whatever is thrown. Good hitters, even in high school, take into account the number of outs, the score, where the fielders are positioned, which bases are occupied and other subtle clues before they ever step into the batter's box.

READING THE SITUATION

How can your team gain the best advantage when at bat during various situations in the game? Teach your players to do the following:

- Know the game situation.
- Know what pitchers have been throwing in various counts during the game and maintain a chart to show the pitch that opposing pitchers throw on each count.
- Know the position of the fielders. For example, if the corners are playing back, a drag bunt might be in order.
- Track the ball as it comes in to the plate and respond accordingly. For example, do not try to pull an outside pitch.

WATCH OUT!

The following circumstances may distract your athletes:

- A good pitcher who is unconventional in his approach, such as one who throws a 3-0 changeup or a 2-0 curveball.
- Being overanxious at the plate. Sometimes pitches look so tantalizing that batters become greedy and swing too hard.

ACQUIRING THE APPROPRIATE KNOWLEDGE

To become good situational hitters, your athletes must know about the following:

Rules

Your athletes need to know several main rules when they are hitting in various situations:

- Rules that pertain to the strike zone
- Rules about interference as a hitter
- Rules about check swings

REMINDER!

When evaluating the game situation and determining what type of swing to make, you and your players must know your team strategy and game plan. Make sure that you and your players consider the questions on page 150.

Physical Playing Conditions

The physical playing conditions significantly affect the game. Thus, you and your players must pay attention to the following physical conditions when trying to determine the best way to hit the ball:

- The condition of the infield. For example, long grass is better for bunting, whereas a hard field can lead to many high bounces on ground balls, which may become hits.
- The surface quality between the bases.
- The slope of the surface on the foul line. For example, if the surface near the foul line slopes toward foul territory, laying down a successful bunt may be harder.

Strengths and Weaknesses of Opponents

You and your players must account for your opponent's strengths and weaknesses to know how your batter should hit the ball. Teach your players to consider the following about your opponents:

- How quickly do the infielders react when a hitter shows bunt?
- Do fielders shift according to the pitch count, such as shifting to the batter's pull side in anticipation that he will pull the ball?
- Does the catcher notice subtle shifts in the batter's stance or position in regard to the plate? An alert catcher will especially affect your ability to use the bunt successfully.
- Has the catcher fallen into a pattern with his pitch calling—fastball, curve, fastball, curve and so on?
- Is the pitcher particularly strong? Against a good pitcher, your team may try to take more pitches to wear him out. The sooner you get to the number 2 pitcher, the better.

At a Glance

The following parts of the text offer additional information on situational hitting.

Self-Knowledge

In addition to being aware of your opponent's strengths and weaknesses, you and your players need to have knowledge about your own team's ability. When trying to determine the best place to hit in various situations, teach your players to be aware of the following:

- How good is the hitter's bat control? You may want to have a disciplined hitter with good bat control in the middle of your lineup.
- How good is the hitter at laying down a bunt?
- Does the hitter have good knowledge of the strike zone?
- Does the hitter understand the best position to place the ball in various situations, and does he have the capability to do this?

Decision-Making Guidelines

When trying to determine how to hit the ball in various situations, you and your players should be sure to consider the previous information. Also consider the following guidelines:

- Have hitters look only for their favorite pitch to hit, for example, and not swing at anything else when the count is in their favor, at 1-0 or 2-0.
- Make sure that hitters know to swing at a curveball only if they have a two-strike count.
- Use the drag bunt more often if the infield corners are playing back.
- Make sure that your batters look for a pitch that they can drive to the right-field side of the diamond when you have a runner at second.
- Make sure that batters look for a pitch up in the strike zone that they can hit to right field, or hit hard, when your team has a runner on third. A ground ball to the right side is as good as a deep fly ball in this situation.
- Have hitters swing from the heels when they get a 2-0 pitch in the strike zone.
- Have your batters hit to the right side when your team has a runner on second with no outs.
- Have your batters take a strike when you are behind late in the game.
- Have the first batter in any inning behave like a leadoff hitter, trying to work the count deep and draw a walk.

Getting Out of a Rundown

You've taught your players to be aggressive on the bases and always to think one base ahead. During the game, a batter tries to take an extra base and hesitates or a good left-handed pitcher's pickoff move to first base fools a runner. In either case, the runner can be caught in no-man's land between bases and find himself in a rundown. When these situations occur, players need to be able to find a way out of the rundown and get back to base safely or, failing in that, help other runners advance to the next base.

READING THE SITUATION

How can your players get out of a rundown? Teach your players to do the following:

- Know the game situation.
- Recognize that the ball has beaten them to the next base.
- Determine whether they are more than 30 feet from the base that they previously touched.
- Pay attention to the defender who has the ball and decide whether they should go forward or retreat to the base from which they came.

WATCH OUT!

The following circumstances may distract your athletes:

- The runner thinks that the outfielder is going to throw the ball to the base ahead, but instead he throws behind the runner.
- The runner does not pay attention to a fielder sneaking in behind him and is picked off.
- On a bunt situation the runner starts to run before the ball is bunted, the batter misses the ball and the catcher throws behind the runner.

ACQUIRING THE APPROPRIATE KNOWLEDGE

To get out of a rundown, your athletes must understand the following:

REMINDER!

When trying to get out of a rundown, your players must know your team strategy and game plan. Don't forget to consider the questions on page 150.

Rules

You and your athletes need to know several main rules when they are in a rundown situation:

- Rules about interference and obstruction
- Rules about establishing and leaving a baseline

Physical Playing Conditions

The physical playing conditions will significantly affect the game. Thus, your players must pay attention to the following physical conditions when they are in a rundown:

- The surface quality between the bases. Your players will likely need to make quick cuts and will need to know where they can achieve their best footing.
- The strength of the wind.

Strengths and Weaknesses of Opponents

Players must account for opponent's strengths and weaknesses to know how to get out of a rundown. Teach your players to consider the following about their opponents:

- Do the fielders react to the rundown situation by shortening up the distance between the bases? When defenses do this, they shorten their throws and gain an advantage in the rundown.

- Do the fielders hustle to their backup positions when the rundown begins? If they do, the runner's ability to get out of the rundown decreases.
- Do fielders stand in the baseline without having the ball? If they do, the runner may have an opportunity to brush up against a fielder and draw an obstruction call.
- Do fielders not run hard at the player who is picked off? If they don't run hard, the runner should attack because he may have an opening.
- Do fielders fake throwing when they are running down a picked-off runner?
- Does the defense make predictable movements, based on your knowledge of the way they play in this situation?

At a Glance

The following parts of the text offer additional information on getting out of a rundown.

Self-Knowledge

In addition to being aware of your opponent's strengths and weaknesses, you and your players need to have knowledge about your own team's ability. When facing a rundown, teach your players to be aware of the following:

- How good is the runner at sensing when a player is about to throw the ball?
- How good is the runner at changing directions rapidly?
- How good is the runner at sensing that a player will be impeding a running lane?

Decision-Making Guidelines

When in a rundown, you and your players should be sure to consider the previous information. While the decision is ultimately yours, you should strive to empower the players to make this decision on their own when the opportunity presents itself, as players need to be ready for this task. Also consider the following guidelines:

- When a runner is caught in a rundown with other runners ahead or behind, the runner's first goal should be to get out of the rundown and be safe either at the next base or the base originally occupied. If he can't get back or advance safely, his next goal is to stay in the rundown and create distraction to allow other runners to advance.
- When another runner or runners are on base, the player in the rundown can create a distraction by running to the outfield side of the baseline or falling down. This action may give the other runner or runners an opportunity to advance.

chapter 6

Defensive Tactical Skills

This chapter will cover the defensive tactical skills that you and your players must know in order to be successful. In this chapter, you will find:

Defensive Positioning

Defensive positioning is not only playing people in the right position on the field but also being able to adjust quickly to changing situations as the game develops. For example, assume that your pitcher has been cruising along into the late innings when he suddenly loses his control and command and allows several runners to reach base. Even after making a pitching change, the floodgates remain open, and the other team slowly turns your safe lead into a close game. You, as a coach, must now get your team from a posture of just trying to get outs into a mind-set of protecting the lead. At points like these, your team will benefit greatly if you have taught your defense to assume the proper alignment based on the situation in the game.

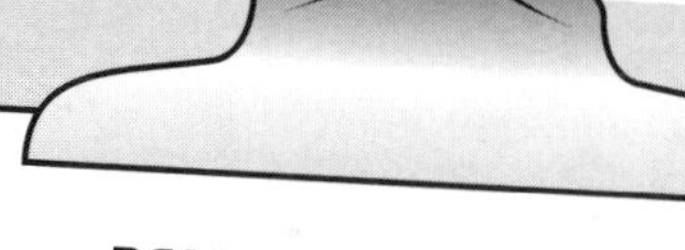

READING THE SITUATION

How do you and your players gain advantage through your defensive positioning? Teach your players to do the following:

- Know the game situation.
- Study the positioning of the runner or runners on base.
- Be aware of what the pitcher throws when ahead or behind in the count to determine whether to move to the left or the right.
- Move into backup or cutoff position according to the situation after the ball is hit.

WATCH OUT!

The following circumstances may distract your athletes:

- Size of the opposing batter
- Hitters who adapt to changing pitching situations (for example, a good hitter who moves up in the box looking to pull a curveball that most hitters would hit to the opposite field)

ACQUIRING THE APPROPRIATE KNOWLEDGE

To use modifications in team defense, you and your athletes must understand the following:

REMINDER!

You and your players must understand the team strategy and game plan. Don't forget to consider the questions on page 150.

Rules

You and your athletes need to know several main rules when you are considering defensive adjustments:

- Rules about interference and obstruction
- Rules about force plays
- Rules about when a pitcher becomes an infielder

Physical Playing Conditions

The physical playing conditions will significantly affect the game. Thus, you and your players must pay attention to the following physical conditions when contemplating the best defensive positioning to use in various game situations:

- Surface quality of the outfield. Play conservatively when the outfield is wet.
- The condition of the infield surface.
- The surface quality of the outfield. Your players need to be aware of holes, ridges and dips in the surface. Likewise, they need to be aware of how long the grass is and whether it is wet.
- The depth of the warning track.
- The effect of the sun. Your players should work at finding a position that diminishes the effect of the sun in their eyes by repositioning their bodies or by shading their eyes.

- The strength and direction of the wind. For example, when the wind is blowing strongly toward home, outfielders should not play as deep as normal.

Strengths and Weaknesses of Opponents

You and your players must account for your opponent's strengths and weaknesses to know the best way to gain an advantage with defensive positioning. Teach your players to consider the following about your opponents:

- Does the opposing team play with an aggressive baserunning approach, or do they use a conservative approach? If they play with an aggressive approach, some runners may take foolish chances that your team may be able to capitalize on.
- How strong is the batter? The opposing team may be more conservative when they have a strong batter up.
- How good is the batter at changing his swing to adapt to changing situations? For example, if he is good at laying down the bunt when the situation calls for it, his coach may ask him to do that. So, be ready.
- How fast and how proficient at stealing is the runner or runners on base?
- Do opposing players pay attention to how far they can lead off the base? If they are not paying attention, you may be able to get an easy out.

Self-Knowledge

In addition to being aware of your opponent's strengths and weaknesses, you and your players need to have knowledge about your own team's ability. When considering different defensive positioning, teach your players to be aware of the following:

- How quick are your outfielders at moving toward the ball?
- How adept are your outfielders at diving for the ball? Their skill at coming in on the ball will affect how deep they can play.
- How good is your team at backing up various plays? Players have to back up every base where a play might occur.
- How good is your team at shifting according to the game situation? The better you are at this, the more advantage you will gain.
- How good is your pitcher's control?
- How fast is the pitcher's move in pickoff situations? How good are your infielders at holding runners on base?
- How fast is the pitcher's throw home? How strong and accurate is your catcher's throwing?

Decision-Making Guidelines

When deciding how to gain the best advantage with defensive positioning, you and your players should be sure to consider the previous information. While the decision is ultimately yours, you should strive to empower the players to make this decision on their own when the opportunity presents itself, as players need to be ready for this task (see "Positioning in the Outfield"). Also consider the following guidelines:

- Use dive plays less often when you have slow-footed outfielders and are in the late innings. A prudent approach may be to allow the opposition to have singles and force them to play station-to-station baseball rather than risk having the ball get past slow outfielders who might have trouble running it down.

(continued)

POSITIONING IN THE OUTFIELD

Throughout the rich lore of baseball, there are many examples of defensive positioning shifts employed by major league teams in attempts to exploit batter weaknesses. When Ted Williams—a dead-pull hitting lefty—was in his prime, opposing teams often employed the Williams Shift. This involved playing the right fielder almost on the right-field foul line, the center fielder in right center and the left fielder in shallow left field about 20 feet behind where the shortstop normally plays. More recently, teams have employed similar tactics to thwart Barry Bonds, playing the right fielder and center fielder both in deep right field and placing the second baseman in straight away shallow right field! While you may not have to use such drastic methods to stop opponents, you should coach your players to move according to changing game situations.

As the game develops, outfielders should be keeping mental notes on all hitters and play them according to what they have done previously. Outfielders should also shift automatically according to the count on the hitter. For example, a 2-0 count is normally considered a pull count, so if the batter is left-handed, outfielders should take a few steps toward the pull side before the pitch. The opposite would be true with a 0-2 count. In that scenario, outfielders should take a few steps toward the hitter's weak, or nonpull, side because the pitcher has the advantage in the count. The batter will be more careful with his swing and will slow it down, increasing the chances that he will hit the ball to the opposite field. The following table designates how many steps to each side a player should take depending on the count.

Count on batter	Number of steps to move to pull side	Number of steps to move to opposite-field side
0-0		
1-0	2 or 3	
2-0	5	
2-1	2 or 3	
3-0	7 or 8	
3-1	5	
3-2	2	
1-1		
2-2		2
0-2		3 or 4
1-2		2 or 3

The pitcher's arsenal also determines where outfielders should position themselves. If a pitcher with a good curveball is throwing, outfielders should shift toward right field when a right-handed batter is at the plate because the ball will be going away from the batter and will most likely be hit in center field or on the right-field side. Likewise, if the pitcher is a flamethrower, outfielders should play to the opposite-field side because the batter will have trouble getting the bat around and won't be able to pull many pitches.

A final consideration is that positioning relates to the score. With a big lead, outfielders can play a little deeper—in effect giving up the single but preventing the extra-base hit. Or, with runners in scoring position in close ball games, outfielders may want to play a little shallower so that they can reduce the runner's chances of scoring.

- Take advantage of hitters who stubbornly refuse to change their swings to adapt to changing situations. The defense may be able to make easy plays because they will be able to get good jumps on the balls that such batters hit.
- Use more risk when your team is far ahead in the game. In this situation, you may decide to go for every ball no matter what because the strategy is simply to get outs and not worry about what the offense is doing. In this kind of late-game situation, outfielders should not be afraid to dive for balls.
- Have outfielders play farther back than normal and closer to the foul line when your team has a one-run lead or the score is tied. Here, the goal is to prevent the tying or perhaps winning run to reach scoring position at second base. Playing deeper holds line drives to singles in most cases and forces the offense into other tactics to advance runners to second.
- If the pitcher is ahead in the count or throws an off-speed pitch, the batter may become defensive and look to make contact with the ball rather than take a full swing. The hitter may be late on the swing and hit to the opposite field.
- If the team has a fast runner at the plate, he may try to use a drag bunt for a base hit. In this situation, the third baseman should move in a few steps to try to take the bunt away from the batter. The third baseman should watch the batter's feet. If the back foot moves or if the batter's hands move up the bat, the third baseman should charge the plate. If the offensive team is good at the fake bunt and slash technique, however, the third baseman should be cautious about moving in.
- If the offense reacts to your positioning, you need to assess whether you need to make an adjustment. For example, some teams with hitters who exercise good bat control may sense that you are giving them singles in the outfield and may choke up and try to make better contact. In effect, they hit with less power but more control and may try just to get as many runners as possible.
- Position infielders two steps closer to second base than normal when most of the balls are hit up the middle of the diamond.
- Realize that high school hitters usually do not have much power to the opposite field. Thus, you may have the off outfielder, the one who is opposite the pull strength of the hitter, take advantage of this fact by playing straight away and shallow. This positioning cuts off the bloop hit that often falls in when a player hits to the opposite field.
- Instruct infielders to cut all throws from the outfield late in a game when you have a lead to prevent trailing runners from advancing farther.
- Position the corner players, the third baseman and first baseman, away from the foul line, even in late innings! Too many times, defenses give up hits between short and third or between first and second because their corner infielders are not in position to cut off balls.

At a Glance

The following parts of the text offer additional information on defensive positioning.

Defending the First-and-Third Double Steal

The first-and-third double steal is an attempt by the offense to have the runner at first try to steal second, hoping that the defense will make a play for him, allowing the runner on third base to steal home. The defense will need to thwart the steal of second while not allowing the runner at third to advance. Assume that it's the top of the seventh and your opponent has put runners on first and third. Your team is ahead by 1 run, but the opposition runners are both fast and savvy, and their coach practices aggressive baserunning. All this makes it likely that the opposition will run the first-and-third double-steal play. If they try to steal second base with the back runner and you concede it to them, you put the winning run in scoring position and jeopardize your team's chances of winning. The first-and-third double steal is one of the most difficult plays to defend in high school baseball because it puts enormous pressure on the defense, especially in later innings. This tactical situation has many options. Teams have to be prepared for every eventuality so that with proper execution, they can suck the air out of any opposing team that tries this play.

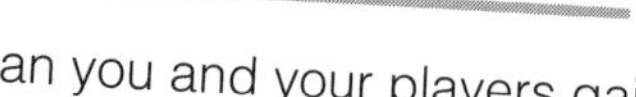

READING THE SITUATION

How can you and your players gain the best advantage when in a first-and-third double-steal situation? Teach your players to do the following:

- Know the game situation.
- Pay attention to the runner at first base to see whether he is taking an abnormally big lead because that may indicate that the double steal is on.
- Know what pitch will be thrown.
- Be aware of how big a leadoff the runner at third base is taking to determine whether he may try to steal home on a throw to second base.

WATCH OUT!

The following circumstances may distract your athletes:

- The offensive team uses the fake break to second or the bluff run as a tactic.
- The runner at first base breaks early in the pitcher's motion.
- The offense employs a delay steal.
- The lead runner fakes an early break to draw a throw and allow the runner at first to reach second easily.

REMINDER!

When defending the first-and-third play, you and your players must understand the team strategy and game plan. Don't forget to consider the questions on page 150.

ACQUIRING THE APPROPRIATE KNOWLEDGE

To defend the first-and-third play successfully, you and your team must understand the following:

Rules

You and your athletes need to know several main rules when you are in a first-and-third situation:

- Rules about interference and obstruction, especially during rundown situations
- Rules about balks
- Rules about when a pitcher becomes an infielder

Physical Playing Conditions

The physical playing conditions will significantly affect the game. Thus, you and your players must pay attention to the following physical conditions when contemplating how to gain the best advantage when facing a first-and-third situation:

- The condition of the ball. For example, if you are playing in a light rain, the ball becomes slippery, making it difficult to grip and throw.
- The strength and direction of the wind. For example, a strong wind blowing toward home may affect the catcher's ability to make a powerful throw.

Strengths and Weaknesses of Opponents

You and your players must account for your opponent's strengths and weaknesses to know how to gain the best advantage when in a first-and-third situation. Teach your players to consider the following about your opponents:

- How quick are the base runners? For example, if the base runners are especially quick you may want to concede second base and trust your pitcher or fielders to make plays and get outs.
- Are the runners getting careless in their primary leads or taking too big a lead? In this situation, the fake to third and throw to first play by the pitcher may work.

Self-Knowledge

In addition to being aware of your opponent's strengths and weaknesses, you and your players need to have knowledge about your own team's ability. When considering how to gain the best advantage when you are in a first-and-third situation, teach your players to be aware of the following:

- How good is your team at executing a pitchout?
- How good is your team at holding runners at first base?
- How good is your team at making strong, accurate throws?
- How good is your team at tagging runners?
- How good is your team at selling fake cuts or throws to the opposing team?
- How strong is the peripheral vision of the second baseman and shortstop? Having good peripheral vision will enable them to reduce the leads of the runners and get a jump on them when they make their break.
- How good is the third baseman at being able to tell when the runner is too far from third base—in no man's land—and call for a cut and the throw to third by the shortstop?
- How good is the communication among fielders? Everybody has to yell, especially when a runner makes a move to a base.

Decision-Making Guidelines

When deciding how to gain the best advantage when facing a first-and-third situation, you and your players should be sure to consider the previous information. "Play Options to Defend the First-and-Third Double Steal" includes sample plays that will guide you in determining how to gain the best advantage when facing this situation. Consider the following additional guidelines:

- Go for outs over stopping the run when you have a big lead. When you have a lead you may concede the run and just try to throw out the runner at second, especially if you have a strong-armed catcher or a pitcher who is quick to the plate.

(continued)

PLAY OPTIONS TO DEFEND THE FIRST-AND-THIRD DOUBLE STEAL

There are many defensive options available to you and your team to use when defending against the first-and-third double steal. But, you, as a coach, should be careful not to become too complicated in your schemes to stop this aggressive offensive strategy. You should decide on no more than three or four options and practice them frequently until your team becomes proficient in the execution of them. It is also best to have your catcher call the plays on the field using a set of prearranged signs. Following are four simple plans of attack that, when mastered, can be used to stop the double steal:

Play #1

The catcher throws straight through to second base. The second baseman covers the base. The shortstop breaks to a position in front of second base where he can cut the ball and a make a throw home if necessary (the shortstop, because he probably has the stronger throwing arm, is the best choice for cutoff responsibility). The pitcher fakes a cut of the catcher's throw and pivots to his glove side to try to hold the runner at third. The pitcher should hit his glove with his throwing hand so that it makes a loud sound, like a ball hitting leather, and then give a good arm, head and shoulder fake to third base to decoy the runner.

Play #2

This play is the same as play #1 except that this time the pitcher cuts off the catcher's throw and wheels to his glove side to catch a sleeping runner at third base. In this tactic, the pitcher should crouch down on the catcher's throw to make it appear as if the ball is going to go through to second base.

Play #3

The catcher gives a good head and shoulder fake as if to throw to second base and then throws to third. To make the play work, the pitcher has to go through with the fake and the other infielders have to cover their bases as in play #2. Also, when making his first step with the right foot on the throw, the catcher must keep the instep pointed to third base instead of turning it towards second as he normally would. This stance enables him to have his shoulders in the proper position to make a good throw to third.

Play #4

This play can trap an overaggressive runner at third into thinking that the throw is going to go to second base and get him to break toward home plate. The pitcher and the third baseman react normally as in play #1. The shortstop covers second base instead of moving in for the cut. The second baseman takes two hard steps toward second, as if he is going to cover the base, and then plants and sprints directly toward home plate. The catcher, instead of throwing to second base, throws directly toward the chest of the sprinting second baseman. When executed properly, the second baseman receives the ball close to the pitcher's mound and is in excellent position to throw out the runner trying to advance from third. If the runner stops and tries to retreat, the second baseman is also in good position to throw to third base and get the runner into a rundown.

- Use the pitchout to try to determine what play the offense may be running before deciding which defense to employ.
- Make sure that your players know their individual responsibilities in this situation. For example, you may require your second baseman to move several steps closer to second base and several steps closer to the baseline between first and second to guard against the steal. The shortstop may have to move closer to the infield grass in case he has to make a cut and throw to home plate to get the runner breaking from third.
- The third baseman and first baseman must know their jobs in the first-and-third situation. Your third baseman may be required to act as a sentry and let the pitcher know whether the runner on first base is taking too big a lead or if he is breaking early toward second—running toward second before the pitcher has come to his set position. The first baseman must hold the runner on and let the catcher know if the runner is stealing by yelling, "Going!" when the runner leaves. Players must know their responsibilities and communicate well with one another.
- Players must keep a close eye on the runner trying to steal second. He may end up running into the tag rather than stopping and getting into a rundown before the runner on third has made a break for the plate.

At a Glance

The following parts of the text offer additional information on the first-and-third double steal.

Throwing Basics	p. 64
Catching a Throw	p. 72
Reacting As a Catcher	p. 90
Pitcher Stretch Mechanics	p. 102
Infield Basics	p. 124
First-and-Third Play	p. 158
Getting Out of a Rundown	p. 174
Pitcher Pickoffs	p. 190
Catcher Pickoffs	p. 194
Rundowns	p. 202

Defending Bunt Situations

Suppose it's the bottom of the seventh and your team has a 1-run lead over the home team. Your pitcher has just walked the leadoff hitter, putting the tying run on first base and bringing the possible winning run to the plate. In this situation, most teams will probably try to bunt the runner to second base and scoring position. Suddenly, although you have the lead, the pressure is on your defense and your tactical expertise. Most teams, usually through lack of practice and confidence, attempt to accomplish too much when confronted with the sacrifice bunt. Too often they try to make a superhuman play to get the lead runner out, and in failing to do so, complicate the situation. The result is that the offense now has two runners on base and the bunt situation still exists!

The key to effective and successful bunt coverage tactics is to train the defense in one line of thought—get an out! Usually, the best and the easiest place to make this out is at first base. Remember, as mentioned earlier, the chances that a runner will score from second base with one out are only slightly better than the chances that he will score from first base with no outs. Go with the percentages, take the easy out and concentrate on the next hitter.

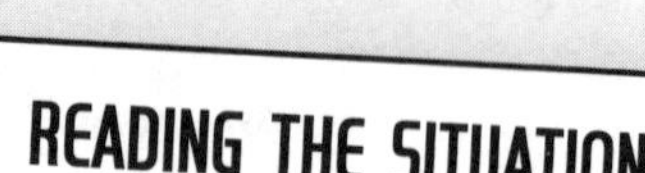

READING THE SITUATION

When deciding whether you are in a bunt situation, you and your players should do the following:

- Know the game situation.
- Watch the runner's lead at first base, especially when one of the batters in the bottom third of the order is at bat.
- Have the pitcher throw a pickoff throw to first base and watch the batter to see how he reacts. If he moves his hands down the bat or leans forward, he may be getting ready to bunt.

WATCH OUT!

The following circumstances may distract your athletes:

- Someone other than the catcher calling the base. Instruct bench personnel and other infielders not to yell when the ball is being fielded.
- The batter fakes a bunt, and the runner steals the base.
- The batter squares to bunt, pulls the bat back and then takes a swing. For that reason, you should not give away the bunt defense too early.

REMINDER!

When defending against the bunt, you and your team must understand the team strategy and game plan. Don't forget to consider the questions on page 150.

ACQUIRING THE APPROPRIATE KNOWLEDGE

To defend against the bunt, you and your athletes should understand the following:

Rules

You and your athletes need to know several main rules when you are defending against the bunt:

- Rules about the 45-foot lines on plays at first base
- Rules about catcher interference and obstruction
- Rules giving fielders the right to field the ball over the runner's right to the baseline

Physical Playing Conditions

The physical playing conditions will significantly affect the game. Thus, you and your players must pay attention to the following physical conditions when contemplating the best way to defend against the bunt:

- The slope of the field surface on or near the foul line. For example, if the surface on or near the foul line slopes toward foul territory, it may be in the fielder's best interest to let the ball roll foul rather than field it and attempt to make a play.
- The condition of the infield surface.
- The condition of the dirt in front of home plate. For example, a soft surface will deaden the ball significantly, making it harder to field.

Strengths and Weaknesses of Opponents

You and your players must account for your opponent's strengths and weaknesses to know how to defend against a probable bunt situation. Consider the following about your opponents:

- How good is the offense at laying down the bunt?
- Is the offense known for trying to use the push bunt and hit the ball past the charging fielders? The tendency to do this would most likely affect the positioning of the second baseman and the pitcher.
- Does the offense have good knowledge of the strike zone? If not, you may be able to force the bunter into popping up.

Self-Knowledge

In addition to being aware of your opponent's strengths and weaknesses, you and your players need to have knowledge about your own team's ability. When defending against the bunt, teach your players to be aware of the following:

- How well does your team handle slowly hit balls?
- Does the catcher make good decisions about who should field the ball?
- How good is the communication among all infielders before the pitch and after the ball has been bunted?
- Can your team throw accurately while on the run?
- Can the pitcher throw high strikes? Typically, high pitches are harder to bunt than low pitches are.
- Do the players on your team have the ability to adjust quickly when a ball is mishandled? Even if the catcher calls "two, two, two," if the fielder misplays the ball, he should automatically throw to first.
- Is your team aware of the priority system for fielding bunts? The third baseman has priority over everyone; the catcher has priority over the pitcher and first baseman, and the pitcher has priority over the first baseman.
- How well do your outfielders react and back up the bases in bunt situations?

(continued)

DEFENDING AGAINST THE BUNT IN THREE BASIC SITUATIONS

You and you team will encounter the bunt in three basic situations. Consider the following defensive tactics:

One Runner on Base

If the opposing team has only a runner on first base, the pitcher must try to hold the runner close with repeated pickoff attempts and must try to throw strikes to the batter high in the zone. The first baseman needs to hold the runner on base and break toward the plate on the pitch. (If the pitcher and first baseman communicate on the number of pickoff throws that the pitcher will make to first base before throwing home, the first baseman can get a faster break on the pitch.) The second baseman must move a few steps toward second base before the pitch is thrown and must break hard for first base as soon as the batter shows bunt. The shortstop then breaks to cover second base. The third baseman plays 15 to 20 feet in front of the base on the grass and charges the plate when the batter shows bunt. The catcher fields the bunt if it's close to the plate; if not, he loudly calls the name of the player who should field the ball and make the throw. If the third baseman fields the bunt, the catcher must be ready to move to cover third base. In all situations the outfielders move in to back up the bases.

Two Runners on Base

If the opposing team has runners on first and second, the pitcher holds the runner close to second base with pickoff throws or by stepping off the rubber and looking at the runner. On a bunt, he must cover the entire third-base side of the infield. The first baseman positions himself on the grass, charges as soon as the batter shows bunt but has no priority in fielding the bunt. The second baseman breaks for first base, and the shortstop works on holding the runner close by simultaneously slapping his glove and making a jab step toward second to decoy the runner into not getting a good jump. He covers second base when the ball is bunted. The third baseman plays about 10 feet in front of the base and does not charge. Instead he covers the base for a potential play. One exception to this would be the wheel, or rotation defense, an advance option. Another would be if the ball was bunted hard on the third-base side, he would have to charge and make the throw to first. If the priority calls for the third baseman to charge the bunt, he cannot do so until he sees the batter bunt the ball. If he moves too early, he gives the runner at second a chance to steal or get a good jump. In this situation the catcher must cover the plate.

Runner on Third or Runners at Second and Third

If the opposing team has a runner at third base or runners at both second and third base, you are in what is called a squeeze bunt situation. In this situation, the first baseman plays in on the grass, and the second baseman cheats toward first base and covers the base if the batter squares to bunt. The shortstop cheats in and breaks to third base on the bunt in case the runner on third is caught in a rundown. The third baseman communicates with the pitcher about the number of pickoff throws to use, plays about 8 to 10 feet behind the base and breaks quickly to the base just as the pitcher lifts his leg. This will help hold the runner from breaking early. If no pickoff is being thrown, the third baseman continues charging home. If the ball isn't bunted, he must return quickly to the base for a possible pickoff throw from the catcher. If the batter squares to bunt, the pitcher throws high and tight.

Decision-Making Guidelines

When deciding how to gain the best advantage in a possible bunt situation, you and your players should be sure to consider the previous information. "Defending Against the Bunt in Three Basic Situations" includes specific examples that will help you be better prepared when defending bunts. Also consider the following guidelines:

- Develop a priority system for handling bunts. Have your catcher take the responsibility to make the call about which base to throw to.
- Make sure that you get one, sure out in a bunt situation. For example, your team may try to get the lead runner only if (a) the ball is bunted firmly and directly at a charging infielder, (b) the lead runner has been held close to the base or did not get a good jump and (c) the ball is fielded cleanly.

At a Glance

The following parts of the text offer additional information on defending bunt situations.

Pitcher Pickoffs

The pickoff play is not necessarily designed to pick off the runner. Its intention is to keep runners close to the base, keep them off balance and stop them from getting good stealing jumps. An off-balance runner is of no use to an aggressive offense.

Assume that a game has reached the late innings. Your team has played well so far and you hold the lead, but the opposition has just gotten the tying run to second base. If the runner is allowed to get a good lead, he can score easily on a base hit, even one to left field. The infielders must keep the runner from getting too big a lead. How do you hold this runner close to the base so that he can't score on a routine base hit?

The solution to this dilemma lies in using various pickoff tactics to keep runners close to the base. Keep in mind that you should use these moves at all times during the game. A team shouldn't worry about runners getting big leads only late in the game. If that's the only time they're concerned about holding runners, then they should be worried about it!

WATCH OUT!

The following circumstances may distract your athletes:

- Runners who take short leads when they are going to steal and long leads when they are not in order to draw throws from the pitcher
- Bluff runs
- Delayed steals
- Fake bunts and steals
- Runners who take a deep lead at second base

READING THE SITUATION

Whenever runners are on base, defenses should pay attention to cues that may indicate that they are stealing or trying to get a big lead at second so that the runner can score. Teach your players (especially infielders) to:

- Know the game situation.
- Watch the runner to see if he pays inordinate attention to the third-base coach while he is giving signs. This often signals that a play is on.
- Watch the runner to see if he is edgy or nervous, or getting to his primary lead faster than usual.
- Watch the runner to see if he is showing tension. When they are stealing, runners often clench their fists or otherwise tighten muscles, a tendency that an observant infielder can spot.

REMINDER!

When trying to stop the running game, you and your team must understand the team strategy and game plan. Don't forget to consider the questions on page 150.

ACQUIRING THE APPROPRIATE KNOWLEDGE

To hold runners successfully, you and your athletes must understand the following:

Rules

You and your athletes need to know several main rules when trying to hold runners:

- Rules about pitchers pausing during the stretch before throwing to the plate
- Rules about when pitchers have to throw and when they do not
- Rules about infielders obstructing runners

Physical Playing Conditions

The physical playing conditions will significantly affect the game. Thus, you and your players must pay attention to the following physical conditions when contemplating whether to use the pickoff from the pitcher to stop the running game:

- Surface quality between the bases where the runners may try to steal. For example, if the surface is poor, the runner may be less likely to attempt the steal.
- Wind speed and direction. For example, a strong wind may reduce the accuracy of your throws, so you may want to reconsider using pickoff attempts.

Strengths and Weaknesses of Opponents

You and your players must account for your opponent's strengths and weaknesses to know whether it is a good idea to use pitcher pickoffs to try to stop the running game. Teach your players to consider the following about your opponents:

- How good are the runners at disguising their intent to steal?
- How good are the runners at reacting to pickoff moves?
- Is the team that you are playing against one that works together to dare pitchers to throw over to the base often? Some teams operate on the assumption that the more throws a team makes to a base, the more chance they have of committing an error and allowing the runner to advance.
- Is the opposition a good bunting team that rarely steals bases? If so, then using pickoffs is not so much to stop runners from stealing as it will be to keep them from getting good secondary leads.
- Do the runners have more weight on the right foot than on the left? When they do this, they lean away from the base and cannot return as quickly on a pickoff throw.
- Are the runners lazy returning to the base after their secondary leads, or do they tend to turn their heads away from the ball at this time? If so, catchers may be able to pick off behind the runner.

Self-Knowledge

In addition to being aware of your opponent's strengths and weaknesses, you and your players need to have knowledge about your own team's ability. When considering using the pitcher pickoffs, teach your players to be aware of the following:

- How good is your team at catching the ball and making tags?
- How good are your shortstop and second baseman at disguising the intent to break to the base for a quick pickoff at second? How good are they at working together as a unit to hold runners close?
- How dominant is your pitcher? If your pitcher is dominant, then pickoff plays become less important because you expect your pitcher to have command over his pitches and be able to challenge hitters successfully, giving them fewer chances to run.
- How good is your team at communicating with one another, especially nonverbal communication between the fielders and the pitcher, such as turning an opened glove to the pitcher as a sign that a timed pickoff is on?

(continued)

PLAY OPTIONS FOR PITCHER PICKOFFS

Several options are available for pickoff plays. Consider the following sample plays:

Play #1

Straight pick at first from a right-handed pitcher. On this play, the pitcher should have two moves with his feet: his bad move, in which after coming set with his hands, he steps back off the rubber with his right foot and then turns and throws deliberately to first, and his good move, in which he takes a small, quick step toward third with his right foot, wheels quickly, steps to first with his left foot and throws. With the good move, pitchers should practice quick movements with their feet. The quicker the feet move, the better the move will be.

Play #2

Pick at first with the first baseman playing behind the runner. In this play, the first baseman stands several steps behind the runner after he has assumed his primary lead. As the pitcher comes to his set position, the first baseman takes a hard, quick step directly at the runner's back and then pushes off to move toward first base. If the pitcher sees a gap between the first baseman and the runner, he steps off and makes a pickoff throw. (Using the good move in this situation is not a good idea because if miscommunication occurs and the first baseman does not continue toward the bag, the pitcher would be forced to throw to the uncovered base. Failure to throw would result in a balk.) If the runner returns to the base or shortens up, the pitcher throws home and the first baseman returns to his fielding position.

Play #3

Pickoff at second base. The defense can use many timed plays here. Both the second baseman and shortstop can move to cover the base or to decoy the runner into thinking that one is going to cover while the other moves in for the pickoff throw when the runner relaxes. You should find a play that you feel comfortable with and work on it to perfect its execution. The key is to get all infielders counting in their heads in the same rhythm so that they break toward the base at the right time and the pitcher pivots and throws at the right time. A simple "one one thousand, two one thousand" rhythm works well in most cases. When first practicing these timing plays, the pick at second for example, infielders and pitchers should count aloud to be certain that they are working at the same rhythm.

Play #4

The daylight play at second with the shortstop. The mechanics for this are similar to what the first baseman does when playing behind the runner. The shortstop takes one or two quick, hard steps toward the runner in his primary lead and then breaks quickly for second. If the pitcher sees a gap, or daylight, between the fielder and the runner, he pivots and makes a quick pickoff throw to the base.

Play #5

Picks at second base. The pitcher has two options for footwork on his move. The pitcher can step toward home with his right foot, pivot and then step to second with his left foot and execute a throw. The second move, often called the inside move to second, occurs when the pitcher lifts his stride leg as if to pitch and then suddenly kicks that leg toward second while turning his pivot foot toward the base so that his body is facing that way. He then throws the ball. The key to this move is to have the pitcher use the same motion that he normally does on a pitch and then whirl and throw. If the pitcher always uses the glide stride and then suddenly starts using a leg lift with a runner on second, he would give away the pickoff.

With a runner on second base, the shortstop and second baseman must try to hold the runner close. They can use the open-glove signal for the pitcher to throw to the base on a timed count or use the daylight play from the shortstop whenever the runner gets too big a lead.

Decision-Making Guidelines

When deciding whether or not to use pitcher pickoff moves to stop the running game, you and your players should be sure to consider the previous information. "Play Options for Pitcher Pickoffs" includes sample plays that will help you to gain the best advantage when facing this situation. Also consider the following guidelines:

- Your pitcher should present different looks to runners to keep them off balance and prevent them from getting good jumps. Pitchers can accomplish this in several ways:
  - Never throwing a pickoff to the base from the same spot in the stretch motion twice in a row. If the pitcher comes to his final set position and then throws to first base, the next time he throws to first should be from a different point in the stretch, such as when the hands first come together or as the hands are moving down to the final set position.
  - Employing the glide stride to throw to home. By quickening the stride, the pitcher effectively delivers the ball to the plate in less time and gives the catcher more time to deliver the ball to second on a steal attempt.
  - Stepping off the pitcher's rubber with the back foot frequently after coming set to keep the runner off balance. An arm fake or a quick head jerk toward the base can occasionally accompany this action.
  - Varying the number of head turns to first before throwing a pitch. The pitcher can also vary the amount of time that he keeps his head turned, long sometimes and very briefly at other times.
  - Any combination of the previous looks.
- Your middle infielders must be in backup position on every throw back to the pitcher in case the throw gets past him. The third baseman should always back up throws from the first baseman back to the pitcher. If a runner is on third and gets too large a lead, the third baseman should move closer to the base to force him back.

At a Glance

The following parts of the text offer additional information on pickoffs by the pitcher.

Catcher Pickoffs

Unlike the pitcher's pickoff at first base, which can be used at any time without a signal, catcher pickoffs are usually designed plays that are called in advance either by the catcher or the coach to keep the runner close or get an out. Teams that run aggressively will often try to get the edge on a defense even when they are not stealing. Sometimes they will take bigger secondary leads in the event that the ball is hit to get a better head start toward the next base. Other times, especially in bunt situations, aggressive runners will try to get a jump on the attempted bunt and edge closer to the next base. In situations such as these, the catcher must sense the anticipation by the offense and react quickly and accordingly. A defense that wants to contain an aggressive running game must employ both catcher pickoffs and pitcher pickoffs.

READING THE SITUATION

How do you and your players decide when to use catcher pickoffs? Teach your players to:

- Know the game situation.
- Watch for signs.
- Watch for runners who are slow getting back to the base from their secondary leads after a pitch.
- Watch for runners who do not look in toward home plate while returning to the base after they have taken a secondary lead.
- Watch the base runner on a missed bunt attempt to see if he takes an abnormally big secondary lead, anticipating that the batter will bunt the ball.

WATCH OUT!

The following circumstances may distract your athletes:

- With multiple runners on base, the trailing runner pretends to be slow getting back to the base to entice a throw from the catcher.
- Runners who tend to use tricks to draw throws, such as pretending to fall or lose their balance.
- Batters who swing through the ball on steal attempts, thus interfering with the catcher's field of vision.

REMINDER!

When considering whether to use pickoffs from the catcher, you and your players must understand the team strategy and game plan. Don't forget to consider the questions on page 150.

ACQUIRING THE APPROPRIATE KNOWLEDGE

To use catcher pickoffs successfully, you and your athletes must understand the following:

Rules

You and your athletes need to know several main rules when you are using pickoffs from the catcher to stop running plays:

- Rules about catcher obstruction
- Rules about the catcher remaining in the catching box
- Rules about pitchouts

Physical Playing Conditions

The physical playing conditions will significantly affect the game. Thus, you and your players must pay attention to the following physical conditions when contemplating whether to use catcher pickoffs:

- Surface quality at home. For example, if the surface quality is poor, your catcher may have a difficult time executing the throw.
- Surface condition between the bases where the runner may try to steal.
- Wind speed and direction.

At a Glance

The following parts of the text offer additional information on pickoffs by the catcher.

Strengths and Weaknesses of Opponents

You and your players must account for your opponent's strengths and weaknesses to know whether it is a good idea to use catcher pickoffs. Teach your players to consider the following about your opponents:

- Do the base runners return quickly to bases, and are they always on the lookout for picks? If so, the pickoff will probably not be successful.
- When do the base runners take their secondary leads? If they take very long secondary leads, your success rate will be higher.

Self-Knowledge

In addition to being aware of your opponent's strengths and weaknesses, you and your players need to have knowledge about your own team's ability. When considering the use of catcher pickoffs, teach your players to be aware of the following:

- Does your catcher throw strongly and accurately?
- How good is the team at decoying a runner into thinking that there will not be a pickoff?
- Is communication among teammates effective, especially through nonverbal signs from the catcher to the infielders?

Decision-Making Guidelines

When deciding whether to use catcher pickoffs, you and your players should be sure to consider the previous information. Also consider the following guidelines:

- If the runner on base is slow and does not look to the catcher when returning to the bag, and the catcher can execute the quick sidearm snap throw or the jump pivot to first base, then the catcher pickoff may be effective.
- If the catcher senses that the other team will try to steal, he might want to use the pitchout because it allows the defense to get the ball to second base more quickly than normal.
- If a bunter misses a ball, the catcher should throw behind the runner. When runners are anticipating the bunt, they tend to have their momentum moving toward the next base. This makes them prime targets for the back pick, either at first or at second.
- If the game is close and in the late innings, the catcher should be wary about pickoffs at third base because miscommunication or errant throws always lead to runs.

Double-Play Defenses

Often called the pitcher's best friend, the double play occurs when two outs result from one batted ball. Usually, the double play refers to outs made with ground balls to the infielders. Imagine that with a runner on first and less than two outs, the batter hits a ground ball toward the middle of the infield. This situation sounds ideal for a double play. But teams must realize that not every ground ball is a double-play ball because many factors come into play before a team can successfully turn two. In amateur baseball, lack of arm strength and accuracy often make turning a double play difficult. The key in a double-play situation is to get one out for sure!

READING THE SITUATION

How can you and your players know when you can try to turn two? Teach your players to do the following:

- Know the game situation.
- Know the type of pitch being thrown.
- Watch to see in which direction the ball is hit and whether it is hit hard enough to turn two.
- Assess whether they have time to turn two if the fielder bobbles the ball.

WATCH OUT!

The following circumstances may distract your athletes:

- Sliding runners. The NFHS stresses that an automatic double play will be called if a runner deliberately slides into a fielder attempting a double-play pivot, but even a "fair" slide can be distracting to high school players.
- If the feeder does not show the ball to the pivot man, the fielder will have difficulty seeing it and may have to make quick adjustments with the glove hand.
- On come-backers, balls hit back to the pitcher, that the pitcher throws to second base, two fielders may attempt to cover the base. Only the fielder with coverage responsibility should cover the base.

REMINDER!

When trying to turn the double play, you and your team must understand the team strategy and game plan. Don't forget to consider the questions on page 150.

ACQUIRING THE APPROPRIATE KNOWLEDGE

To turn the double play, you and your athletes must understand the following:

Rules

You and your athletes need to know several main rules when you are trying to turn the double play:

- Rules about interference and obstruction
- Rules about having the foot on the base when catching the ball
- Rules about tagging the runner if the force play is no longer in effect

Physical Playing Conditions

The physical playing conditions will significantly affect the game. Thus, you and your players must pay attention to the following physical conditions when in a possible double-play situation:

- Irregular field conditions, which cause the ball to hop erratically
- The condition of the infield surface
- The condition of the ball

Strengths and Weaknesses of Opponents

You and your players must account for your opponent's strengths and weaknesses to be prepared for turning the double play. Teach your players to consider the following:

- How fast is the runner on base?
- Does the runner on base get a good secondary lead and jump when the ball is hit?
- Is the batter left-handed? If so, he will be quicker to first.

At a Glance

The following parts of the text offer additional information on double-play defenses.

Self-Knowledge

In addition to being aware of your opponent's strengths and weaknesses, you and your players need to have knowledge about your own team's ability. When considering whether to try to turn two, teach your players to be aware of the following:

- How quick is your team with their feet? How well do they transfer the ball from their gloves to their throwing hands?
- How well does the team communicate, particularly among the infielders and especially between the second baseman and the shortstop?
- How fast are your players' releases on their throws?
- How well can the players use soft hands in catching the ball?
- How good are the players at making accurate three-quarter-arm flip throws? The timing and execution of the double play depends on these throws.
- How good are the players at keeping their bodies under control at the base?
- How well can the team read the situation to determine whether the ball is hit hard enough to get a double play? Communication among the infielders is particularly important here.

Decision-Making Guidelines

When deciding whether to try to turn two, you and your players should be sure to consider the previous information. Also consider the following guidelines:

- Take the easy play at first base or second base when it is late in the game and your team needs outs. In this situation, it may be better for you to go for only one out.
- Go for one out when the ground conditions slow the progress of the ball.
- When your infielders are not playing double-play depth, rarely go for the double play.
- Infielders should always throw the ball to the base that is in the direction in which they are moving. For example, if a ball is hit to the left of the second baseman, the best play may be to throw in the direction of movement, in this case, first base. Trying to stop momentum, turn and throw the ball to second is difficult for high school players.

Determining the Best Pitching Options

The game between the hitter and the pitcher is like a game of cat and mouse, with each player trying to gain the edge over the other. Given this framework, you need to arm your pitching staff with enough information to approach a game productively. You should take into account many things—the individual make-up of the pitcher, the strengths and weaknesses of the opposition, the number of runners on base and their locations, etc.—when forming a strategy. You will need to provide your pitchers with a blueprint of flexibility that leads to success.

WATCH OUT!

The following circumstances may distract your pitchers:

- The batter starts with an open stance and steps into the plate.
- The batter crowds the plate but then strides away when swinging.
- The batter has learned to conceal a weakness with his stance. For example, a batter may crowd the plate to make the pitcher think that he is weak on pitches to the outside part of the plate in the hopes that the pitcher will throw inside to his strength.

READING THE SITUATION

Pitchers must be knowledgeable about hitters. They should study their stances, stride lengths and where they stand in the box, looking for indicators that might help in how they pitch to them. When trying to determine the best pitching options, teach your players to do the following:

- Communicate effectively with proper signs.
- Look to see whether the batter is short or tall.
- Study the position of the batter in the box.
- Watch to see whether the batter crowds the plate.
- Study the stride of the batter.
- Watch to see whether the batter drops his back shoulder or whether he has an uppercut swing.
- Watch to see whether the batter steps toward third or toward first.
- Be aware of the batter's bat speed and know whether his barrel or his hands move first.
- Try to get a sense of whether the batter wants to pull the ball.

REMINDER!

When trying to determine the best pitches to use in various situations, you and your team must understand the team strategy and game plan. Don't forget to consider the questions on page 150.

ACQUIRING THE APPROPRIATE KNOWLEDGE

To determine the best pitch to use in various situations, you and your athletes should understand the following:

Rules

You and your athletes need to know several main rules when you are trying to determine the best pitch to use in various situations:

- Rules that define the strike zone, as well as the actual strike zone of the umpire on a given day
- Rules about quick pitches and the amount of time allowed between pitches

- Rules about throwing at a hitter
- Rules about defacing the ball

Physical Playing Conditions

The physical playing conditions will significantly affect the game. Thus, you and your players must pay attention to the following physical conditions when trying to determine which pitches are best to use:

- The slope of the mound. For example, a mound with a slope that is steeper or gentler than what the pitcher is used to will affect his pitches.
- The strength and direction of the wind. For example, if the wind is blowing from center field straight to home plate, the curve will not break as much. Your team may want to consider using the changeup instead.
- The condition of the ball.

Strengths and Weaknesses of Opponents

You and your players must account for your opponent's strengths and weaknesses to know what pitches are best to use in various situations. Teach your players to consider the following:

- Do the batters have good short-to-long swings? If so, getting inside pitches past them may be difficult.
- Do the batters tend to keep their hands back? If so, fooling them with breaking balls may be difficult.
- Where does the batter stand in the box? If he stands toward the front, throwing him fastballs will give your pitcher the best advantage. On the other hand, if he stands in the back of the box, throwing breaking pitches will be best.
- Is the batter overanxious? If so, an off-speed pitch could work well.
- Does the batter have good knowledge of the strike zone?
- Does the batter stand far back from the plate, or does he step in the bucket (for a right-handed hitter that would be stepping toward third with his stride foot)? If so, your pitcher may be effective on the outside part of the plate.
- Does the batter drop his back shoulder or have an uppercut swing? If so, a high pitch may be most effective.
- How is the batter's stride? If the batter has a big stride, pitch high to him. On the other hand, if the stride is narrow, pitch low to him.
- Does the batter take a lot of extra time moving through his preswing routine between every pitch? If he does, be ready to throw a pitch as soon as he is in the batter's box. Make him rush the hit.
- Does the batter appear anxious to hit? If so, make him wait. Take the maximum amount of time between pitches allowable. Step off the rubber often.
- Does the batter lunge at pitches? If so, throw him slow-breaking pitches.
- Does the batter crowd the plate or have an extremely closed stance? If he does, throw fastballs to the inside portion of the strike zone.

(continued)

Self-Knowledge

In addition to being aware of your opponent's strengths and weaknesses, you and your players need to have knowledge about your own team's ability. When trying to determine the best pitches to use in various situations, teach your players to be aware of the following:

- How good is your pitcher at delivering pitches in the strike zone?
- How good is your team at sensing when hitters adapt to certain pitches or situations? Is your team able to change the pitching plan on the fly?
- How good is the communication between the catcher, coach and pitcher?
- How good is the team at identifying the need to change pitching rhythm to throw hitters off? An earlier note stated that pitchers need to destroy timing. Pitchers can accomplish this simply by not always throwing within the same time frame: They may throw a pitch, wait 20 seconds, throw another, wait 10 seconds, throw a third pitch, wait 15 seconds, throw another pitch and so on. Varying the time between pitches can prevent batters from getting comfortable.
- How good is the team at remembering the pitches that have been pitched in various situations and adjusting accordingly? Knowing that a pitch once retired a good hitter, the pitcher can be certain that the hitter will remember the pitch and be looking for it the next time. Pitchers should never return to the scene of the crime! More often than not, against a good hitter, that sort of thinking can ruin a good pitching performance and destroy a game plan.

Decision-Making Guidelines

When determining the best pitches to use in various situations, you and your players should be sure to consider the previous information. Also consider the following guidelines:

- Have pitchers pitch every pitch with a purpose, even the five warm-up pitches between innings. If a pitcher throws strikes during his warm-ups, the umpire senses that the pitcher has command over his pitches and is more likely to give him the borderline strike.
- Have pitchers establish the fastball early in the game to let batters know that they can control it and throw it for strikes. With that in mind, the batter will be looking for the fastball in counts that he thinks are in his favor. Then, if the pitcher can throw a curveball in such a situation, he will have an advantage.
- Have pitchers work the "L." This could best be described as the inside 6 inches of the strike zone, from top to bottom, closest to the batter and the 6 inches at the bottom of the strike zone from one edge of the plate to the other, as shown in figure 4.35 on page 95. If pitchers can locate most of their pitches in reasonable proximity to that L area, they will have success
- Consider asking pitchers to get two of the first three pitches in for strikes, instead of asking that every first pitch be a strike. This approach may alleviate the pressure that a pitcher puts on himself.
- Work toward having an average number of pitches per inning. For example, you may try to have only 15 pitches per inning. With that construct, some pitchers may challenge themselves further by working hard to have two or three 10-pitch innings or a certain number of ground-ball outs each contest.
- Caution pitchers and catchers to avoid getting into a pattern with their pitch selection such as two fastballs followed by a curve and then two more fastballs and another curve. Even if a pitcher has problems throwing a certain pitch for a strike on a given day, he must still use it to

at least let the batter know that he has the option to use it. For example, if a pitcher's breaking pitch is not working, don't abandon it entirely. The pitcher should still throw it, but focus on throwing it to a spot where it can't be hit. Eventually the pitch may come around and then the pitcher will be even more commanding.

- Consider having pitchers work on their least effective pitches when the team is either way ahead or way behind in a game. Nothing can substitute for game situations to make a pitcher more confident in a pitch. If you have decided to leave a pitcher in the game in a blowout, there is no better time to work on a bad curveball or a lousy changeup.
- The strikeout should rarely be considered part of team strategy for a pitcher. Try to convince pitchers that the perfect inning is three pitches. To strike out the side, he has to throw at least nine pitches, or six more than perfect. Persuade pitchers to make hitters hit the ball to a fielder.
- If the count is favorable for the batter—3-0, 2-0, 2-1, 3-2—the pitcher is vulnerable and needs to be careful because he has to throw a strike, but not too good a strike, to avoid dire consequences. On the other hand, if the count is 0-1, 1-1, 0-2 or 1-2, the pitcher holds the upper hand and can afford to be delicate in his pitch location without fear of walking the hitter or serving up a room-service fastball.
- If the opposing team has runners in scoring position, pitchers should take more time and focus more than usual. In a squeeze bunt situation, for example, pitchers need to be deliberate and try to pick up any clue that may tip the other team's hand.
- If a runner is on third with less than two outs, the pitcher should try to get a ground-ball out or a strikeout.
- If a hitter rips a fastball hard but foul, the pitcher's next pitch should be a changeup. The hitter will be so eager after getting good wood on the previous pitch that he will be way out in front and will usually hit the ball weakly.
- If the batters keep their hands back, fooling them with breaking balls may be difficult.

At a Glance

The following parts of the text offer additional information on determining the best pitching option.

Pitcher Basics	p. 94
Pitcher Stretch Mechanics	p. 102
Throwing a Fastball	p. 106
Throwing a Curveball	p. 108
Throwing a Changeup	p. 112
Aggressive Baserunning	p. 152
Situational Hitting	p. 172
Defensive Positioning	p. 178
Pitcher Pickoffs	p. 190

Rundowns

A pickoff throw or judicious use of the cutoff by an infielder catches a player off base, but then 15 throws later, he winds up safe at the next base! Probably no other play in baseball can make an otherwise good team look as if it belongs in the center ring of a circus than an improperly executed rundown. A rundown occurs when a pitcher's pickoff move catches a player off base or when a throw catches a base runner between bases on an aborted attempt to advance to the next base on a hit. When this kind of play occurs, defensive players need to know the proper way to force the runner into a sure out, at the base farthest from home plate if possible. Done properly, only one throw will be necessary and the runner will be out.

WATCH OUT!

The following circumstances may distract your athletes:

- The trapped base runner veers out of the baseline, requiring the tagger to lunge.
- The trapped base runner falls down, hoping that the player with the ball trying to make a tag will miss him.
- The trapped runner deliberately tries to run in line with the throw hoping to get hit.

READING THE SITUATION

How can you and your players gain the best advantage when in a rundown situation? Teach your players to do the following:

- Know the game situation.
- Study the player caught in the rundown and recognize that he is at least 30 feet from his last base.
- Watch the player to see whether he has hesitated or stopped running.
- Run hard toward the player.
- Close in on the player from both sides to reduce the throwing distance.
- Immediately assume proper backup positions, making sure to follow the ball after throwing it.
- Make adjustments, as necessary, depending on whether another runner is on base.

ACQUIRING THE APPROPRIATE KNOWLEDGE

To perform a successful rundown, you and your athletes must understand the following:

Rules

You and your athletes need to know two main rules when you are in a rundown situation:

- Rules about interference and obstruction
- Rules about establishing and leaving the baseline

REMINDER!

When handling a rundown situation, you and your players must understand the team strategy and game plan. Don't forget to consider the questions on page 150.

Physical Playing Conditions

The physical playing conditions will significantly affect the game. Thus, you and your players must pay attention to the following physical conditions when in a rundown situation:

- The strength and direction of the wind.
- The surface quality between the bases.
- The position of the sun in relation to the runner. For example, the sun may affect fielders' ability to see the quick throws that they need to make in a rundown situation.

Strengths and Weaknesses of Opponents

You and your players must account for your opponent's strengths and weaknesses to know how to gain the most in a rundown situation. Teach your players to consider the following:

- How fast is the runner?
- Does the runner routinely pay attention to his calls from his coaches, or does he tend to ignore his coaches' instructions?
- How good does the runner disguise his intent to break toward one of the bases?
- How good is the runner at sensing when a ball will be thrown and being able change directions quickly?
- Is the runner known for attempting to get an obstruction call by trying to run into players who do not have the ball?

At a Glance

The following parts of the text offer additional information on rundowns.

Throwing Basics	p. 64
Catching a Throw	p. 72
Aggressive Baserunning	p. 152
Getting Out of a Rundown	p. 174
Defensive Positioning	p. 178
Pitcher Pickoffs	p. 190

Self-Knowledge

In addition to being aware of your opponent's strengths and weaknesses, you and your players need to have knowledge about your own team's ability. When considering how to gain the best advantage when you are in a rundown situation, teach your players to be aware of the following:

- Are the players involved in the rundown good at getting the runner out with a few throws?
- How strong is the communication, both verbal and nonverbal, between the tosser and the receiver?
- How good are the players at making quick flip throws while on the run?
- How good is the team at catching and tagging?
- How good are the players at cooperating with one another and backing each other up?

Decision-Making Guidelines

When deciding the best way to gain an advantage in a rundown situation, you and your players should be sure to consider the previous information. "Executing the Rundown in Two Situations" describes two plays that will also guide you in gaining the best advantage in this situation. Also consider the following guidelines:

- Get the trapped base runner running full speed.
- Never fake a throw while running.
- The player with the ball should run hard after the trapped base runner, while holding the ball in the throwing hand. The receiver on the other end of the rundown should shorten up the distance between the trapped base runner and the next base. He should raise both hands clearly and call, "Now!" when he feels that the ball should be thrown. The player with the ball should make a quick wrist toss to the receiver and create a good angle so that the base runner will not be in the way of the throw. After throwing the ball, the tosser should veer to his right so that he will be out of the way if the runner stops and begins back to the original base. He should then follow the throw and become a backup at the base thrown to.
- When a rundown starts and no other runners are on base, all defensive players should hustle toward the bases where the rundown is occurring to back up in case they are needed.

Wild Pitches

Wild pitches and passed balls are balls thrown from the mound that the catcher cannot catch and that roll far enough away from home plate to allow runners to advance on the bases. No matter how good a pitcher is at locating his pitches or how good a catcher is at receiving and blocking, balls will occasionally get past the catcher and travel toward the backstop. If a base runner is on third base, the offense has a good chance to score an easy run. When the ball gets past the catcher, the entire infield must respond quickly to minimize the damage.

WATCH OUT!

The following circumstances may distract your athletes:

- Fans are distracting players.
- Opposing players and coaches are yelling.
- Everyone on the field is moving quickly to a new position.
- Base runners are moving.

REMINDER!

When reacting to a wild pitch or passed ball, you and your players must understand the team strategy and game plan. Don't forget to consider the questions on page 150.

READING THE SITUATION

On most passed balls or wild pitches, runners will be able to move up at least one base. The key to the defensive strategy is to prevent them from advancing farther or, with a runner on third base, possibly to make a putout at the plate. With this in mind, teach your players to do the following:

- Know the game situation.
- Know when the ball gets past the catcher and begins rolling toward the backstop.
- Know what the other runners do on the wild pitch (when more than one runner is on base).
- Watch for aggressive runners who try to advance more than one base, and know the shortstop's responsibility in this situation (as discussed on page 152).

ACQUIRING THE APPROPRIATE KNOWLEDGE

To recover quickly from a wild pitch or passed ball, you and your athletes must understand the following:

Rules

To react properly to wild pitches, you and your athletes need to know several rules and strategies, both written and unwritten:

- Rules about dead ball and live ball
- Rules about interference and obstruction

Physical Playing Conditions

The physical playing conditions will significantly affect the game. Thus, you and your players must pay attention to the following physical conditions when trying to recover from wild pitches and passed balls:

- The composition of the backstop. For example, if the backstop is made of a hard surface, the catcher must be aware of the angle and speed at which the ball will rebound.
- The distance from the backstop to home plate.

Strengths and Weaknesses of Opponents

You and your players must account for your opponent's strengths and weaknesses to know how to recover after a wild pitch or passed ball. Teach your players to consider the following:

- Are the runners especially quick or aggressive?
- Do the runners have the ability to read when the ball is in the dirt and get good jumps?
- Does the hitter recognize immediately that the ball is far enough past the catcher for the runner to advance and communicate that fact quickly to the runner?

At a Glance

The following parts of the text offer additional information on wild pitches and passed balls.

Self-Knowledge

In addition to being aware of your opponent's strengths and weaknesses, you and your players need to have knowledge about your own team's ability. When considering the best way to recover from wild pitches and passed balls, teach your players to be aware of the following:

- How good is the catcher at scooping up the ball and getting quickly into throwing position?
- How good is the catcher at making quick snap throws?
- Do all players know their backup and fielding priorities?

Decision-Making Guidelines

When deciding the best way to recover from a wild pitch or passed ball, you and your players should be sure to consider the previous information. Also consider the following guidelines:

- Take less risk in stopping runners who are advancing when your team is leading by a large margin. In this situation, you may simply want to get the ball back to the pitcher near the mound.
- Catchers must keep in mind the importance of blocking every ball in the dirt throughout the game, not only when a runner is on third. This mind-set prevents them from being lazy when it counts.
- Pitchers should charge home plate all the while, yelling to the catcher and pointing in the direction of the ball. If a runner is on third, the pitcher must let the catcher know if the runner is trying to advance by shouting, "Coming, coming, coming" or "He's coming." If the runner is not running, the pitcher should yell, "No throw" or "No, no, no" to let the catcher know that there is no play.
- The second baseman should sprint to second base and cover the bag if the wild pitch or passed ball occurs on a ball four or strike three and the batter–runner might try to advance to that base.
- The shortstop becomes the key to the defensive strategy during a wild pitch or passed ball. As soon as the ball gets past the catcher, the shortstop, usually the quickest and most sure-handed infielder in amateur baseball, should sprint to a position near the pitcher's mound in line with the catcher and any possible throw to home plate. From this position, he backs up any errant throws and, if more than one runner is on base, can stop further advancement.
- The first baseman should bust to home plate for backup on the first-base side of the infield. If the wild pitch or passed ball is ball four or strike three and the batter is running to first, the first baseman, after seeing that the shortstop is in backup position, should return to first base in case a rundown occurs.
- The third baseman should stay at third base, especially if several runners are on base when the wild pitch or passed ball occurs. The outfielders should move in to back up the bases.

PART IV

Planning for Teaching

Part IV helps you apply what you learned in the previous chapters to developing a plan for the upcoming season. By having a good season plan that outlines your practices for the year and then creating specific practice plans that make up your season plan, you will be ready to coach and get the most out of your season.

In chapter 7 you learn how to create your season plan, which is a framework for the practices that make up your season. Besides presenting the six essential steps to developing the season plan, this chapter provides a sample games approach season plan. A sample traditional approach season plan can be found in the *Coaching Baseball Technical and Tactical Skills* online course.

After you have your season plan, you must create what is called a practice plan, which outlines how you will approach each practice. Chapter 8 helps you do this by explaining the important components of a good practice plan and then providing you with a sample of the first eight practices of your season based on the games approach season plans. A sample traditional approach practice plan can be found in the *Coaching Baseball Technical and Tactical Skills* online course.

chapter 7

Season Plans

John Wooden, the great UCLA basketball coach, followed a simple coaching philosophy that emphasized execution over winning. He felt that if his Bruins concentrated on executing the basics, winning would follow. In that regard, his well-planned practice sessions created a foundation for 10 national titles in a 12-year span in the 1960s and 1970s. As Wooden said, "Failure to prepare is preparing to fail." Before the first practice of the season, you should review your coaching philosophy and reflect on the upcoming year. By doing so, you can avoid the pitfalls of previous years and set goals for the one to come. No matter what the sport, a good coach makes plans.

Planning begins with formulating a sound coaching philosophy. Do you pursue a conservative approach to the game or an aggressive one? When a runner reaches first, do you bunt him to second, or do you have him try to steal the base instead? Will you let batters swing at the first pitch, or will you tell them to take that first pitch? These and myriad other considerations go into the building of a coaching philosophy.

How do you form a philosophy? First, you should always go with your gut feelings. You shouldn't try to adapt a viewpoint that goes against your personal beliefs. You will have difficulty selling something to players that you don't believe in yourself. That being said, you shouldn't be afraid to borrow from successful approaches that have worked for others. Pay close attention to schools or teams that win often. What makes those teams successful? You shouldn't be afraid to ask other coaches how they prepare for a season, run practices or discipline players. A good coach will be flattered and more than willing to share information.

But as you know, gathering information from other coaches or from books provides only the raw material for an aspiring coach. The next step is to process this information and organize it into a useful plan. Good coaches are good teachers. Just as a teacher wouldn't think about walking into a classroom without a lesson plan, a coach shouldn't begin a season without a plan. You need to organize information into a working whole, or a season plan, by skillfully analyzing, observing and prioritizing.

Six Steps to Instructional Planning*

Chapter 1 of Rainer Martens' *Successful Coaching, Third Edition* provides a framework for creating and implementing coaching values. You may want to read that chapter and begin to refine your coaching philosophy.

After you have articulated your philosophy, you can begin planning for the season ahead by following a simple six-step procedure called "Six Steps to Instructional Planning," as shown here:

Step 1: Identify the skills that your athletes need.

Step 2: Know your athletes.

Step 3: Analyze your situation.

Step 4: Establish priorities.

Step 5: Select methods for teaching.

Step 6: Plan practices.

Step 1: Identify the Skills That Your Athletes Need

To help athletes become excellent baseball players, you need to know what skills players need to play baseball. Not all these skills will be within the reach of most high school players, so you must filter this all-encompassing list. First, you need to isolate the skills the team needs to be successful, as shown in column one of figure 7.1.

Figure 7.1 provides an overview of the basic to intermediate skills needed in baseball, based on the skills mentioned in chapters 3 through 6 as well as information on communication and physical, mental and character skills from Rainer Martens' *Successful Coaching, Third Edition.* At this stage, you should examine the list of skills and add others if desired. Step 4 of the planning process will explain further how you can put this list to work for yourself.

Step 2: Know Your Athletes

Before going into a season, you should be familiar with your athletes. If you trained the team the year before, you can just review the list of returning players and evaluate them—their strengths, their weaknesses, how much they still have to learn and so on. If you are a new coach with no knowledge of the skill level of a team, the process is more difficult. You should review the guidelines for evaluation discussed in chapter 2 before attempting this process. You may want to conduct a tryout camp on the first day of practice or before the season, if the rules allow. The camp could be conducted much like a major league tryout camp with one exception, replacing the 60-yard dash with the first-to-third sprint, a test that

---

*Adapted, by permission, from R. Martens, 2004, *Successful Coaching*, 3rd ed. (Champaign, IL: Human Kinetics), 237.

Figure 7.1 Identifying and Evaluating Skills

STEP 1	STEP 4							
	Teaching priorities			Readiness to learn		Priority rating		
Skills identified	Must	Should	Could	Yes	No	A	B	C
Offensive technical skills								
Preparing to Hit	M	S	C	Yes	No	A	B	C
Swing and Follow-Through	M	S	C	Yes	No	A	B	C
Bunting Basics	M	S	C	Yes	No	A	B	C
Sacrifice Bunting	M	S	C	Yes	No	A	B	C
Drag Bunting	M	S	C	Yes	No	A	B	C
Running Basics	M	S	C	Yes	No	A	B	C
Running to First Base	M	S	C	Yes	No	A	B	C
Rounding the Bases	M	S	C	Yes	No	A	B	C
Stealing Second Base	M	S	C	Yes	No	A	B	C
Stealing Third Base	M	S	C	Yes	No	A	B	C
Bent-Leg Slide	M	S	C	Yes	No	A	B	C
Headfirst Slide	M	S	C	Yes	No	A	B	C
Defensive technical skills								
Throwing Basics	M	S	C	Yes	No	A	B	C
Catching a Throw	M	S	C	Yes	No	A	B	C
Catcher Basics	M	S	C	Yes	No	A	B	C
Catcher Throwing	M	S	C	Yes	No	A	B	C
Catcher Blocking	M	S	C	Yes	No	A	B	C
Reacting As a Catcher	M	S	C	Yes	No	A	B	C
Pitcher Basics	M	S	C	Yes	No	A	B	C
Pitcher Stretch Mechanics	M	S	C	Yes	No	A	B	C
Throwing a Fastball	M	S	C	Yes	No	A	B	C
Throwing a Curveball	M	S	C	Yes	No	A	B	C
Throwing a Changeup	M	S	C	Yes	No	A	B	C
Outfield Basics	M	S	C	Yes	No	A	B	C
Challenging Outfield Plays	M	S	C	Yes	No	A	B	C
Infield Basics	M	S	C	Yes	No	A	B	C
Fielding Ground Balls	M	S	C	Yes	No	A	B	C
Double Plays	M	S	C	Yes	No	A	B	C
Fielding Pop-Ups in the Infield	M	S	C	Yes	No	A	B	C
Offensive tactical skills								
Aggressive Baserunning	M	S	C	Yes	No	A	B	C
Baserunning From Second	M	S	C	Yes	No	A	B	C
Scoring From Third	M	S	C	Yes	No	A	B	C
First-and-Third Play	M	S	C	Yes	No	A	B	C
Using the Bunt	M	S	C	Yes	No	A	B	C
Knowing When to Steal Second	M	S	C	Yes	No	A	B	C
Knowing When to Steal Third	M	S	C	Yes	No	A	B	C
Hit and Run	M	S	C	Yes	No	A	B	C
Situational Hitting	M	S	C	Yes	No	A	B	C
Getting Out of a Rundown	M	S	C	Yes	No	A	B	C

(continued)

Figure 7.1 ***(continued)***

STEP 1	STEP 4							
	Teaching priorities			Readiness to learn		Priority rating		
Skills identified	Must	Should	Could	Yes	No	A	B	C
Defensive tactical skills								
Defensive Positioning	M	S	C	Yes	No	A	B	C
Defending the First-and-Third Double Steal	M	S	C	Yes	No	A	B	C
Defending Bunt Situations	M	S	C	Yes	No	A	B	C
Pitcher Pickoffs	M	S	C	Yes	No	A	B	C
Catcher Pickoffs	M	S	C	Yes	No	A	B	C
Double-Play Defenses	M	S	C	Yes	No	A	B	C
Determining the Best Pitching Options	M	S	C	Yes	No	A	B	C
Rundowns	M	S	C	Yes	No	A	B	C
Wild Pitches	M	S	C	Yes	No	A	B	C
Physical training skills								
Strength	M	S	C	Yes	No	A	B	C
Speed	M	S	C	Yes	No	A	B	C
Power	M	S	C	Yes	No	A	B	C
Endurance	M	S	C	Yes	No	A	B	C
Flexibility	M	S	C	Yes	No	A	B	C
Quickness	M	S	C	Yes	No	A	B	C
Balance	M	S	C	Yes	No	A	B	C
Agility	M	S	C	Yes	No	A	B	C
Other	M	S	C	Yes	No	A	B	C
Mental skills								
Emotional control—anxiety	M	S	C	Yes	No	A	B	C
Emotional control—anger	M	S	C	Yes	No	A	B	C
Self-confidence	M	S	C	Yes	No	A	B	C
Motivation to achieve	M	S	C	Yes	No	A	B	C
Ability to concentrate	M	S	C	Yes	No	A	B	C
Other	M	S	C	Yes	No	A	B	C
Communication skills								
Sends positive messages	M	S	C	Yes	No	A	B	C
Sends accurate messages	M	S	C	Yes	No	A	B	C
Listens to messages	M	S	C	Yes	No	A	B	C
Understands messages	M	S	C	Yes	No	A	B	C
Receives constructive criticism	M	S	C	Yes	No	A	B	C
Receives praise and recognition	M	S	C	Yes	No	A	B	C
Credibility with teammates	M	S	C	Yes	No	A	B	C
Credibility with coaches	M	S	C	Yes	No	A	B	C
Character skills								
Trustworthiness	M	S	C	Yes	No	A	B	C
Respect	M	S	C	Yes	No	A	B	C
Responsibility	M	S	C	Yes	No	A	B	C
Fairness	M	S	C	Yes	No	A	B	C
Caring	M	S	C	Yes	No	A	B	C
Citizenship	M	S	C	Yes	No	A	B	C

Adapted, by permission, from R. Martens, 2004, *Successful Coaching*, 3rd ed. (Champaign, IL: Human Kinetics), 250-251.

provides a better measure of a player's speed, balance and quickness. Next, you could position players in deep center field and have fly balls and ground balls hit to them. Players would then throw to third base and home. This test gives you a picture of a player's arm strength and ability to read balls in the air. Finally, you could put all players at the shortstop position to field ground balls and throw to first, providing you with an indication of the players' footwork. Later, players with stronger arms could try out for specific positions like catcher or pitcher. Completing a form such as "Basic Infielder Skills Evaluation" on page 13 would give you a good idea of a player's fielding skills and potential ability. Armed with this knowledge, you could then reevaluate the skills identified in step 1 to ensure that they are the appropriate skills for the team.

Step 3: Analyze Your Situation

You also need to analyze your situation in preparing for a season. Before embarking on grandiose schemes like buying new uniforms or traveling great distances to play games, you need to consider the amount of help that you will get from the community, including parents and school and civic officials. You must be aware of budgetary concerns and have clear goals regarding fundraising if any is needed. Practice facility availability is also a concern. A program self-evaluation form, as shown in figure 7.2, can help you with this process.

You must remember to consider many factors other than technical and tactical skills before planning for a season. Note that as the season progresses, time available for practice diminishes. Be sure to teach all the basics early.

During the first 2 weeks of season, practice is held six times a week, but during the following 8 to 10 weeks, only 3 days are open for training, subject to rainouts or rescheduling. Moreover, on any given practice day, key players may be absent for school-related reasons or if they are fatigued and in need of rest. Any of these factors could necessitate a change of plans.

Step 4: Establish Priorities

You must institute a set of priorities before a season. Given the limited practice time available to most high school teams, you cannot do everything possible within the game of baseball. You should also consider the abilities of the athletes before establishing priorities. Refer to figure 7.1, paying special attention to the column under "Step 4." Here you examine the list of essential skills and evaluate them to establish practice priorities for the season. First, you must give each skill a priority according to its importance. Ask yourself, "Is this a skill that I 'must,' 'should' or 'could' teach?" You should then ask, "Are my athletes ready to learn this skill?" The results from step 2 may help you with this phase. Finally, based on those two factors—the teaching priority and the athlete's readiness to learn—you can give each skill a priority rating in column 4. The A-rated skills would be those that you feel are essential to teach, so you should cover them early and often. Likewise, you should teach as many B-rated skills as possible. Finally, depending on the ability and rate of progression of the players, you could teach C-rated skills.

Although most of the skills have been tabbed as must-teach skills, circumstances may arise that make teaching some skills impractical at various times during the season. For example, you might feel that teaching the first-and-third play to your offensive unit is essential and that teaching your defense to defend against the double steal is vital as well. But the team may not be ready or able to learn the complicated assignments necessary to mastering these tactical skills. Players may have difficulty reading the play and picking up on the cues to execute the play properly. Some may be easily distracted or have trouble acquiring the necessary knowledge. Players at key positions may lack the physical ability to be effective. In

Figure 7.2 Evaluating Your Team Situation

How many practices will you have over the entire season, and how long can practices be?

How many contests will you have over the entire season?

What special events (team meetings, parent orientation sessions, banquets, tournaments) will you have and when?

How many athletes will you be coaching? How many assistants will you have? What is the ratio of athletes to coaches?

What facilities will be available for practice?

What equipment will be available for practice?

How much money do you have for travel and other expenses?

What instructional resources (videos, books, charts, CDs) will you need?

What other support personnel will be available?

What other factors may affect your instructional plan?

Reprinted, by permission, from R. Martens, 2004, *Successful Coaching*, 3rd ed. (Champaign, IL: Human Kinetics), 247-248.

this case, you might come up with a conservative approach to these two tactical skills and delay teaching complicated responses.

Step 5: Select Methods for Teaching

Next, you should choose the methods that you want to use in daily practices to teach the skills that you have decided are necessary. Take care in implementing this important step. The traditional approach to practice involves using daily drills to teach skills, interspersed with batting practice and infield practice. This approach emphasizes technical skill development, the thinking being that the more a player drills the little skills, the better he becomes at performing them in games.

This traditional method might cover the techniques of baseball adequately and even approximate most of the tactical situations that a team will face during games, but it does have several glaring shortcomings. First, traditional practice sessions overemphasize techniques at the expense of tactics. Second, too much direct instruction occurs. Typically, a coach would explain a skill, show how to perform it and then set up situations in which players could learn the skill.

Recent educational research has shown, however, that students who learn a skill in one setting, say the library, have difficulty performing it in another setting, like the classroom. Compare this finding to the common belief among coaches that young players today don't have baseball sense, the basic knowledge of the game that players used to have. For years, coaches have been bemoaning the fact that players don't react as well to game situations as they used to, blaming everything from video games to the increasing popularity of other sports. But external forces may not be entirely to blame for the decline in baseball logic. Bookstores offer dozens of drill books to help coaches teach the technical skills of baseball, and teams around the country practice those drills ad infinitum. If drills are so specific, numerous and clever, why aren't players developing that elusive baseball sense? Perhaps just learning techniques and performing drill after drill creates not expertise, but only the ability to do drills.

An alternative way to teach baseball skills is the games approach. As outlined in chapter 1, the games approach allows players to take responsibility for learning skills. A good analogy is to compare the games approach in sports to the holistic method of teaching writing. Traditional approaches to teaching students to write included doing sentence-writing exercises, identifying parts of speech and working with different types of paragraphs. After drilling students in these techniques, teachers assigned topics to write about. Teachers used this method of teaching for years. When graduating students could not write a competent essay or work application, educators began questioning the method and began to use a new approach, the holistic method. In the holistic method of teaching writing, students wrote compositions without learning parts of speech or sentence types or even ways to organize paragraphs. Teachers looked at the whole piece of writing and made suggestions for improvement from there, not worrying about spelling, grammar or punctuation unless it was germane. This method emphasized seeing the forest instead of the trees.

This forest versus trees approach is applicable to teaching baseball skills as well. Instead of breaking down skills into their component parts and then having the athletes put the pieces back together, you can impart the whole skill and then let the athletes discover how the parts relate. This method resembles what actually occurs in a game, and learning occurs at game speed. These latter two concepts are crucial to understanding the games approach.

This method does not take you out of the equation; in fact, you must take a more active and creative role. You must shape the play of the athletes to get the desired results, focus the attention of the athletes on the important techniques and enhance the skill involved by attaching various challenges to the games played.

You can use the games approach to teach almost any area of the game. Instead of having pitchers and catchers throw to each other and simply chart their progress, you can create games around the pitchers' bullpen work and encourage competition. Instead of just holding an infield workout during a practice session, you can make the workout more gamelike by shaping, focusing and enhancing. Working on a double play, for example, might be more real if base runners were involved or if fielders were timed with a stopwatch each time. If infielders cannot complete the double play in 4.4 seconds or less, you will have to work on the infielders' positioning and quickness to ensure that they are capable of actually turning two.

Step 6: Plan Practices

At this stage of the planning process, you should sketch a brief overview of what you want to accomplish during each practice for the season. Using the information compiled in the previous five steps, you can sketch an outline for an entire season, both practices and games, which can be called the season plan. Figure 7.3 shows a sample season plan for the games approach, using a 12-week season plan that includes a 2-week period for postseason playoffs. For a sample traditional approach season plan, please refer to the *Coaching Baseball Technical and Tactical Skills* online course.

This plan presumes that the first 2 weeks of the season will be devoted primarily to practice, with games beginning in the 3rd week. The early practices are more detailed and complete. After games begin, practice plans become more open ended so that you can focus on problems that may have occurred in past games and can develop practices according to the game plan (see chapter 9).

The game plan should include a review of the previous game, scouting reports and the team's overall strategy. Approaching practices in this manner helps you fine-tune practices to prepare for upcoming games. The main objective of practices at this point in the season is to focus on the game plan, but when time permits, you should revisit key skills so that the learning process continues all season long.

Although the plan in figure 7.3 is shown in isolation, you can and should employ both approaches when considering your season planning. You may feel more comfortable teaching bunting with the traditional approach but may find that the games approach works better for you when teaching the first-and-third double-steal play. Remember to work through the six steps yourself to create a season plan best suited for your team.

After completing the season plan, you can further refine step 6 of the process by adding specifics to your individual workouts. The next chapter helps you in this procedure by showing the components of a good practice session and providing a sample of the games approach to practices.

Figure 7.3 Games Approach Season Plan

		Purpose	Skills
WEEK 1—PRESEASON	**Practice 1**	Introduce and review defensive tactical skills.	Double-Play Defenses
	Practice 2	Continue review of defensive tactical skills further; introduce and review situational hitting.	Situational Hitting
	Practice 3	Introduce the tactics of bunting (offense and defense); go over the tactics involved with wild pitches.	Defending Bunt Situations • Using the Bunt • Wild Pitches
	Practice 4	Introduce the tactics of aggressive baserunning.	Aggressive Baserunning
	Practice 5	Introduce the tactics of stealing (offense and defense).	Knowing When to Steal Second • Knowing When to Steal Third • Pitcher Pickoffs • Catcher Pickoffs
	Practice 6	Introduce the tactics of pitching.	Determining the Best Pitching Options
WEEK 2—PRESEASON	**Practice 7**	Introduce the tactics of defensive positioning.	Defensive Positioning
	Practice 8	Focus on intermediate tactical skills that will help the team score runs and prevent the opponent from scoring.	Aggressive Baserunning • Baserunning From Second • Scoring From Third • First-and-Third Play • Defending the First-and-Third Double Steal
	Practice 9	Focus on tactical skills to prepare players for game day.	Getting Out of a Rundown • Rundowns • Hit and Run • Defensive Positioning
	Practice 10	Focus on intermediate running tactics.	Using the Bunt • Sacrifice Bunting • Drag Bunting • Stealing Second Base • Stealing Third Base • Pitcher Pickoffs • Defending Bunt Situations • Catcher Pickoffs
	Practice 11	Build pitchers' tactical awareness and seasonal strategy.	Determining the Best Pitching Options • Pitcher Basics • Pitcher Stretch Mechanics • Situational Hitting • Double-Play Defenses • Throwing a Fastball • Throwing a Curveball • Throwing a Changeup • Fielding Pop-Ups in the Infield • Challenging Outfield Plays
	Practice 12	Prepare for game day.	Review of skills identified in the game plan
WEEK 3—IN-SEASON	**Game 1**		
	Practice 13	Review bunts.	Bunting Basics • Sacrifice Bunting • Drag Bunting
	Game 2		
	Practice 14	Review steals.	Stealing Second Base • Stealing Third Base
	Game 3		
	Practice 15	Review slides.	Bent-Leg Slide • Headfirst Slide
WEEK 4—IN-SEASON	**Game 4**		
	Practice 16	Review pitch selection and tactics.	Throwing a Fastball • Throwing a Curveball • Throwing a Changeup
	Game 5		
	Practice 17	Review baserunning strategy.	Aggressive Baserunning
	Game 6		
	Practice 18	Review skills as necessary.	Baserunning From Second

(continued)

Figure 7.3 ***(continued)***

		Purpose	Skills
WEEK 5—IN-SEASON	**Game 7**		
	Practice 19	Review options at third.	Scoring From Third
	Game 8		
	Practice 20	Review skills as necessary.	First-and-Third Play
	Game 9		
	Practice 21	Review skills as necessary.	Using the Bunt
WEEK 6—IN-SEASON	**Game 10**		
	Practice 22	Review skills as necessary.	Hit and Run
	Game 11		
	Practice 23	Review skills as necessary.	Situational Hitting
	Game 12		
	Practice 24	Review aggressive baserunning options.	Getting Out of a Rundown
WEEK 7—IN-SEASON	**Game 13**		
	Practice 25	Review game situations and tactics.	Defensive Positioning
	Game 14		
	Practice 26	Review skills as necessary.	Defending the First-and-Third Double Steal
	Game 15		
	Practice 27	Review skills as necessary.	Defending Bunt Situations
WEEK 8—IN-SEASON	**Game 16**		
	Practice 28	Review skills as necessary.	Pitcher Pickoffs
	Game 17		
	Practice 29	Review catching strategy.	Catcher Pickoffs
	Game 18		
	Practice 30	Review skills as necessary.	Wild Pitches
WEEK 9—IN-SEASON	**Game 19**		
	Practice 31	Review skills as necessary.	Double-Play Defenses
	Game 20		
	Practice 32	Review pitch selection.	Determining the Best Pitching Options
	Game 21		
	Practice 33	Review skills as necessary.	Rundowns
WEEK 10—IN-SEASON	**Game 22**		
	Practice 34	Review skills as necessary.	Defending the First-and-Third Double Steal
	Game 23		
	Practice 35	Review skills as necessary.	Situational Hitting
	Game 24		
	Practice 36	Review skills as necessary.	Determining the Best Pitching Options
	Playoffs		

chapter 8

Practice Plans

To get the most out of your practice sessions, you must plan each practice. Completing the season plan, as described in the last chapter, helps you do this. But you have to take that season plan a step further and specify what you will be covering at every practice.

As described in *Successful Coaching, Third Edition*, every practice plan should include the following:

- Date, time of practice and length of practice session
- Objective of the practice
- Equipment needed
- Warm-up
- Practice of previously taught skills
- Teaching and practicing new skills
- Cool-down
- Coaches' comments
- Evaluation of practice

The following games approach practice plans were developed based on the season plan from chapter 7 (as shown in figure 7.3 on page 217). Early practices focus on baseball as a whole, including essential tactical skills. Then, as players need to refine technical skills, those skills are brought into the practices. When athletes play focused games early in the season, they quickly discover their weaknesses and become more motivated to improve their skills so that they can perform better in game situations. For a sample traditional approach practice plan, please refer to the *Coaching Baseball Technical and Tactical Skills* online course. Additionally, sample drills and games, as mentioned in both the games and traditional approach practice plans, can also be found in the *Coaching Baseball Technical and Tactical Skills* online course.

PRACTICE 1

Date:

Monday, March 13

Practice Start Time:

3:20 p.m.

Practice Length:

2 hours, 40 minutes

Objectives:

- Begin team conditioning.
- Players demonstrate basic throwing and catching techniques.
- Players demonstrate proper running form in running through first base.
- Players become aware of the importance of repeating basic skills daily.
- Players react aggressively to baserunning situations.
- Players learn relaxation techniques.

Time	Name of activity	Description	Key teaching points	Related skills
3:20–3:30	Prepractice meeting and team building	Explain procedures for choosing varsity and earning team cap; review expectations of players, contained in team manual.	• Hustle. • Teamwork.	
3:30–3:50	Warm-up	Ballet Class and stretching for flexibility.	• Arm pump and knee lift. • Full range of motion in stretches.	• Running Basics, page 44
3:50–4:00	Conditioning	1-mile timed run.	• Proper running form.	
4:00–4:01	Water break			
4:01–4:21	Throwing and catching	Explain proper procedures for throwing and catching by introducing "Whoosh!" drill—progress through all four stages using dowels; in second part replace dowels with taped baseballs and continue stages.	• Proper arm action, balance and footwork. • Soft hands when receiving.	• Throwing Basics, page 64 • Catching a Throw, page 72
4:21–4:46	Daily drill sets for catchers	Catcher's Toolbox—catchers move through stages as outlined in drill.	• Soft hands. • Balanced stance. • Shifting from sign stance to receiving stance. • Framing.	• Catcher Basics, page 74 • Reacting As a Catcher, page 90

Time	Name of activity	Description	Key teaching points	Related skills
4:21–4:46	Daily drill sets for pitchers	Pitcher's Toolbox—pitchers move through stages as outlined in drill.	• Staying closed. • Late rotation. • Follow-through. • Tight abdominal muscles.	• Pitcher Basics, page 94
4:21–4:46	Daily drill sets for infielders	Infielder's Toolbox—infielders move through stages as outlined in drill.	• Fielding position. • Watching the ball into the glove. • Forehand and backhand. • Gather and throw skills. • Proper footwork.	• Infield Basics, page 124
4:21–4:46	Daily drill sets for outfielders	Outfielder's Toolbox—outfielders move through stages as outlined in drill.	• Drop step and crossover. • Catching above eye level. • Blocking ground balls. • Shifting position.	• Outfield Basics, page 114
4:46–4:47	Water break			
4:47–5:02	Drill: Bobble and Go!	Baserunning situations, running through first and rounding first.	• Running form. • Thinking one base ahead.	• Aggressive Baserunning, page 152
5:02–5:12	Cool-down	20-yard sprints out of batter's box; stretch main muscle groups.	• Complete stretches.	
5:12–5:20	Coaches' comments	Reminders; end-of-practice comments; discuss criteria for earning team cap.	• General comments. • Positive points. • Take notes on player comments about cap's criteria.	
5:20–5:25	Team breathing and visualization exercises	Begin explanation of relaxation and importance of visualization; begin breathing exercises to teach relaxation; players lie on their backs as tension free as possible with eyes closed; coach teaches players how to breath to release stress by sequentially relaxing body parts from feet to head.	• Focus on inhaling. • Work from feet up to head.	
5:25–6:00	Coaches' meeting	Meet in coaches' office.	• Assess the day's workout. • Discuss next practice.	

PRACTICE 2

Date:

Tuesday, March 14

Practice Start Time:

3:20 p.m.

Practice Length:

2 hours, 25 minutes

Objectives:

- Continue conditioning.
- Continue training proper arm action in throwing.
- Players become more proficient in basic technical infield, catching, outfield and pitching skills.
- Through challenge games, players begin to understand and react appropriately to tactical defensive situations.
- Players learn proper defensive positioning in specific offensive situations listed in the playbook.

Time	Name of activity	Description	Key teaching points	Related skills
3:20–3:33	Prepractice meeting and team building	Go over practice routine for the day.	• Hustle. • Teamwork.	
3:33–3:45	Warm-up	Ballet Class and stretching for flexibility.	• Slow stretches. • Full range of motion.	• Running Basics, page 44
3:45–3:54	Conditioning	1-mile timed run.	• Driving arms. • Beating previous time.	• Running Basics, page 44
3:54–3:55	Water break			
3:55–4:10	Throwing and catching	Whoosh!—progress to taped balls.	• Proper arm action • 12 o'clock–6 o'clock rotation.	• Throwing Basics, page 64 • Catching a Throw, page 72
4:10–4:30	Daily drill sets for catchers	Catcher Challenge—catchers work in partners to develop framing, receiving and footwork skills; add variation 1.	• Quick feet. • Quickly transferring ball into throwing position.	• Catcher Basics, page 74
4:10–4:30	Daily drill sets for pitchers	Dueling Pitchers—game variation of Pitcher's Toolbox; add stretch mechanics.	• Shorten delivery time. • Quickly getting ball to the plate from the stretch.	• Pitcher Stretch Mechanics, page 102
4:10–4:30	Daily drill sets for infielders	Goalie—infielders work in partners to develop fielding position, forehand, backhand, gather and throw skills.	• Transferring ball from glove to throwing hand. • Quickly getting ball into throwing position.	• Fielding Ground Balls, page 132

Time	Name of activity	Description	Key teaching points	Related skills
4:10–4:30	Daily drill sets for outfielders	Five Alive—outfielders work on drop step, crossover and blocking ground balls.	• Think "First three steps hard and fast" on every ball. • Direct route to the ball.	• Outfield Basics, page 114
4:30–5:00	Batting practice	Coaches throw; players move through five closed and open stations—tees, soft toss, swing trainer or Speed Stik, on deck, live; coaches fungo to infielders and outfielders.	• Short, compact swing; hitting fundamentals. • Evaluate swings.	• Preparing to Hit, page 20 • Swing and Follow-Through, page 26
4:30–5:00	Bullpens	Pitchers, paired with catchers, rotate out of bullpen to throw 12 pitches to catcher; coach charts pitches, sets up situations.	• Form. • 50% speed. • Work inside, outside, up and down.	• Pitcher Basics, page 94 • Throwing a Fastball, page 106 • Throwing a Curveball, page 108 • Throwing a Changeup, page 112 • Determining the Best Pitching Options, page 198
5:00–5:15	Drill: Situations	Play four to five innings to practice defensive situations.	• Emphasize fielding priorities. • Every base gets covered. • Every player moves on every play.	• Defensive Positioning, page 178 • Aggressive Baserunning, page 152
5:15–5:20	Cool-down	Sprints from first to third for time; pitchers run foul lines.	• Running form on sprints. • Emphasize watching third-base coach. • Economical turn at second.	• Running Basics, page 44 • Aggressive Baserunning, page 152
5:20–5:25	Coaches' comments	End-of-practice comments from staff; hand out criteria for earning team cap.	• Positive points. • Motivate for next practice.	
5:25–5:30	Team breathing and visualization exercises	Continue breathing exercises from previous practice.	• Long, easy breaths. • Focus on exhalations.	
5:30–5:40	Team meeting	Review criteria for earning team cap; take nominations from players; hand out ballots; vote.	• Team members facilitate the meeting.	
5:40–5:45	Coaches' meeting	Staff meet after practice.	• Discuss practice. • Begin to narrow list of candidates for varsity.	

PRACTICE 3

Date:
Wednesday, March 15

Practice Start Time:
3:20 p.m.

Practice Length:
2 hours, 25 minutes

Objectives:

- Catchers improve their throwing ability.
- Players learn how to use cutoffs.
- Players learn how to read the bunt and respond to get one sure out.
- Put players in various defensive situations to improve their tactical skills.
- Players strengthen understanding of roles in various hitting situations.
- Pitchers understand the importance of using the strike zone effectively.

Time	Name of activity	Description	Key teaching points	Related skills
3:20–3:30	Prepractice meeting and team building	Review practice outline; remind players about first team ballot after practice.		
3:30–3:50	Warm-up	Ballet Class; flexibility exercises; 1-mile timed run.	• Slow stretching. • Good form.	• Running Basics, page 44
3:50–3:51	Water break			
3:51–4:05	Throwing and catching	Same as previous practices; begin long toss.	• Proper arm action and footwork. • 12 o'clock–6 o'clock spin. • No lollipop throws.	• Throwing Basics, page 64 • Catching a Throw, page 72
4:05–4:25	Daily drill sets for catchers	Catcher Challenge (variation 1)—increased distance between partners, full throw, working on catcher throwing positioning after each stop.	• Reacting. • Throwing.	• Catcher Throwing, page 82
4:05–4:25	Daily drill sets for pitchers	Dueling Pitchers—game variation of Pitcher's Toolbox.	• Hiding curve. • Moving ball in, out, up, down.	• Pitcher Basics, page 94 • Throwing a Curveball, page 108 • Determining the Best Pitching Options, page 198
4:05–4:25	Daily drill sets for infielders	Goalie (variation 1, with triangles)—working in groups of three, same rules as previous practice.	• Quick feet. • Quick transfer of ball from glove to throwing hand.	• Fielding Ground Balls, page 132

PRACTICE 3

Time	Name of Activity	Description	Key teaching points	Related skills
4:05–4:25	Daily drill sets for outfielders	Five Alive (variation 1)—add wall play into game; play off wall to relay man.	• Playing angles on ball off wall. • Getting into position.	• Challenging Outfield Plays, page 120
4:25–4:26	Water break			
4:26–4:46	Game: Bunt Game	Batters placed in bunting situations; fielders charge and react; situations change as game develops.	• Bunting skills. • Fielding skills.	• Using the Bunt, page 160 • Defending Bunt Situations, page 186
4:46–5:15	Game: Bingo, Bango, Bongo	Runner on base; batter reacts to situation created by runner; if successful, gets his BP swings; runs out last one.	• Batting skills.	• Situational Hitting, page 172
4:46–5:15	Bullpens	Pitchers throw 15 to 20 pitches to catcher; coach charts pitches.	• Arm action on breaking ball. • Follow-through. • 50 to 75% velocity only.	• Throwing a Fastball, page 106 • Throwing a Curveball, page 108 • Throwing a Changeup, page 112
5:15–5:25	Cool-down	Cone drill plyos; hot box drills for infielders; pitchers run foul lines; running downhill.	• Lengthening stride in downhill runs.	
5:25–5:30	Coaches' comments	End-of-practice summary.	• Positive points.	
5:30–5:35	Team breathing and visualization exercises	During relaxation, show players how to use recall of past performances to enhance visualization training.	• Emphasize re-creating a successful baseball moment. • Focus on all senses.	
5:35–5:40	Team meeting	Review criteria for earning team cap; take nominations from players; hand out ballots; vote.	• Team members facilitate the meeting.	
5:40–5:45	Coaches' meeting	Meet in coach's office.	• Discuss practice. • Begin to narrow list of candidates for varsity.	

PRACTICE 4

Date:

Thursday, March 16

Practice Start Time:

3:20 p.m.

Practice Length:

2 hours, 30 minutes

Objectives:

- Incorporate tactical awareness into running.
- Incorporate tactical awareness into pitching challenges—working corners, throwing high in bunt situations and so on.
- Work on double-play tactics in infield games.
- Catchers react to tactical challenges in games.
- Incorporate defensive positioning tactics with aggressive baserunning.

Time	Name of activity	Description	Key teaching points	Related skills
3:20–3:35	Prepractice meeting and team building	Review practice outline.	• Remind players to be aggressive.	
3:35–3:50	Warm-up	Ballet Class; flexibility exercises; 1-mile timed run.	• Slow stretching. • Good form.	• Running Basics, page 44
3:50–4:15	Drill: Bobble and Go!	Runners react to outfielders and coach; outfielders hit cutoff; coaches signal for bobble.	• Baserunning. • Conditioning.	• Rounding the Bases, page 48 • Aggressive Baserunning, page 152
4:15–4:17	Water break			
4:17–4:30	Throwing and catching	Same as previous practices; continue long toss.	• Proper arm action.	• Throwing Basics, page 64 • Catching a Throw, page 72
4:30–4:40	Daily drill sets for catchers	Catcher Challenge (variation 1)—increased distance between partners; full throw; work on catcher throw positioning after each stop.	• Reacting and throwing.	• Catcher Throwing, page 82
4:30–4:40	Daily drill sets for pitchers	Dueling Pitchers—game variation of Pitcher's Toolbox; concentrate on stretch position in all drills.	• Proper arm action. • Glide stride. • Holding runners.	• Pitcher Basics, page 94 • Determining the Best Pitching Options, page 198

PRACTICE 4

Time	Name of activity	Description	Key teaching points	Related skills
4:30–4:40	Daily drill sets for infielders	Goalie (variation 2)—add line-drive throws, double-play pivots and throwing to first base.	• Fielding and throwing.	• Infield Basics, page 124 • Fielding Ground Balls, page 132 • Double-Play Defenses, page 196
4:30–4:40	Daily drill sets for outfielders	Five Alive (variation 2)—add throwing to second.	• Fielding and throwing.	• Outfield Basics, page 114
4:40–5:05	Drill: Situations	Batters hit (bunt, swing away and so on) according to game situation; runners react to where ball is hit and fielders make plays on runners; start with runners in different position; add get-an-out variation in which catcher reacts to bunt to get the out.	• Aggressive running. • Catcher throwing.	• Situational Hitting, page 172 • Defensive Positioning, page 178 • Defending Bunt Situations, page 186 • Using the Bunt, page 160
5:05–5:20	Scrimmage	Divide teams; play two innings with three outs; rotate pitchers after three outs.	• Coach evaluates players for later discussion.	
5:05–5:20	Bullpens	Pitchers not throwing in scrimmage work on pitches; chart all pitches.	• Glide stride. • Varying timing to the plate. • Stepping off.	• Pitcher Pickoffs, page 190 • Determining the Best Pitching Options, page 198
5:20–5:25	Cool-down	Run sprints from first to third and from second to home from secondary lead; coach hits fungoes to start.	• Getting good jump when ball is hit.	• Aggressive Baserunning, page 152
5:25–5:35	Coaches' comments and team building	End-of-practice comments; take more nominations for team caps.	• Positive points from practice. • Areas of improvement. • Players state nominations.	
5:35–5:40	Team breathing and visualization exercises	Continue teaching relaxation technique.	• Focus and recall of past events while breathing. • Introduce concept of rehearsal.	
5:40–5:50	Coaches' meeting	Meet in coach's office.	• Further refine varsity and JV lists. • Discuss player evaluations. • Review practice plans.	

PRACTICE 5

Date:

Friday, March 17

Practice Start Time:

3:20 p.m.

Practice Length:

2 hours, 40 minutes

Objectives:

- Players increase tactical abilities at all positions.
- Players work on reading and reacting to the ball off the bat.
- Players execute pickoff plays under enhanced situations.
- Pitchers work on learning to work the ball low in the strike zone.
- Players react to various plays at game speed.

Time	Name of activity	Description	Key teaching points	Related skills
3:20–3:35	Prepractice meeting and team building	Award caps to those named on ballots; announce that Thursdays will be changeup days when pitchers throw changeups only.	• Emphasize skills exhibited by players who earned caps.	
3:35–3:55	Warm-up	Ballet Class and flexibility exercises.	• Hold stretches for 20 seconds.	• Running Basics, page 44
3:55–3:57	Water break			
3:57–4:10	Throwing and catching	Same as previous practice.	• Proper arm action. • Proper footwork.	• Throwing Basics, page 64 • Catching a Throw, page 72
4:10–4:20	Daily drill sets for catchers	Catcher Challenge (variation 2)—balls in dirt, high, low, inside, outside; assume missed bunt, pickoff plays and so on.	• Reacting. • Throwing to second.	• Catcher Pickoffs, page 194
4:10–4:20	Daily drill sets for pitchers	Dueling Pitchers—game variation of Pitcher's Toolbox.	• Changeup grip. • Release point.	• Determining the Best Pitching Options, page 198
4:10–4:20	Daily drill sets for infielders	Goalie (variation 2)—practice playing the ball.	• Direct route to the ball to get there quickly.	• Infield Basics, page 124 • Fielding Ground Balls, page 132
4:10–4:20	Daily drill sets for outfielders	Five Alive (variation 2)—playing the ball.	• Direct routes, no L routes. • Running on balls of feet. • Crow hop. • Proper footwork.	• Challenging Outfield Plays, page 120

PRACTICE 5

Time	Name of activity	Description	Key teaching points	Related skills
4:20–4:40	Game: Cat and Mouse	Work on pickoff plays.	• Shape various pickoff situations; focus players' attention on tactical decision-making.	• Pitcher Pickoffs, page 190
4:40–5:05	Scrimmage	Divide teams; play two innings with three outs; rotate pitchers after three outs.	• Coach evaluates players for later discussion.	
4:40–5:05	Bullpens	Pitchers not throwing in scrimmage work on pitches; chart all pitches.	• Glide stride. • Varying timing to the plate. • Stepping off.	• Determining the Best Pitching Options, page 198
5:05–5:15	Drill: Situations	Continue from previous practice; incorporate different situations.	• Emphasize options available on each situation. • Freeze play to show positive or negative reactions.	• Defensive Positioning, page 178
5:15–5:30	Cool-down	Players at each base get sign, take primary lead and react to pitcher; stretching.	• Jab step. • Good drive toward second.	• Aggressive Baserunning, page 152
5:30–5:40	Coaches' comments and team building	Comments on practice; more nominations for caps; vote.	• Teamwork shown during the day.	
5:40–5:45	Team breathing and visualization exercises	Continue breathing and focusing exercises; remind players to do on their own several times daily.	• Rehearsal for action.	
5:45–6:00	Coaches' meeting	Meet on field.	• Further refine varsity and JV roster list. • Review evaluations. • Remind coaches to be positive at all times.	

PRACTICE 6

Date:

Saturday, March 18

Practice Start Time:

8:30 a.m.

Practice Length:

4 hours

Objectives:

- Build on tactical skills at all positions.
- Focus on cutoff executions with infielders and outfielders.
- Work with pitchers on moving the ball around the strike zone.
- Fine-tune sliding techniques.
- Work on first-and-third execution.
- Work on situational hitting, and hit and run.

Time	Name of activity	Description	Key teaching points	Related skills
8:30–8:35	Prepractice meeting and team building	Award caps; remind players that varsity and JV teams will be decided at the end of practice; collect goals from each player.	• Emphasize positive contributions of other team members.	
8:35–8:50	Warm-up	Ballet Class and flexibility exercises.	• Emphasize running form; full range of motion in stretches.	• Running Basics, page 44
8:50–8:51	Water break			
8:51–9:05	Throwing and catching	Same as previous practices; long toss with one hop.	• Proper arm action. • Follow-through.	• Throwing Basics, page 64 • Catching a Throw, page 72
9:05–9:15	Daily drill sets for catchers	Catcher Challenge (variation 2)—add throw to second.	• Good positioning to stop the ball. • Quick, accurate release to second.	• Catcher Basics, page 74 • Catcher Pickoffs, page 194
9:05–9:15	Daily drill sets for pitchers	Dueling Pitchers—game variation of Pitcher's Toolbox; vary routine from previous days.	• Working breaking pitches away.	• Pitcher Basics, page 94 • Determining the Best Pitching Options, page 198
9:05–9:15	Daily drill sets for infielders	Goalie (variation 2)—add line-drive throws; stopping ball and throwing to first base.	• Good positioning to stop the ball. • Quick, accurate release to first. • Going back on pop-ups.	• Infield Basics, page 124 • Fielding Pop-Ups in the Infield, page 146

PRACTICE 6

Time	Name of activity	Description	Key teaching points	Related skills
9:05–9:15	Daily drill sets for outfielders	Five Alive (variation 3)—add base runner; catcher throws to first or second based on the situation.	• Decision making.	• Outfield Basics, page 114
9:15–9:45	Hitting stations	Use whole complex—tees, hit-run triangle drills with Wiffle balls, soft toss, live hitting in cages.	• Short-to-long swings. • Keeping hands inside the ball. • Slow, easy, early load.	• Hit and Run, page 170
9:15–9:45	Bullpens	Pitchers throw 20 pitches to catcher; vary windup and stretch; emphasize mixing fastballs, curves, changes; coach charts all pitches.	• Getting ball in correct zones. • Boxing, tilting, duplicates.	• Throwing a Fastball, page 106 • Throwing a Curveball, page 108 • Throwing a Changeup, page 112 • Determining the Best Pitching Options, page 198
9:45–10:30	Scrimmage	Divide teams; play two innings with three outs; rotate pitchers after three outs.	• Aggressive baserunning.	• Determining the Best Pitching Options, page 198 • Situational Hitting, page 172
10:30–10:40	Game: 21 Outs	Runner reads pitcher and steals or returns according to signs, sliding; catcher gives signal for either pitchout or pickoff.	• Walking in rhythm when pitcher looks back. • Getting good jump.	• Stealing Third Base, page 54 • Pitcher Pickoffs, page 190
10:40–10:50	Game: Globetrotter	Runners on corners respond to plays by pitcher and catcher; coach at first and third to assist.	• Clear signs from catcher. • Communication between fielders. • Positioning. • Cuts.	• Defending the First-and-Third Double Steal, page 182 • First-and-Third Play, page 158
10:50–10:55	Cool-down	Four-Corner Sprints—straight steal at first, delay steal at second, tag and go at third, getting out of the box at home.	• Jumps and hustle.	
10:55–11:00	Coaches' comments and team building	Coaches comment on practice; take nominations for caps, discuss rededicating attitudes for next week, remind players to practice breathing at home.	• Progress made during the week; point out positives from the day.	
11:00–12:30	Coaches' meeting	Meet for lunch.	• Discuss roster of varsity and JV. • Make final decisions on team makeup.	

PRACTICE 7

Date:

Monday, March 20

Practice Start Time:

3:20 p.m.

Practice Length:

2 hours, 25 minutes

Objectives:

- Fine-tune tactical skills on extra-base hits.
- Increase catcher understanding of tactical skills related to steal situations.
- Work entire team on tactical awareness in bunt situations.
- Increase awareness of aggressive baserunning skills.
- Players should become more aware of the importance of goals.
- Continue work on using the cutoff and relay system.

Time	Name of activity	Description	Key teaching points	Related skills
3:20–3:35	Prepractice meeting and team building	Award caps; announce varsity and JV; remind players that coaches will be discussing their goals with them individually during practice today.	• Positive contributions of all players. • Highlight some goals players have cited.	
3:35–4:05	Warm-up	Ballet Class; flexibility exercises; throwing and catching.	• Range of motion in stretches. • Catching with two hands.	• Running Basics, page 44 • Throwing Basics, page 64 • Catching a Throw, page 72
4:05–4:06	Water break			
4:06–4:15	Daily drill sets for catchers	Catcher Challenge (variation 3)—focus on signaling and steal protection.	• Quick feet. • Quickly getting ball into throwing position.	• Catcher Pickoffs, page 194
4:06–4:15	Daily drill sets for pitchers	Dueling Pitchers—game variation of Pitcher's Toolbox.	• Moving ball around the zone. • Locating pitches.	• Determining the Best Pitching Options, page 198
4:06–4:15	Daily drill sets for infielders	Goalie (variation 4)—review playing the ball.	• Quick crossover. • Direct route to ball. • Squaring up to the plate. • Good feeds at second.	• Double-Play Defenses, page 196
4:06–4:15	Daily drill sets for outfielders	Five Alive (variation 3)—review finding the cutoff.	• Throwing to chest and head area of receiver.	• Defensive Positioning, page 178

PRACTICE 7

Time	Name of activity	Description	Key teaching points	Related skills
4:15–4:40	Situational batting practice	Use whole complex—stations for tees, soft toss, Speed Stik, one-knee drills, live; for live bat, place runners at various bases; they react to runner and count; make it a game by awarding points for successful execution; coach charts all pitches.	• Reacting to the situation created. • Short-to-long swings. • Looking middle or away.	• Situational Hitting, page 172
4:40–5:05	Defensive situations	Focus on ball between infield and outfield; two fungo hitters (LF and RF); triple drills with outfielders; covering bases on steals; cutoffs and relays.	• Communication between infield and outfield. • Hitting cutoff man. • Outfielder catching low and infielder catching high.	• Defensive Positioning, page 178 • Defending the First-and-Third Double Steal, page 182 • Rundowns, page 202
5:05–5:20	Bunt Game	Fielders take active role; read the situation and respond.	• Bunt defenses.	• Defending Bunt Situations, page 186
5:20–5:30	Game: Globetrotter	Same as previous practice.	• Communication.	• Defending the First-and-Third Double Steal, page 182
5:30–5:35	Cool-down	First-to-third sprints from 12-foot lead for time; tag up and score from third; use outfielders and fungo hitter, no throws; stretch main muscle groups.	• Economy of turn at second. • Listening to coach at third.	
5:35–5:40	Coaches' comments and team building	Introduce and define game plan; reiterate season plans; nominate for caps if necessary; remind players of relaxation drills; introduce the concept of team goals and formation of same by practice #9.	• Importance of preparing for opponents. • Evaluate correlation of team's technical skill and team tactical approach.	
5:40–5:45	Coaches' meeting	Divide player goal sheets among coaches for individual review at next practice.	• Discuss and evaluate practice.	

PRACTICE 8

Date:

Tuesday, March 21

Practice Start Time:

3:20 p.m.

Practice Length:

2 hours, 20 minutes

Objectives:

- Increase tactical skills at all positions.
- Continue to practice gamelike situations with situational hitting in BP and creating running situations at the same time.
- Emphasize the importance of not playing the opposition but instead concentrating on getting outs.
- Begin preparation of the first game plan.

Time	Name of activity	Description	Key teaching points	Related skills
3:20–3:32	Prepractice meeting and team building	Award caps; discuss aggressive play.	• Examples of outstanding leadership.	
3:32–3:50	Warm-up	Ballet Class; flexibility exercises; throwing.	• One-bounce long toss.	• Running Basics, page 44 • Throwing Basics, page 64 • Catching a Throw, page 72
3:50–4:00	Game: Globetrotter	Four-corner throwing using multiple balls.	• Proper form. • Quick footwork. • Focus and concentration.	• Throwing Basics, page 64 • Catching a Throw, page 72
4:00–4:10	Daily drill sets for catchers	Catcher Challenge—review passed balls; covering home on home-to-first double plays.	• Footwork around the plate. • Always pivoting to the left to go back to the ball on wild pitch.	• Wild Pitches, page 204
4:00–4:10	Daily drill sets for pitchers	Dueling Pitchers—game variation of Pitcher's Toolbox; review breaking pitches and changing speeds.	• Location and movement in the zone.	• Determining the Best Pitching Options, page 198
4:00–4:10	Daily drill sets for infielders	Goalie—add challenging plays such as slow rollers and backhands.	• Quick feet. • Focusing on target on difficult throws.	• Defensive Positioning, page 178

PRACTICE 8

Time	Name of activity	Description	Key teaching points	Related skills
4:00–4:10	Daily drill sets for outfielders	Five Alive (variation 4)—add *Sports Center* phase; review diving catches, long runs and long reaches.	• Hustle. • First three steps hard and fast. • Getting to the ball.	• Defensive Positioning, page 178
4:10-4:15	Drill: Bobble and Go!	Same as practice #4; incorporate sliding into second.	• Hard first steps when rounding first. • Deciding to take second. • Good sliding form.	• Rounding the Bases, page 48
4:15–5:00	Game: 21 Outs	Various scenarios to put players in game settings; emphasize situational hitting, sliding, pickoffs, cuts and double-steal defense.	• Throwing strikes. • Getting outs.	• Determining the Best Pitching Options, page 198 • Defending the First-and-Third Double Steal, page 182 • Defensive Positioning, page 178
5:00–5:20	Bullpens	Pitchers in game setting work out of stretch position; runners stationed at each base work on reading and reacting to pitcher pickoff moves; work on getting jumps and other aggressive running strategies.	• Pitchers work on glide stride. • Various timings on stretch.	• Pitcher Pickoffs, page 190
5:20–5:25	Cool-down	Sprints from first to third; stretches.	• Looking in to plate after third step.	
5:25–5:30	Coaches' comments and team building	Discuss positive aspects of practice, review season and game plans, comment on goal preparations, remind players that they will decide team goals at next practice.	• Contributions of players who have not been mentioned in the past few days.	
5:30–5:40	Coaches' meeting	Meet in coach's office.	• Review points discussed with players regarding goals. • Congratulate staff members on hard work so far. • Review season checklist.	

PART V

Game Coaching

You can plan, and you can practice all day long. But if your team does not perform to the best of its ability during your games, what good has all that planning done for you? Part V will help you prepare for game situations.

Chapter 9 teaches you how to prepare long before the first game, including issues such as communication, scouting your opponent and creating your game plan. Chapter 10 teaches you how to be ready to make decisions during and after the game, such as how to deal with removing pitchers, making substitutions and setting a batting order.

After all the preparation that you have made, game day is when it really becomes exciting, especially if you and your team are ready for the challenge.

chapter 9

Preparing for Games

Everything covered so far—the techniques, the tactics, the practice and season plans—occurs in the weeks leading up to the first game. All this means little, however, unless you can assemble these parts to focus your team on the next game. You must prepare a game plan that tailors the overall strategy to gain the best advantage in the upcoming contest. Following are areas that you should consider when crafting a game plan.

Communication

As a coach, you must communicate well at many levels—with players, team captains, assistant coaches, school and community officials, parents, umpires and the media. You must be aware of your nonverbal communication, which can be just as loud as what you say with your mouth.

Players

When you communicate well, you engage your players in the learning process. When players become partners and have a stake in their own development, you become a facilitator, not merely a trainer. This is the key to the games approach and what makes it such a valuable approach to coaching. Although shaping, focusing and enhancing play is difficult, it is ultimately more rewarding because it allows players to take ownership of their development.

As part of the communication process, you should assemble a team manual that covers basic defensive alignments, notes on the season plan, aggressiveness, team signs and signals, basic techniques and summarized versions of tactics. Distribute this resource to players several weeks before the first day of practice. Many sources available to coaches contain diagrams that show defensive positioning tactics. The manual should not be too long, because the longer it is, the less apt the athletes are to read it. Meet with players often and encourage them to study the manual thoroughly.

Before the beginning of a season, you should prepare a list of expectations, which outlines the policies you expect players to follow. The term *expectations* is preferable to the term *rules,* which conveys a sense of rigidity. Following are basic expectations which form a guide upon which you can expand to fit your own circumstances.

TEAM EXPECTATIONS

- Exhibit the positive attitude of a team player. Be a team player; never do anything that could destroy team morale.
- Conduct yourself with honor, dignity, humility and graciousness. Be humble in victory and gracious in defeat.
- Try to reach your potential consistently and set challenging goals for yourself each day, each week and each month of the season.
- Be on time for team meetings, practices, transportation departures and other team-related activities.
- Be at practice every day.
- Exhibit passion for the game and work hard each day.
- Commit yourself to the idea that we will be the hardest working team in the state.
- Respect fellow players, equipment, the game and yourself by having pride in our school, our team and your appearance.
- Be respectful to umpires, opposing players, coaches, fans and other field personnel at all times.
- Accept adversity and deal positively with it.
- Be able to accept harsh criticism and practice self-discipline.
- Understand that no player is guaranteed playing time. The coaching staff will decide on playing time based on established criteria.
- Understand that everything the coaching staff does has a purpose—to make the team better!
- Adhere to the school Athletic Code and all state policies and procedures. Avoid profanity, gambling, smoking and alcohol and drug use.
- Prepare yourself mentally for each game. Focus only on the game or practice after you reach the field.

The term *expectations* also communicates to players that they are responsible for living up to them. The coaching staff must reinforce expectations daily so that they become second nature to the team. Any breaches of discipline that arise should be handled immediately and even handedly. You must treat all players alike, starters no differently than subs. Finally, you should make sure that your list of expectations covers any exigency that may occur in your local situation.

You may decide to have the team elect captains, who can then assist you in communicating to the team. Emphasize to captains that their main role is to help make their teammates better players, not order them around. Show captains the many ways to accomplish that—by encouraging teammates, helping them work on their skills, supporting them and modeling good practice habits.

Parents

Before the season begins, you should schedule a preseason meeting with parents of all baseball candidates, separate from the meeting that most schools already sponsor during each sport season. A few weeks before the season begins, mail a letter to the homes of players (see figure 9.1) with an RSVP enclosed. This personal touch will pique the interest of parents and make them feel valuable to the program. A special invitation letter should go to the superintendent, the principal and the athletic director, who should be present to explain school policies, athletic codes and general school issues.

Prepare a simple agenda for this meeting and follow it to keep the meeting on track and to convey to parents a sense of your organizational ability. Besides setting an agenda, you should prepare and distribute a simple list, as shown in "Team Roles and Responsibilities" on page 243, outlining the roles of parents, players and coaches. Parents want to be involved in their child's progress, so stating the method of communication between parent and coach is important.

Staff

Coaches need to communicate well with their assistants. Each season, you should hold a formal preseason meeting with your coaching staff to outline expectations. Discuss season philosophy and specific techniques that you will emphasize, especially if changes have occurred from the previous year or if new members have joined the staff. You should spell out, or even write out, the roles of assistants or volunteer coaches, including how to deal with parents, who should be referred to you. Assistants should be firm and fast in noting breaches of discipline and bringing them to your attention.

Officials

Coaches must also communicate well with officials. You should treat officials as the professionals that they are, even when they are wrong. When questioning a ruling, approach the official slowly and respectfully. Players will model your behavior with umpires. Because most states and leagues provide outlets for official evaluations, you can address shortcomings and commendations of officials through that process.

Community and Media

Involvement with the community and the media demands that you be a good communicator. You speak each day with your demeanor. If you become rattled or easily frustrated, players will assume that demeanor. If you are cool-headed, the players will be calm too. By maintaining composure, you convey an attitude of control under pressure even in intense, challenging situations.

You should be accommodating to the press and instruct players in tactics for talking to media. Players need to understand that the role of the media may come in conflict with the goals and expectations of the team. Players should respectfully

Figure 9.1 Preseason Meeting Invitation

Date: ______________________________

TO: Parents of Prospective Players

RE: Preseason Meeting

My assistant coaches and I cordially invite you to be our guest at a preseason orientation meeting that

will be held on ____________________ (date), 20____ at ______________________________ (location and time).

This informal meeting will provide us with an opportunity to share common concerns—our expectations for your son, what you may expect from us during the upcoming season and what we expect from you.

Please let me know if you will be able to attend by completing the bottom portion of this letter and returning it to school with your son. I look forward to meeting with you and promise that the meeting will be short.

Sincerely,

(name) ______________________________

(position title) ______________________________

✂- -

Name: ______________________________

Child: ______________________________

☐ Yes, I am planning to attend the preseason meeting.

☐ No, I cannot attend the preseason meeting.

Comments: ______________________________

____

____

From *Coaching Baseball Technical and Tactical Skills* by ASEP, 2006, Champaign, IL: Human Kinetics.

TEAM ROLES AND RESPONSIBILITIES

Coach's Roles

- To teach, encourage and motivate
- To be patient and enthusiastic
- To be positive, fair and consistent with players
- To set a good example for players and fans
- To use care in making all player-related decisions
- To conduct daily organized practice sessions in a safe environment
- To establish and keep channels of communication open with players and parents
- To make sure that players know expectations, procedures, policies and lettering requirements
- To provide updated game schedules throughout the season
- To help athletes set goals for themselves and the team

Parent's Roles

- To be positive and to support all team members
- To respect the decisions of the officials and coaches
- To respect the opponent's fans, coaches and players
- To contact the coach through agreed-upon athletic department procedures at the appropriate time and place—not on game day
- To understand that the coaching staff is concerned with making their child not only a better athlete but also a better person, a concern that may take precedence over winning
- To not criticize a coach or team member with destructive comments during a game

Player's Roles

- To exhibit good character both on and off the field, which includes being positive, having a good attitude, being respectful, being disciplined, being honest, displaying good sportsmanship and being resilient
- To work and play hard
- To be a team player by understanding his role on the team
- To challenge himself daily by going beyond what is expected
- To know and follow team and scholastic expectations
- To communicate with the coaching staff regarding any conflict or misunderstanding of expectations
- To be at practice every day or to notify the coach in advance of scheduling conflicts
- To show pride

answer questions that deal with games but defer questions about philosophy or game management to the coaching staff. Players must be careful not to say anything derogatory about an opponent that might find its way onto an opponent's locker room bulletin board.

Scouting an Opponent

The first step in developing a successful game plan is to scout the opponent thoroughly and eliminate the element of surprise from the game equation. Good scouting can make practices more engaging if players are made aware of the reasons why certain plays or alignments might be successful against an upcoming opponent. Players will feel more ownership, a basic characteristic of team building.

Preparing to Scout

Scouting is less prevalent in baseball than it is in some other sports, and coaches are often unable to scout all opponents. Unlike football and basketball teams that play one or two games a week, most baseball teams play at least three games per week at the high school level, making it difficult for a one-coach staff to do it all.

You can transform the liability of having a small staff into an asset if you are willing to use parents as scouts. This approach enables you to make parents feel part of the team, perhaps enhancing coach–parent relationships.

You should prepare your scouts, especially parents, in the nuances of good scouting. Useful scouting includes comments on the style of play of the upcoming foe: Are they aggressive on the bases? Do they like to bunt or steal? Do they like to get ahead with breaking pitches or fastballs? Do the pitchers like to throw to the bases? Do they have any trick plays? You should have scouts use stopwatches to time everything that can be timed during a game.

If scouting a team beforehand is not possible, a comprehensive record of the teams' last contest will be extremely helpful, so keeping scouting records during games is important. Watch the opponent during their pregame warm-up. You can learn much by observing, for example, how quickly outfielders reach balls hit during infield or outfield or how strongly they throw to the bases.

You should also try to scout players during the summer by watching them play in summer leagues. In many high school conferences, games for both varsity and junior varsity are scheduled on the same day, which means that assistant coaches will not be available to scout because they will be coaching. Even if you cannot spare personnel to scout conference opponents, try to have someone available to scout early tournament opponents so that you don't have to rely on last-minute phone calls to other coaches to gather sketchy information.

Scouting Form and Report

You can develop a simple form to improve scouting input. The form shown in figure 9.2 was adapted from a form developed by Dick Siebert at the University of Minnesota and passed down through Tom Meyer, former coach at the University of Wisconsin.

Using one card for every player scouted, whoever is scouting places a small version of one of the symbols in the bottom left corner of the form on the diamond graphic each time the player hits a ball. The lines in the upper left are used to keep track of other at bats and baserunning statistics for the player. The batting order blanks on the right-hand side note where a batter hit in the lineup for each game. Advantages of this old-school method are that it can be added to for each game that the player is watched and it doesn't require technical knowledge.

Scouting forms are available from many sources, or you can design one. Digital scouting programs operate the same way as the card does but may require significant learning before use. They have the advantage of being able to produce detailed statistics regarding any player who has been scouted. These can be printed and distributed immediately.

Figure 9.2 Sample Scouting Form

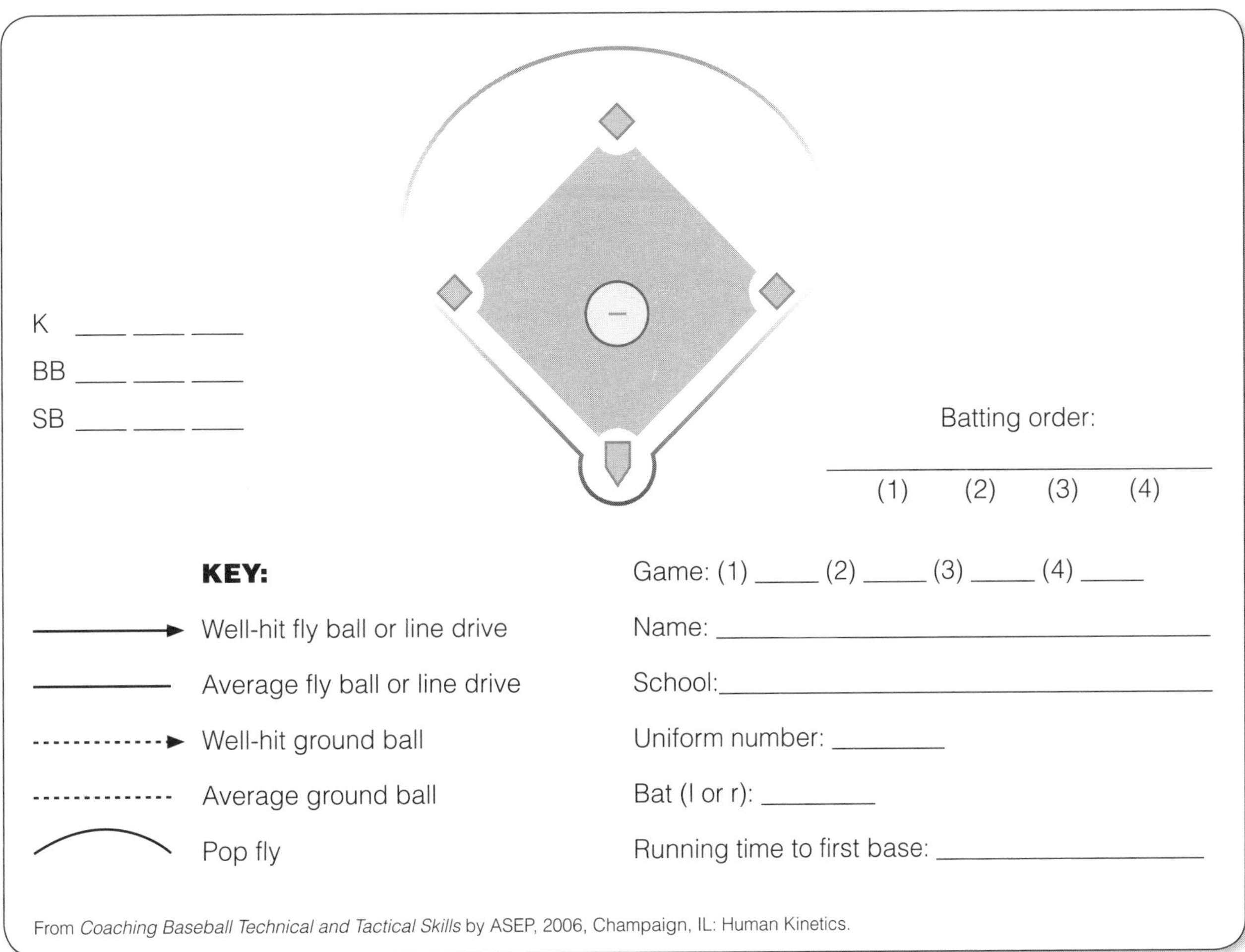
K ___ ___ ___

BB ___ ___ ___

SB ___ ___ ___

Batting order:

(1) (2) (3) (4)

KEY:

Well-hit fly ball or line drive

Average fly ball or line drive

Well-hit ground ball

Average ground ball

Pop fly

Game: (1) ____ (2) ____ (3) ____ (4) ____

Name: ____________________

School: ____________________

Uniform number: ________

Bat (l or r): ________

Running time to first base: ______________

From *Coaching Baseball Technical and Tactical Skills* by ASEP, 2006, Champaign, IL: Human Kinetics.

After gathering this information—running times, hitting tendencies, pitching notes and so on— through use of the scouting form, you can assemble it into a scouting report. You should summarize and share certain bits of information. If an opponent has special players, good hitters or outstanding pitchers, inform your team.

If the scouting report indicates that the opposition is outstanding, you should be careful when discussing the report. A scouting report should focus more on what you can do against the opponent rather than the other way around. Don't make too much of any one player or strategy. Instead, get your players to play their own game one pitch at a time.

Developing a Specific Game Plan

The next item is to develop a game plan for the opponent, formulated by considering the scouting report, your overall strategy and your team's offensive and defensive capabilities. The plan should be specific to the game being played that day, taking into account things like who is hot and injuries.

A sample form to help you prepare is given in figure 9.3. Notice that it covers all contingencies, from the time that players should arrive on the field to who is completing the game charts. Another useful form is the manager's checklist,

Figure 9.3 Game Duty Organizational Chart

Game: ______________________ **Date:** ______________

Arrival time: ______________

Game captains: (1) ______________________ (2) ______________________

Outfield warm-up: ______________

Outfield fungo hitters: (1) ______________________ (2) ______________________

Outfield fungo shaggers: (1) ______________________ (2) ______________________

Catcher to warm-up starter: ______________________

First-base coach: ______________________

Scorekeeper: ______________________

Game notes: ______________________

Pitching chart: ______________________

Count chart: ______________________

Reading opponent's pitcher: ______________________

Reading coach's signs: ______________________

Bullpen catcher: ______________________

Relief pitchers (long): (1) ______________________ (2) ______________________

Relief pitchers (short): (1) ______________________ (2) ______________________

Courtesy runners: (1)______________________(2) ______________________

From *Coaching Baseball Technical and Tactical Skills* by ASEP, 2006, Champaign, IL: Human Kinetics.

Figure 9.4 Manager's Checklist

- ❑ Stopwatches
- ❑ Ice chest and gel ice packs
- ❑ Charts (i.e. pitching or count)
- ❑ Game assignment form
- ❑ Lineup cards (2)
- ❑ Dugout lineup card
- ❑ Scorebook
- ❑ Clipboards (3)
- ❑ Sharpened pencils (6) and black marker (1)
- ❑ Pitch counter
- ❑ Portable home plate (catcher's bag)

HOME GAMES ONLY

- ❑ Game balls (12)
- ❑ Checks for umpires
- ❑ Routinely check first aid equipment and supply

From *Coaching Baseball Technical and Tactical Skills* by ASEP, 2006, Champaign, IL: Human Kinetics.

provided in figure 9.4, which covers details that the team manager should handle before the game to relieve you of those responsibilities. When players are aware of their pregame and game duties, they feel more valuable to the team, even if they are sitting on the bench. Listing the relief pitchers in the game plan helps the players named prepare mentally should they be needed, and having bench players involved in warm-ups between innings keeps them engaged and ready to play. Courtesy runners will not have to be reminded to get on a helmet; they'll be ready when the player for whom they will run is at bat.

Team Building and Motivation

Baseball is a team game. A malfunction by any of the nine parts of the whole can destroy the rhythm of the team. You should therefore spend quality time each day motivating players to behave as a team.

One method is to include some fun elements during practice sessions. For example, after practice one day of the first week, you can conduct a nonbaseball activity such as a basketball game or a bowling tournament and reward the winners with a reprieve from field maintenance the following day. You can make practices fun by incorporating games to stimulate players, or you can allow players to plan a Parent's Day and activities. You may also want to think about pairing returning letter winners with new players during the first week of practice so that the rookies learn the drills and the routine more easily and gain confidence. Instilling in players a sense of pride in their diamond, their dugout and their locker room and making them feel a part of the process gives them self-esteem. Rewarding the whole team every once in a while can be effective, especially after a hard week of practice. These special things help build camaraderie. You should also use daily practices to motivate players. Don't wait until the pregame pep talk to do your motivating. Rah, rah talks and "Win one for the Gipper" speeches are rarely effective.

Another tier of communication in which you should play a direct role is setting individual and team goals. Tell players in advance that you expect them to write out their personal and team goals before the end of the first week of practice. To give them a concrete focus for their goals, create and distribute a simple fill-in-the-blanks form with space to list individual and team goals. But you cannot expect players to formulate realistic goals without assistance. You should spend a few minutes explaining the characteristics of goals—that they should provide direction, be specific, aim high but be achievable and be written. After players submit their goals, discuss them individually with the players.

To make certain that the team is always emphasized above the individual, you need to expend a lot of effort. You must never single out players or hold them above others. Doing so can lead to animosity and destroy team unity. Even when using running as a form of discipline, never run only the offending party. Make the whole team run, and be clear that the team, not the individual, is responsible. You should make team members feel that they have ownership and that their opinion counts. A technique that goes a long way toward building team unity and gives players a voice in decisions is a variation of a technique learned from Mike Dee, successful head coach at the University of Illinois at Chicago. The approach, discussed in "Getting Creative With Caps," gives players a role in deciding who their teammates will be and makes them earn their way onto the squad.

Preparing for the Game

When preparing for a game, you must avoid either overworking your team or not working them hard enough and plan practice sessions accordingly.

Most practice sessions after the 3rd week take place on days between games. The workload should be light to medium. You have to walk a fine line between keeping players in shape and keeping them well rested before games. Overworking a team mentally is also possible.

Structure practices according to the game plan. For example, you can apply your team's hitting philosophy to an upcoming game. If the next opponent features a pitcher who is fast but has control problems, you might work your team more than you usually do on taking pitches. Against a good pitcher, you might use a practice to work on your players' two-strike hitting approach, reasoning that the opponent's pitcher might often get ahead of the hitters. The 0-2 or 1-2 batting practice game would be good preparation for that pitcher.

GETTING CREATIVE WITH CAPS

On the first day of practice, team members are presented with their baseball caps before practice begins. But these caps are not the real team hats. They are the ugliest, least desirable caps that any self-respecting baseball player would want to wear. For example, the 2004 Wisconsin state champions, the Burlington Catholic Central Hilltoppers, were presented on opening day with lime green hats lettered in pink!

After a team meeting and discussion, a criterion was formulated about what players had to do to earn their "real" caps. To earn his Hilltoppers cap, a prospective baseball player had to

- exhibit a positive attitude with both words and body language,
- work hard,
- be ready to practice or play every day,
- be attentive,
- lead by example,
- believe in himself,
- demonstrate character both on and off the field,
- be willing to help his teammates improve,
- avoid making excuses and
- possess a short-term memory and not have rabbit ears.

Players voted on nominated players at the end of practice each day. Ideally, the voting process should be oral and open, but high school players are often intimidated by peer pressure and do not openly speak their minds in a group setting. The Hilltoppers used a paper ballot. If 75 percent of the players said that a teammate had done well enough to have earned his cap, at the start of the next day's practice the player was awarded the cap with the appropriate fanfare. A negative vote on a ballot had to be accompanied with a written comment, thus reducing the tendency to be subjective and vote for buddies. If players hadn't earned their caps by the start of the season, they wore "rent-a-caps" in games and had to return them after the contest.

After the team had been divided into varsity and JV, the same process continued on the JV until all players earned a cap. This process brought the team together in an amazing way. In the end, no one wanted to be the last player to earn a cap, so everyone made an effort.

Using short daily drills on basic mechanics in practice between games will also keep players' techniques sharp. If you have covered all technical aspects in practices leading up to the first game, you should not use daily practices during the season to introduce new techniques, but merely to enhance and hone existing ones. The game plan should favor tactical preparation over technique by about a 2:1 ratio. Drill work should be the same as before with a new twist. Daily use of the games approach helps keep players sharp and focused on the tactics of baseball.

Controlling a Team's Performance

In preparing a game plan, you need to remind players that they can manage only their own play and have no control over the weather, the umpires, the fans and the way the other team plays. But as the coach, you can control other things in the performance arena, particularly the game routine. Established routines for pregame meetings and warm-ups help players feel relaxed.

Pregame Meeting

The pregame meeting, which should take place before the warm-up to embed the players' focus for the day, should emphasize the points worked on in practice and meaningful items from the scouting report. You need to tell players beforehand the uniform of the day and when to report.

Also, for home games, you should address postgame and pregame field preparation activities. Because most teams do not have grounds crews to do the work for them, items such as who puts in the bases, who lines the field and who rakes before and after the game should be spelled out as in the sample "Field Maintenance Checklist" shown in figure 9.5.

Assign all players chores to do before and after games if possible. Infielders should take care of their part of the infield, outfielders should pull weeds in the warning track and catchers should repair the home plate area.

Figure 9.5 Field Maintenance Checklist

Game: ______________________ **Date:** ______________

Stow and plug bases	________	________	________
Sweep home dugout	________	________	________
Sweep visitor dugout	________	________	________
Empty trash	________	________	________
Put equipment in storage closet	________	________	________
Rake mound	________	________	________
Tamp mound	________	________	________
Rake bullpens	________	________	________
Rake batter's box	________	________	________
Police warning track	________	________	________
Rake first-base line	________	________	________
Rake third-base line	________	________	________

From *Coaching Baseball Technical and Tactical Skills* by ASEP, 2006, Champaign, IL: Human Kinetics.

SAMPLE PREGAME ROUTINES

The following sample pregame routines for outfielders and infielders incorporate most of the techniques needed in a game and can be accomplished easily in less than 20 minutes. Every player will have an opportunity to experience most of the plays that he will see during a game, and the routines may have the added effect of awing the opponent.

Outfield Warm-Up

Coach	Outfielders	Others
Hits to each outfielder	LF, CF, RF throw to 2B.	SS, 2B practice cuts and relays to 2B; C, P, 1B, 3B work on fielding bunts, communicating and throwing to first or third.
Hits to each outfielder	LF, CF, RF throw to 3B in turn.	3B occasionally yells, "Cut two," forcing SS to cut and throw to 2B.
Hits ball in gap	LF, CF, RF chase down ball and throw to 3B.	Infielders works on double cut to third base; 1B covers second base.
Hits fly ball to each outfielder	LF, CF, RF throw to home plate.	P backs up home; 3B and 1B act as cutoff.
Hits groundball to each outfielder	LF, CF, RF make do-or-die throws to home plate.	Same as previous; catcher can call, "Cut" and name a base so that the 1B or 3B can cut the ball and throw.

Infield Warm-Up

Coach	Infielders	Others
Hits to third baseman	3B fields ball, throws to 1B and waits for return throw from C; when 3B receives the throw, he pretends to tag a sliding runner and then throws to 2B, who throws to 1B, who in turn throws to the backup C situated in foul territory on the first-base side.	P stands on mound; gets throw from 1B and then throws a medium-speed pitch to the first C in his crouch behind the plate; C throws the ball to the base where the fungo was hit (third base on this hit and to other bases on successive hit balls).
Hits to shortstop	SS follows same routine as 3B. After receiving ball from C, he throws again to 1B, who in turn throws to the backup C.	P pretends to cut throw from C to 2B.
Hits to second baseman	Same routine as before, but 2B receives return throw from C 10 feet in front of the base, pivots and throws to 3B, simulating a first-and-third double-steal cut. 3B throws to the backup C.	P does the same as previous.
Hits to right of first baseman	1B fields and throws to P covering the base; P throws to C at home, who starts the ball around the horn.	P reacts to ball on his left side and moves to cover first.
Hits double-play ground balls to all fielders	Infielders work on 5-4-3, 6-4-3, 4-6-3, 1-6-3, 3-6-1 and 3-6-3 double plays.	
Hits pop-ups to infield	Review communication and priorities on pop-ups. Note effect of wind on ball.	.
Hits final two ground balls to each infielder in sequence, the first a hard-hit grounder and the second a slow roller	Infielders play deep, field first ball and throw to home plate; after throwing they run toward home for the slow roller and throw to 1B. When the slow roller is hit to 1B, he throws to 3B.	One infielder needs to cover third base until 1B has received his two ground balls.
Hits a pop foul over home plate area	C removes mask, finds the ball, turns his back to the infield and fields it.	Players remain lined up near third-base line and cheer on teammates during the finale.

Pregame Warm-Up

The pregame warm-up should be more than a just a warm-up. It should touch on all basic plays and techniques that your team might have to use in a game. Inform players of some basic rules before the first game and the first warm-up:

- To save time, players should never chase a missed ball; other players should shag missed balls.
- Backups should be ready at each position when the first player at the position has fielded and thrown a ball.
- Players should hustle after every ball.

By following the preceding approaches, you can create an atmosphere of organization and certainty around your program. Communicating well, developing a sound game plan and practicing it, and working on controlling your team's performance are steps in the direction of success

chapter 10

During and After the Game

The three-step tactical triangle approach to analyzing a game situation detailed earlier in this book creates a blueprint for you and your players to follow in making decisions during a game. While the game is in progress, you must accurately read the cues presented, apply technical and tactical knowledge on the spot, adjust the game plan accordingly and make decisions immediately. Baseball writer Roger Kahn justifiably compares baseball to "playing chess at 90 miles per hour" (*The Head Game: Baseball Seen From the Pitcher's Mound,* 2000). The logical format of the triangle helps you slow the speed of the game and apply organized, logical thinking to any situation.

During the Game

Coaches make dozens of tactical decisions during a game. For example, suppose that your game plan calls for stealing rather than bunting. The game has reached the sixth inning, and the score is 1-1. The first batter has reached base, and the opposing pitcher has done a great job all day holding runners close. Here you should be willing to discard the game plan and bunt, and then maybe steal third as a surprise move. The ability to adjust and read the game as it develops is a critical application of the tactical triangle. The following sections show how to apply the tactical triangle to several key situations that commonly occur in games.

Removing Pitchers

One of the more difficult decisions for a coach is determining when to go out and talk to a pitcher. All baseball rules limit the number of visits to the mound by a coach during a game, so you should be judicious in making a trip. If a pitcher is obviously struggling or if you notice a major technical problem, do not hesitate to call time and go out to talk with the pitcher. Usually, you will want the catcher to join the conversation. You should not add any undue pressure here by criticizing the pitcher, especially if he is struggling. A good method of communicating during a mound visit is to start with something completely irrelevant to the situation by asking the player something innocuous like, "What did you eat for lunch today?" Although outwardly ridiculous, this question or a similar one serves the purpose of throwing the pitcher off balance and relaxing him. After the pitcher answers, you can turn the conversation over to a discussion of mechanics or tactics, but nothing that would add pressure. Focus the pitcher on the game plan—on or out in three—or on some technical skill that he may be omitting. Telling the pitcher to focus on his front shoulder or where he breaks the ball out of his glove takes his attention away from other things, like the necessity to throw strikes.

Besides knowing when to call productive time-outs, you need to plan for substitutions. Pitches need to be charted and counted throughout a game, and you should know how many pitches you are going to let a player throw before removing him. But more important than pitch count is what you see. For example, a pitcher who drops his elbow below his shoulder in his throwing motion or does not lift his leg as high as he normally does may be fatigued, and you need to recognize those signs and get a relief pitcher warming up.

Substituting Players

You must also be prepared to substitute players. If a pitcher overmatches a hitter, you should not hesitate to pinch hit for that player. If a player is in the lineup for his hitting ability but reaches base in a situation in which you need speed, you should be willing to pull that player for a pinch runner. If you lay the groundwork daily in practice and communicate the idea that players must play roles, then substitution will not cause an ego crisis.

Another way that you can eliminate substitution problems is to have all players learn a second position. Players should practice this second position often during the week. Doing this creates the belief that other players can play every position and that the team will not suffer when the "normal" defense is not in place. By working hard in word and action to make each player feel valuable, you can overcome the "me" attitude prevalent in sport today. You will know that you have been successful when the player taken out of the game becomes the biggest cheerleader for the sub. Working to make every player adept at a second position creates team depth and versatility and contributes to the team-building process.

When planning substitutions, bear in mind the talents of each player. Who is good at going to the opposite field? Hitting curveballs? Who is a better hitter or better fielder? Then when a situation presents itself in a game—when a bunt might be needed, for example—you will have predetermined which player to use to accomplish the task if the starting player is not as adept at doing so. You will want to consider several variables before substituting. What is the score? How many outs does the team have left? Is it worth exchanging an out to advance a base runner? If a runner gets on base, are the hitters that follow capable of driving

SIGNS AND SIGNALS

As we learned in chapter 9, proper communication is vital. Catchers have to communicate with pitchers. Infielders and outfielders must communicate on fly balls. Coaches have to be able to communicate with hitters and base runners without the other team knowing what they are "talking" about. A simple signal method called the touch system is easy to incorporate, undemanding to read, simple to alter on the fly yet hard for opponents to pick up.

In the touch system, different parts of the uniform are assigned to different baseball tactics. For example, touching the left arm might be the bunt sign. If a coach touches this part of the uniform, the player should try to bunt if the next pitch is a strike. The higher the level of play, the more complex the sign system, but no more than six or seven body touches should occur in a sign sequence.

An indicator sign starts the sign sequence. The coach flashes the indicator to alert the player that the real sign will follow. If the indicator is the nose, the coach will touch the nose and follow with the series of signs.

You must make it clear where in the order of the signs the real sign will be given. The real sign may be the first sign after the indicator, the second or the third. The advantage of this system is that you can change the order if you think that opponents are stealing the signs. You simply change from the first sign after the indicator to the second or third. A more complicated method is to use the first sign after the indicator in the first inning, the second sign in the second inning and so forth. When the indicator is not given, players know that no real sign will be given. On those occasions, however, players must continue to watch the coach until the sequence ends.

To cancel a sign, use an easily visible rub-off sign, usually a deliberate rubbing motion over some part of the body, normally the chest or legs.

Following is a sample set of signs using the touch system:

Hit and run.

Take the next pitch.

Sacrifice bunt.

Steal.

Suicide squeeze.

Several other methods of sign-giving can be used. You should not be afraid to ask knowledgeable coaches about how to convey signs. There are several good books on the market that cover the art of sign-giving, as well.

him home? You should adhere to the season plan when considering subbing. Is it time to play the percentages or throw caution to the wind and be aggressive?

You must remain flexible in making substitutions. A pitcher may be breezing along and suddenly hit a wall or lose his control. If the player scheduled for first relief would be overmatched, you will have to adjust and use someone not listed in the game plan. In these cases, you should explain to the player who was scheduled to pitch in relief why you changed the original plan. Make players aware that fluctuating game situations may force you to alter the game plan on the fly, adversely affecting their playing time. Again, openness of communication can soothe feelings.

Batting Order

Another game management issue is the batting order. You should structure the batting order so that it fits your game plan and then communicate the reasons to the players. The leadoff hitter should have a good batter's eye, not strike out often and have some speed. The second hitter should be a good contact hitter and good bunter. A left-hander in this spot is a plus. The number 3 hitter should be the team's best hitter and combine power and speed. The number 4 and 5 hitters should possess some power and be able to drive in runs; speed is not a major consideration. The number 6 hitter is the team's second leadoff hitter. He should have a good eye and some speed. The number 7, 8 and 9 hitters are usually the team's weakest hitters.

When putting together a batting order, consider these points. First, the leadoff hitter usually bats leadoff only once a game. Second, a good fastball hitter in the number 8 or 9 spot can be effective because opposing teams look at these players as weak hitters and don't want to walk them, so they throw "meat" balls. Third, rather than go with the conventional batting order, put players who can go with the pitch behind guys who get on base often.

After the Game

Although postgame activities should follow a familiar routine, your management job is not over. The time immediately after the game offers the best opportunity to teach your team good sportsmanship. This task will not be difficult if you have instructed your players all season long about what makes good character: trustworthiness, respect, responsibility, fairness and caring. Win or lose, you and the captains should thank the umpires for their work. If the umpires have not done an effective job, a simple thank you without elaboration is all that is necessary. You can evaluate the ump later. Nothing positive ever comes from an angry postgame encounter.

Players should line up at home plate to shake hands with the opposing team. Coaches should shake hands with the opposing coaches. Even after an emotional game, you should remain calm and say a kind word to the opposing coach, win or lose. If a problem occurred during the game, you can handle it later with a meeting.

Immediately after shaking hands, players should assemble in the outfield behind the base nearest their team dugout for the postgame meeting with coaches. Holding this meeting at some distance from the dugout avoids the distraction of fans or parents. Before meeting with the team, you and your staff should confer about what you will say about the game just completed. A good rule is to keep all comments positive, even in a loss. You can address the negative points in the prepractice meeting the following day.

After the postgame talk, you should make plans for the treatment of any injury. If a player should be taken to a doctor for a checkup, inform his parents. If a trainer is on site, injured players should report to the trainer or make an appointment to see the trainer before practice the next day. Only after all the preceding items are covered should you allow the media to talk to the players. Letting them interview players before completion of postgame rituals detracts from the team-first atmosphere that should prevail.

You should evaluate the game with your assistants while traveling home on the team bus or while the players are grooming the field. Because the game is fresh, this is a good time for the coaching staff to go over the evaluation rubrics presented earlier, look for specific items that need to be covered and plan the next day's practice.

Long ago, the medieval Japanese poet Basho said, "Every day is a journey and the journey itself is home." In Japan, these words strike deeply into the heart of the baseball experience. There, as here, coaches lead their teams on a daily journey toward their goals—improving, winning, excelling, making the playoffs and so on. But reaching the goal is not the end. If you accomplish all that is set out in these chapters, you will have conveyed to your players that playing the game, playing it well and playing it as a team is more important than all the wins or losses. Yes, victory can be sweet and should be savored, but that sweetness can be fleeting and turn sour if you haven't communicated the other things that matter. The journey itself stands at the heart of coaching. The journey to knowledge is the essence of the game.

index

about asep

Coaching Baseball Technical and Tactical Skills was written by the American Sport Education Program (ASEP) with the assistance of Tom O'Connell, a 30-year veteran coach and 2004 American Baseball Coaches Association Coach of the Year.

ASEP has been developing and delivering coaches' education courses since 1981. As the nation's leading coaching education program, ASEP works with national, state and local youth sport organizations to develop educational programs for coaches, officials, administrators and parents. These programs incorporate ASEP's philosophy of "athletes first, winning second."

ADD TO YOUR LEARNING ARSENAL

When a pitcher adds a pitch to his arsenal, it can take him from being average to "lights out." By participating in the **Coaching Baseball Technical and Tactical Skills online course**, you'll add to your coaching arsenal and make you even more effective in teaching your players the techniques and tactics of baseball.

With your registration, you'll receive a copy of the *Coaching Baseball Technical and Tactical Skills* book and CD-ROMs containing video clips, which you'll refer to while going through the course. Incorporating audio clips, Flash animation, interactive quizzes, downloadable coaching aids, and online test, the course takes you chapter by chapter through the book, providing you with an engaging, interactive learning experience.

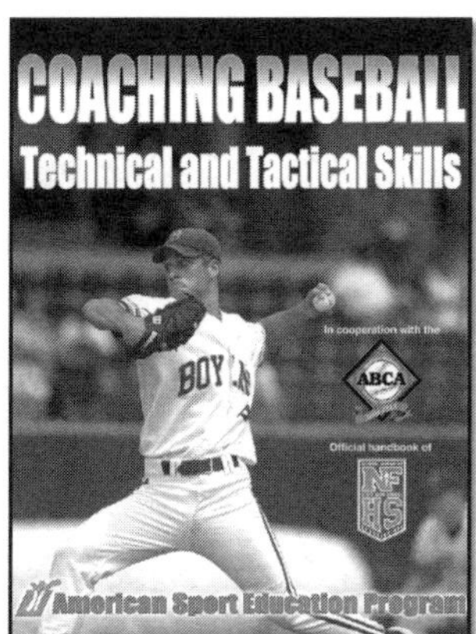

Coaching Baseball Technical and Tactical Skills online course is a component of the NFHS Coaches Education Program. Completion of the course puts you one step closer to earning the program's **Bronze Level** credential.

Register for Coaching Baseball Technical and Tactical Skills online course today! Visit **www.ASEP.com** and select "Course Catalog" from the "Quick Clicks" menu or call ASEP at **800-747-5698**.

The NFHS Coaches Education Program is supported, developed, and delivered through a partnership with the American Sport Education Program, a 25-year leader in the sport education field. The NFHS Coaches Education Program fulfills the coaching education requirements of more than 40 state high school associations.

A DIVISION OF HUMAN KINETICS

It Starts With the Coach

Much is expected of today's high school coach. On any given day, you may play the role of mentor, motivator, mediator, medic, psychologist, strategist, or trainer. Each requiring a separate set of skills and tactics that together make you a "coach."

The **Bronze Level** credential—offered through the NFHS Coaches Education Program—is designed with all of these roles in mind. It includes courses on coaching principles, sport first aid, and sport-specific techniques and tactics, and requires CPR certification. The Bronze Level prepares you for all aspects of coaching and is a recognized and respected credential for anyone who earns it.

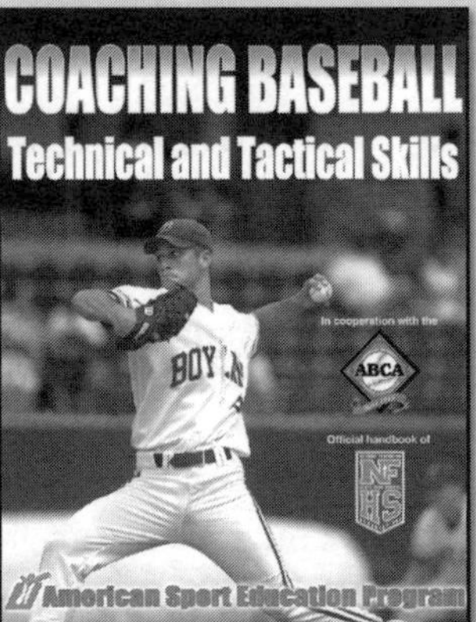

To enroll in any of these courses, visit the ASEP Web site at **www.ASEP.com** or contact your state association.

To learn more about how you can adopt the program for your state association or organization, contact Jerry Reeder, ASEP Sales Consultant, at **800-747-5698, ext. 2325** or e-mail **JerryR@hkusa.com**.

The NFHS Coaches Education Program is supported, developed, and delivered through a partnership with the American Sport Education Program, a 25-year leader in the sport education field. The NFHS Coaches Education Program fulfills the coaching education requirements of more than 40 state high school associations.

A Division of Human Kinetics